IMAGES
of America

THE UPPER KENNEBEC VALLEY

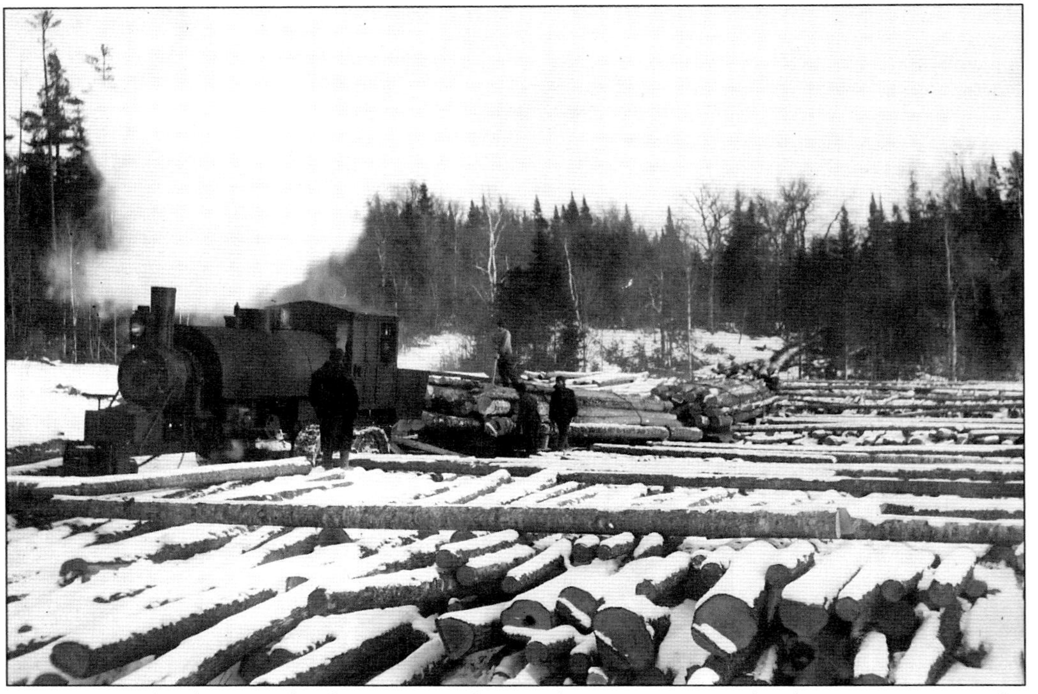

A steam Lombard tractor hauling into Taylor Brothers' Squaretown landing, *c.* 1920–21. The locomotive-like Lombards could haul more than any other tractor in use at that time.

COVER: The summer home of Kate and Alfred Burke in Concord, west of Lily Pond, *c.* 1900. Often the location of large gatherings and picnics, this summer place also had a small stocked private trout pond (south of Lily Pond) for the use of Mr. Burke and his invited friends. The Burkes ran a store on the main street of Bingham for many years.

IMAGES of America

THE UPPER KENNEBEC VALLEY

Jon F. Hall

ARCADIA PUBLISHING

ISBN 978-0-7385-6432-6

Published by Arcadia Publishing
Charleston, South Carolina

Printed in the United States of America

Library of Congress Catalog Card Number: 2009920440

For all general information contact Arcadia Publishing at:
Telephone 843-853-2070
Fax 843-853-0044
E-mail sales@arcadiapublishing.com
For customer service and orders:
Toll-Free 1-888-313-2665

Visit us on the Internet at www.arcadiapublishing.com

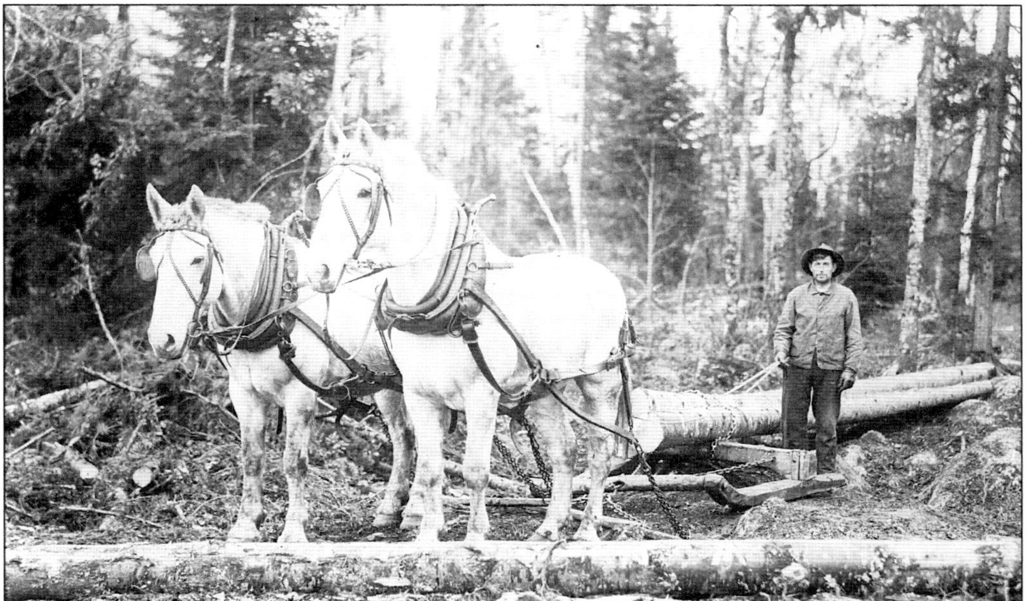

Tom Owens of Bingham with a woods team. This *c.* 1915–20 photograph shows him hauling logs to a collection point.

Contents

Acknowledgments

The Upper Kennebec Valley started with a substantial family collection of photographs from the Bingham, Moscow, and Caratunk areas. It has been greatly expanded from the generosity of local organizations such as the Bingham Union Library, the Madison Public Library, and the Embden Historical Society, and owes a debt of gratitude to Earle G. Shettleworth Jr. and the Maine Historic Preservation Commission. Much useful information has been taken from the published histories of Caratunk, Moscow, Bingham, Solon, Embden, and Madison, and from Mary Calvert's *The Kennebec Wilderness Awakens*. A number of individuals deserve special thanks for both information and photographs, including Howard Mitchell of Caratunk, Robert Hunnewell, first selectman of Bingham, Stanley Hill of Bingham and Concord, Evangeline Thompson of Concord, Amy F. Thorndike of Concord Haven, Virginia Merrill, Ann Padham, and Roland Tozier of Solon, Carol Dolan of the Embden Historical Society, Genevieve Partridge of North Anson, Laton and Joanne Edwards of Madison, and Harold M. Sterling of Yarmouth. Special thanks to Dr. Joyce Bibber of USM for encouraging me to go in this direction.

Others who were generous in sharing photographs and information include Rachel Moore Lopez, Harry Melcher, Mike Morris, Frederick McClintick, Leola Rollins, Leta Howes, Ernest Getchell, Vivian Berry, Dorothy Flanders, Norma Frost, Nellie Macdougall Parks, Marie Wing Cutchin and the estate of Sylvia Reynolds, Eddie Andrews, Arlene Robinson Flannery and the estate of Ruby Robinson, Donna McAllister, D. Kenneth Woodard, Fiorello Ventresco, Shirley Hilton Cornue, Donald Folsom, Gail Pierce, and Betsy Partridge Bolvin.

Though care has been taken to be factually accurate, errors will likely be found, for which I apologize in advance.

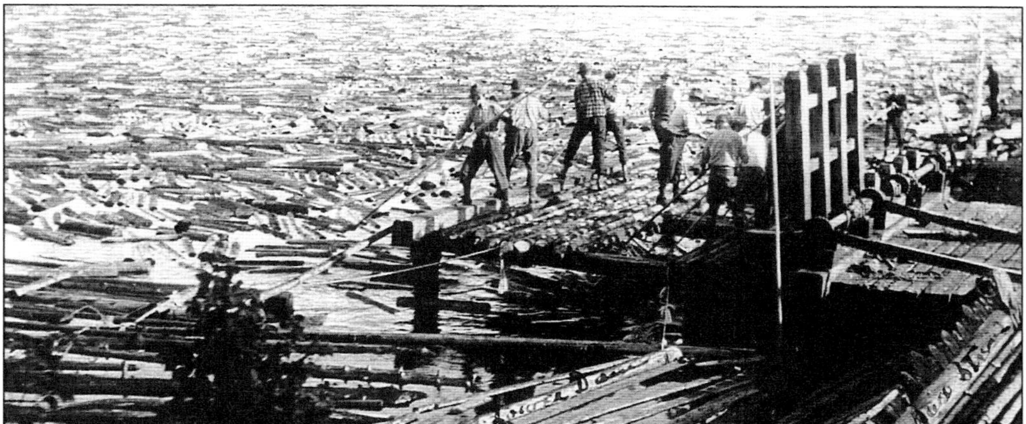

Walter Robinson's crew, Chase Stream, 1925, sluicing 4-foot pulpwood through Robinson's lower dam.

Introduction

The Upper Kennebec Valley, for the purposes of this book, includes the settled towns and plantations starting at The Forks, where the Kennebec River is formed by the East Branch and the Dead River, and follows the downstream course of the river through Caratunk, Moscow, Bingham, Solon, by Concord, Embden, and North Anson on the west bank, stopping at Madison and Anson with the beginnings of heavy industry. The north end of the valley has a landscape of picturesque woods, mountain streams, and lakes. Lumbering has been a major industry since the first European settlers came, following the route of Benedict Arnold's 1775 expedition to Quebec. Below Solon, the valley broadens out with more lush intervale farms and fewer mountains, and the transportation of goods and people becomes easier. Though the area had been long inhabited by Native Americans, its nature changed as European settlers moved north from Massachusetts, New Hampshire, and southern Maine. Little permanent settlement existed before the 1780s, and today the earliest surviving buildings are from the early 1800s. The settlers cleared land for subsistence farming first, then began to exploit the vast woodlands and excellent water-power resources of the Kennebec and its tributaries. They built small mills on the streams first, to supply lumber and grind grain. As the population grew in the mid-1800s, they developed light industries and small manufacturing enterprises. Most produced wood products or woods implements. Eventually, with the arrival of the railroad after the Civil War, small mills exported wooden items and corn shops canned produce. The 1880s through the 1920s saw a great period of prosperity and building in the valley, and heavy industry started in Madison with the building of a large woolen mill and a paper mill. Starting in the 1930s, the railroad, which once extended all the way to Moosehead Lake, shrank back, and many of the old cleared farms were abandoned and became overgrown. Light industry moved southward to easier climates and the Upper Kennebec Valley was left to depend primarily on its woods, lakes, and the river for its livelihood.

This book concentrates on the earlier images of the valley and its inhabitants, starting with mid-1800s daguerreotype and tintype portraits of early settlers and with stereo photographs of towns and farms. It tries to show the visual changes that have occurred over the years and looks particularly for what is no longer here or what has greatly changed over time. The book owes a great deal to the published local histories of the Upper Kennebec Valley towns and to the generosity of longtime inhabitants in sharing their stories and their photographs.

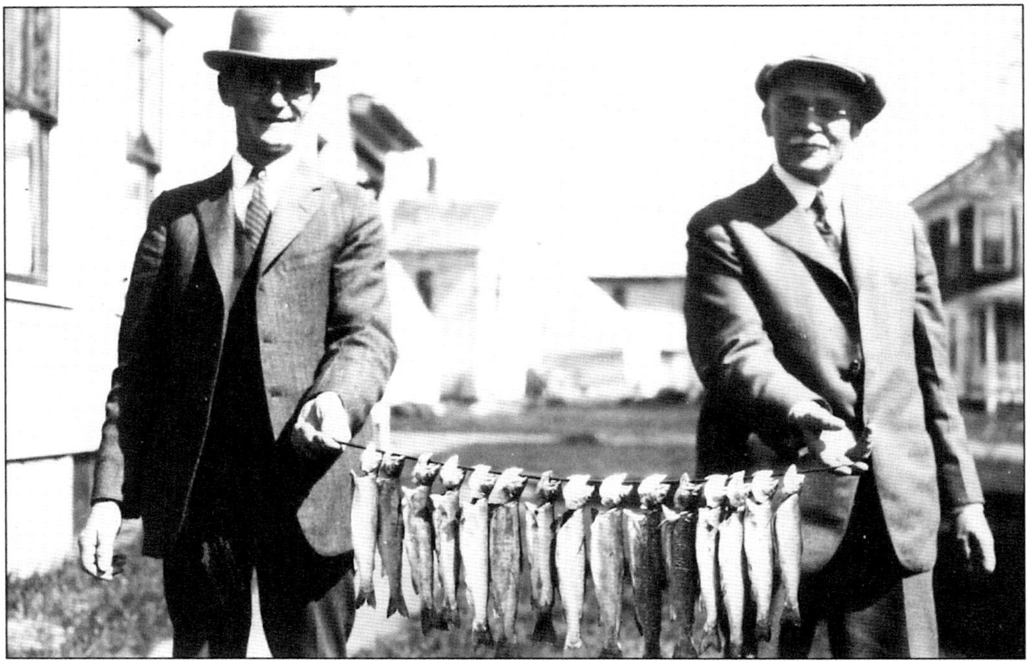

Jack Owens and Eugene D. Parks, with a string of Pleasant Pond trout, *c.* 1930. Eugene was the father of Leah Parks Macdougall. This photo was taken beside the Bingham Congregational Parsonage.

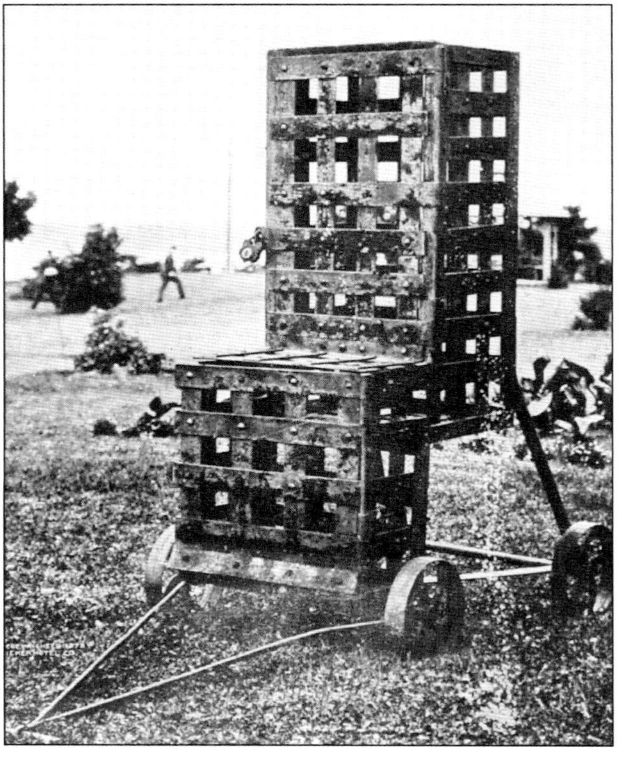

The Tramp Chair, invented by Sanford Baker in 1898. A number of these were made and used in cities and towns around Maine, including Bingham, to discourage "tramps." The "tramp" was locked inside and paraded through the town. It was apparently a very effective deterrent.

One

The Forks and West Forks

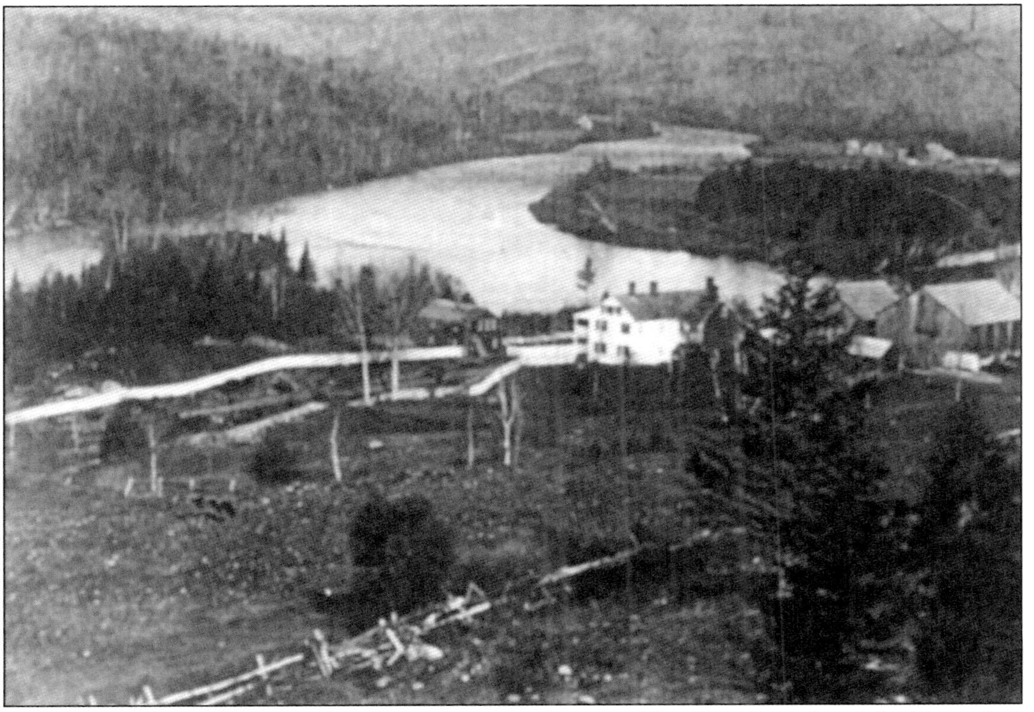

The Forks, where the Kennebec River begins its course. The East Branch of the Kennebec comes in from Moosehead Lake via Indian Pond to join the Dead River, which comes east from Flagstaff Lake and beyond. This c. 1890 photograph also shows the back side of what is now the Marshall Hotel.

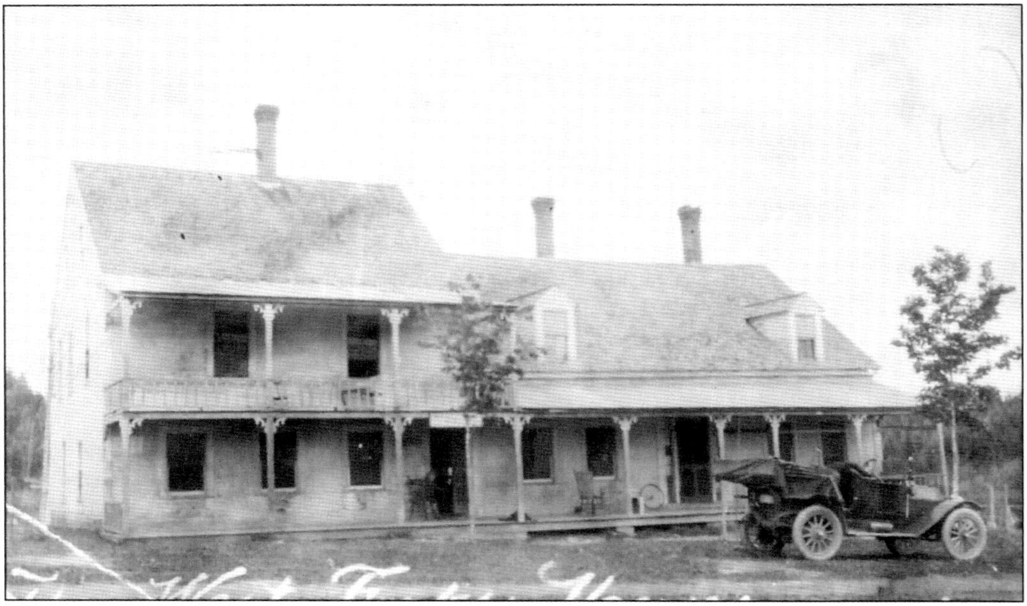

The West Forks Hotel, located north of West Forks village, near the present home of Howard Smith. At the time of this c. 1915 photograph, the hotel was operated by Thomas Berry Sr. and his wife, Myrtia. Eddie Comber operated it after the Berrys. The hotel burned in 1925.

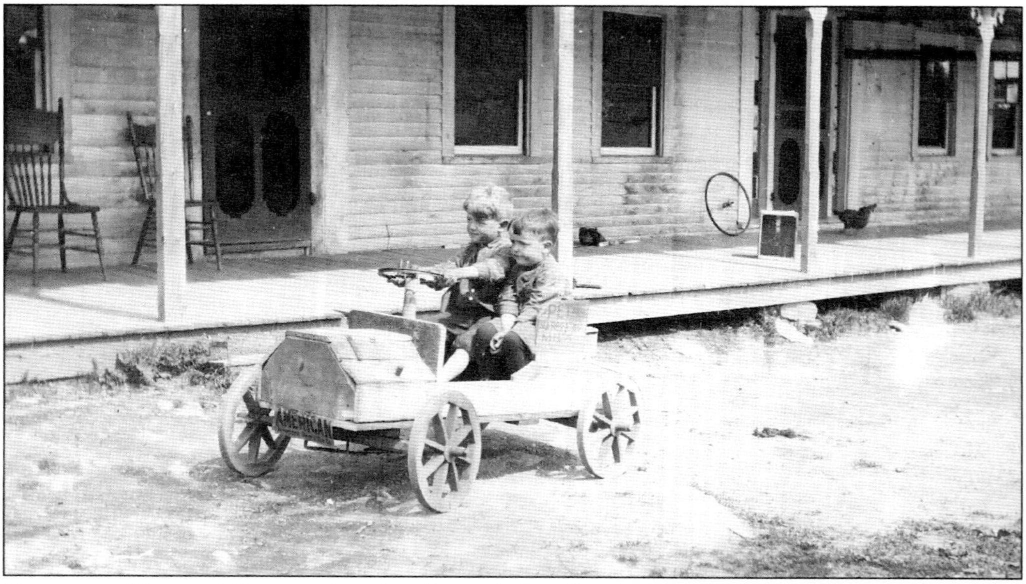

Tommy and Bernard Berry in their locally made "car," in front of the West Forks Hotel, c. 1915. The front plate says "American" and the seat reads "Pet Evaporated Milk." Clearly, much fun could be had in a homemade rig.

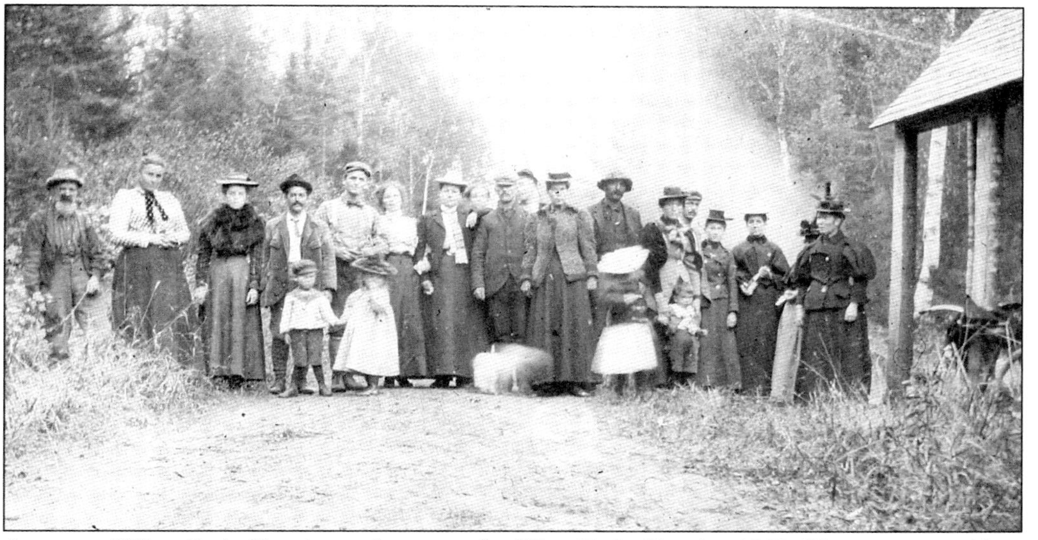

A group of West Forks Families, taken near the West Forks Hotel, c.1900. This group would go into Salmon Stream farm for a couple of weeks in the summer to pick blueberries, taking with them a loaded wagon of supplies, including a cookstove, and return with barrels of berries. From left to right are: (front row) Jeremiah Durgin, Matilda Durgin, Hattie McKay, Charles McKay, William Durgin, Esther Packard, Marie Packard, Bert Durgin, Eva Durgin, Warren Durgin, Minnie Durgin, Danville Durgin, Eva Pierce, Grace Durgin (Bunker), and Delora Pierce; (back row) Eva Durgin and Leamon Pierce; (children) Leslie Durgin, Alma Bloom, Henrietta Durgin, and Jim Dewey Durgin.

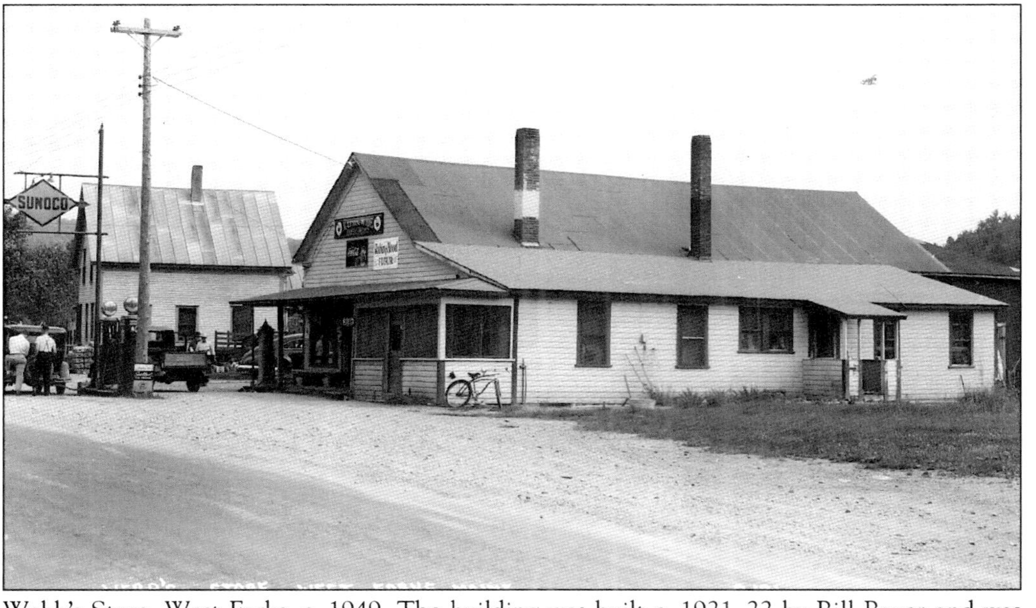

Webb's Store, West Forks, c. 1949. The building was built c. 1921–22 by Bill Bauer and was first used as a dance hall. For several years it was operated as a dance hall and restaurant by Tom and Clarisse Berry. Appleton Webb opened his store here in 1935, and he and his wife, Norma Webb, ran it for many years, leasing it to Bernard and Margaret Berry c. 1952–58. The Webbs' son Edmund and his wife Marie ran the store later. It was closed c. 1970.

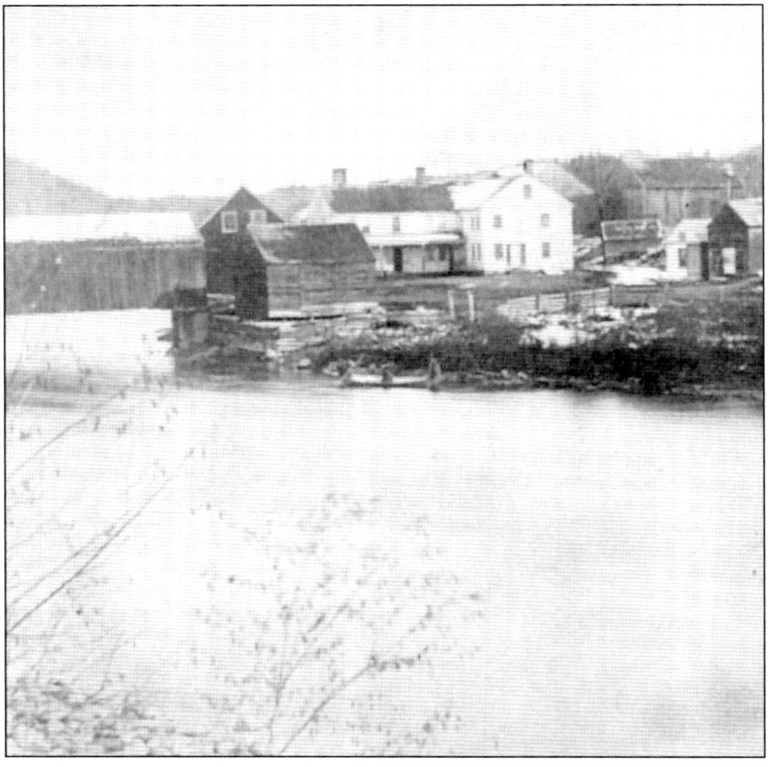

The Murray Hotel at the south end of the covered bridge spanning the East Branch. This *c.* 1875 stereo photo shows the old bridge, which was torn down *c.* 1932 to make way for the first steel bridge. The Murray Hotel preceded the much larger Forks Hotel which stood in the same location.

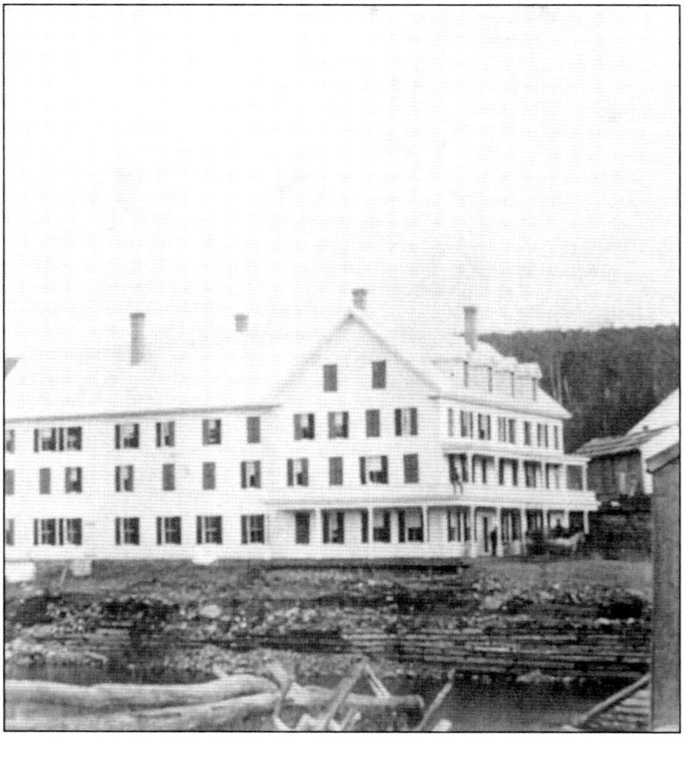

The Forks Hotel. This hotel was built *c.* 1876 by Joseph Clark Jr. and Governor Abner Coburn, the two largest landowners in this part of the valley. At his death, Joe Clark owned 150,000 acres of timberland, valued then at 50¢ per acre. This hundred-room hotel was a very ambitious undertaking for such a remote area; it also shows the great optimism that businessmen had from their success at lumbering, and from the early interest in sport hunting and fishing. The hotel burned in 1906.

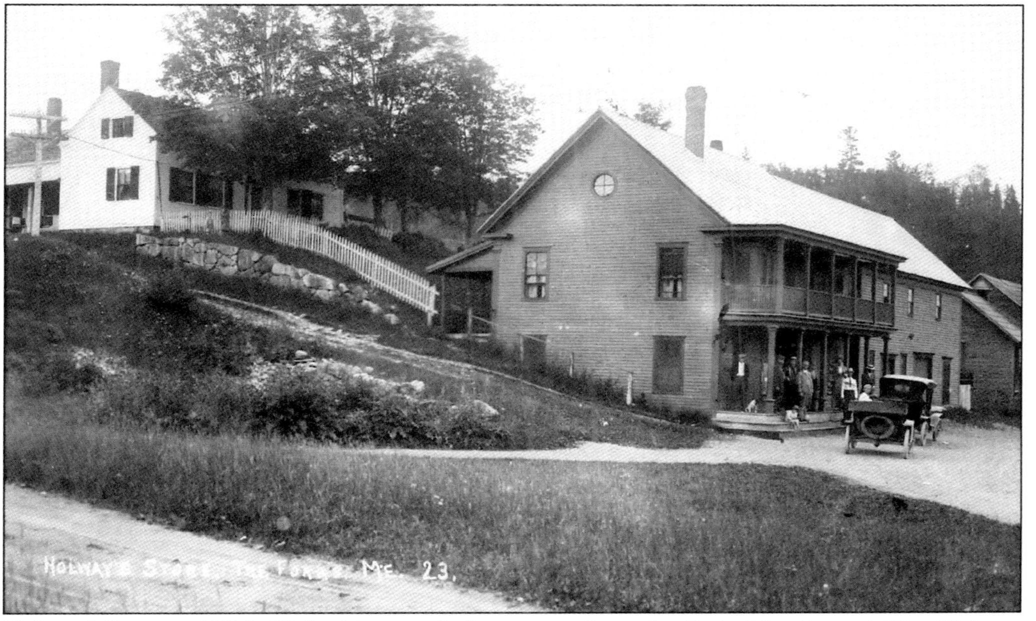

Holway's Store, *c.* 1915–20, looking south from near where the Forks Hotel stood. The Holway family ran this store from the turn of the century to about 1940. The house behind the store, currently the oldest home still standing in The Forks, was built *c.* 1840 by Charles Foster. It is now the home of Crabapple Acres Whitewater.

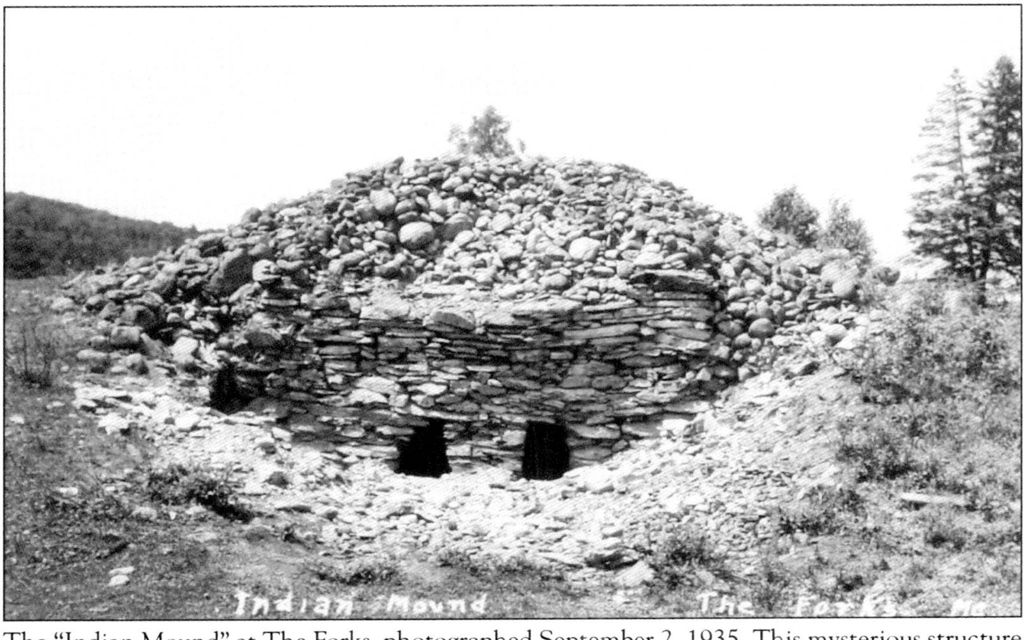

The "Indian Mound" at The Forks, photographed September 2, 1935. This mysterious structure is very ancient and not much understood, but earlier attributions to the "red paint people" are thought to be doubtful.

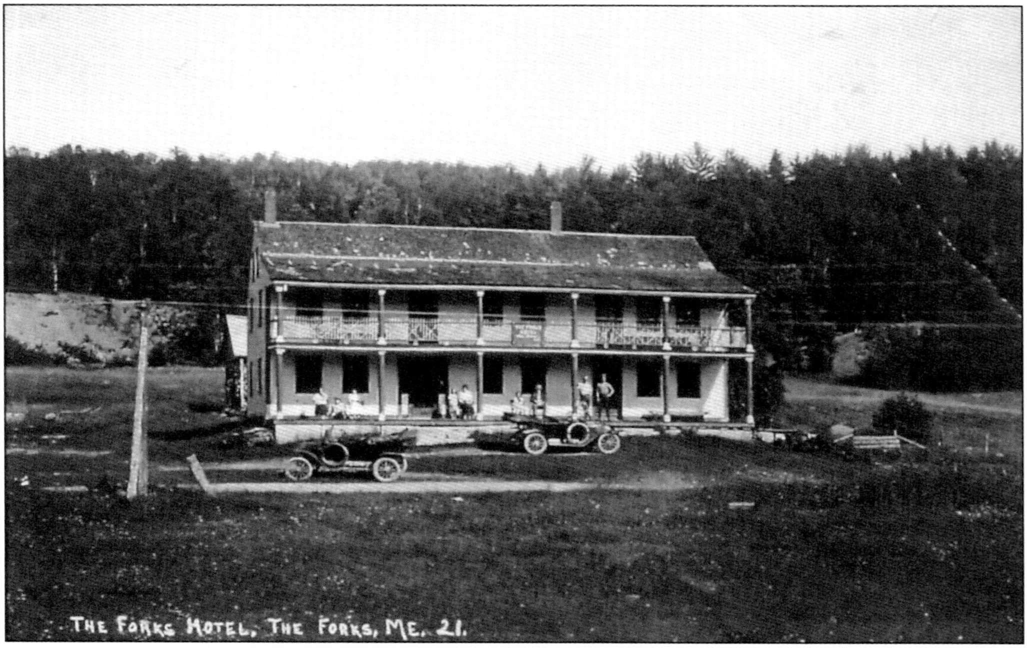

The Forks Hotel (a different hotel, farther south on the River Road), *c*. 1915. This building has been known for a long time now as Marshall Hotel.

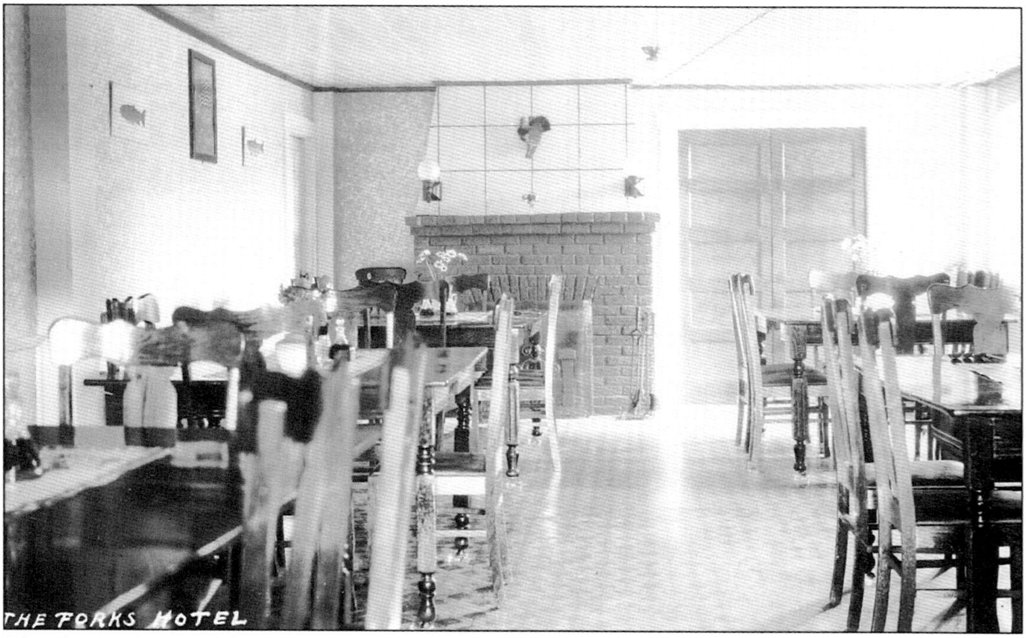

The dining room of the Forks Hotel (now Marshall Hotel), *c*. 1930. The simple decor (two fish and a picture of the flag on the left wall, vases of local wildflowers on the tables) is typical of places catering to local people and sport fishermen. Though electricity was not yet sent into the area by wire, many homes and businesses had their own generators, as was the case here.

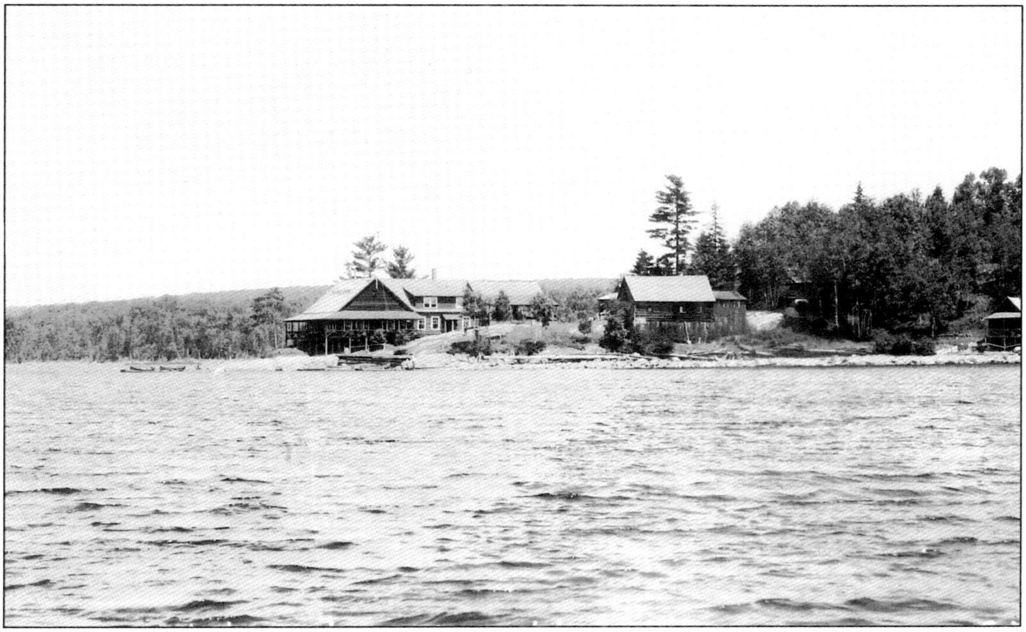

Troutdale Cabins, Lake Moxie. Located along the Somerset Railroad Mountain Division, going to Greenville, Troutdale had its own station. Originally called Mosquito in the logging days, the names of the camps and the station were changed later to appeal more to "sports."

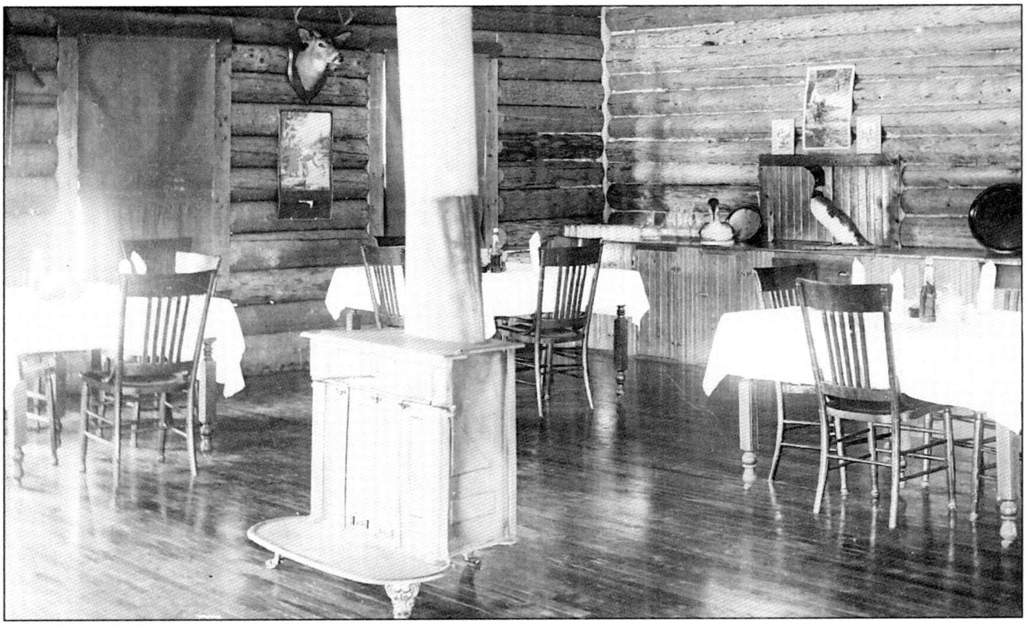

The dining room, Troutdale Cabins. The appealingly simple decor of these rooms and the interiors of many of the individual cabins were a cultivated "rustic" look, often popularized from writings about lumbering, sport fishing, and hunting. After lumbering operations were conducted in a remote area, the lumber camps often became locations for sporting camps.

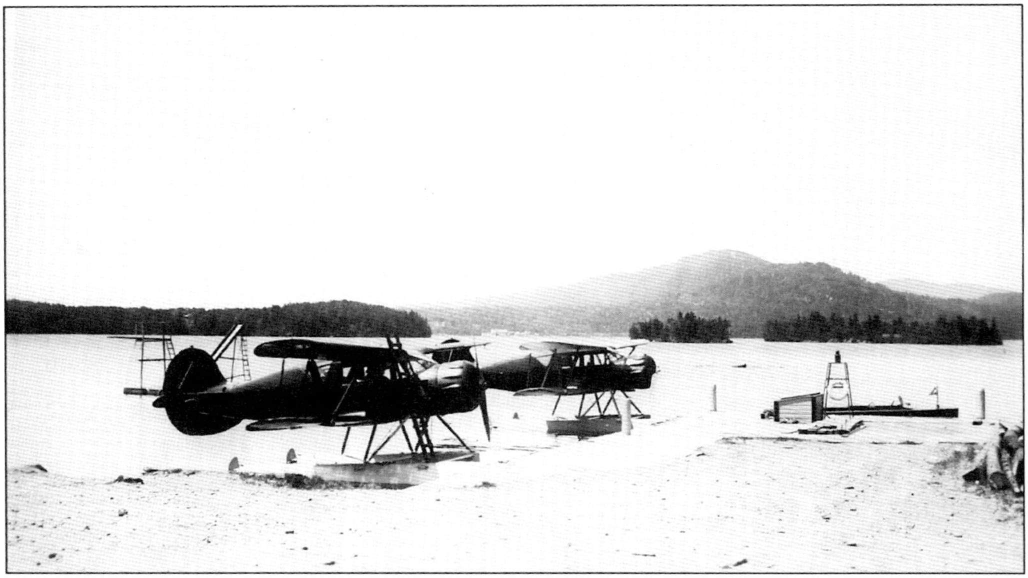

Biplanes on floats at Lake Moxie, late 1930s. Float planes were becoming a popular mode of transport for the more affluent sportsmen, since they made access to remote lakes relatively easy.

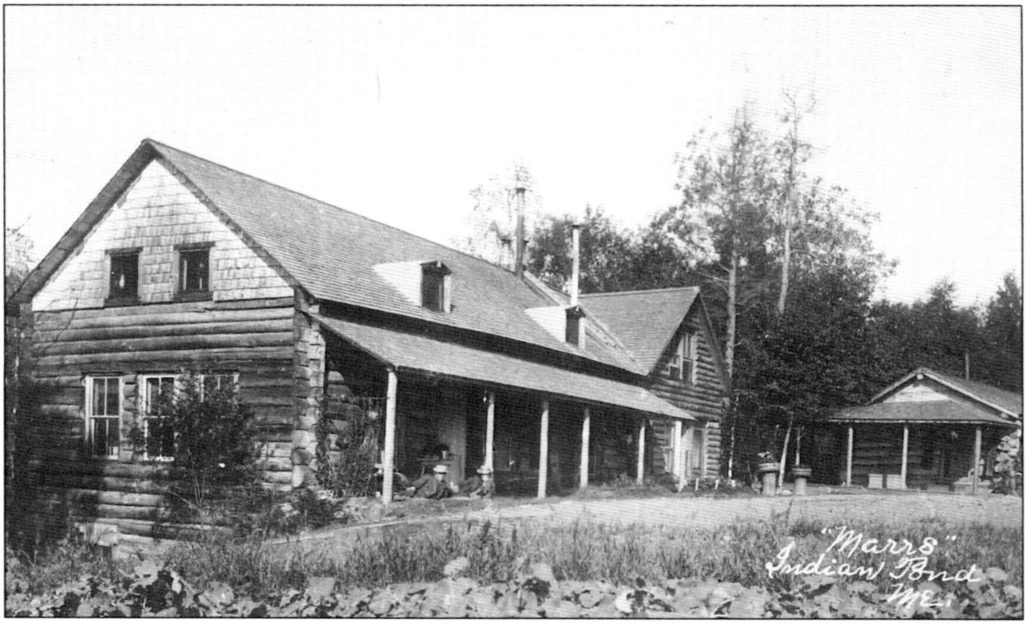

Marr's Camps, Indian Pond, *c.* 1910–20. In 1905, M.J. "Mike" Marr had ten cabins at Indian Pond, two at Indian Stream, and one at Chase Stream. During the heyday of these camps, the railroad fare from Portland to The Forks, round-trip, was $10. The excursion rate in 1889 from Boston to The Forks was $13. At that time, travelers went by stagecoach from Skowhegan north.

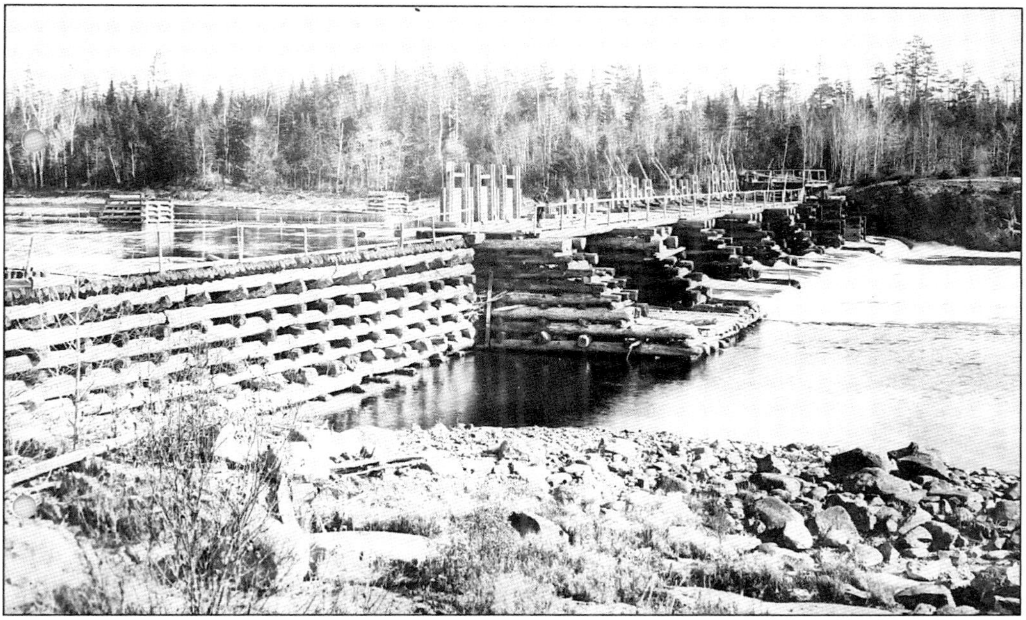

The old dam at Indian Pond, *c.* 1910-20. Because Indian Pond had little current, large crews were needed to raft logs across the pond. This type of dam was replaced by Central Maine Power's Harris Station hydroelectric dam, which was built *c.* 1952–55.

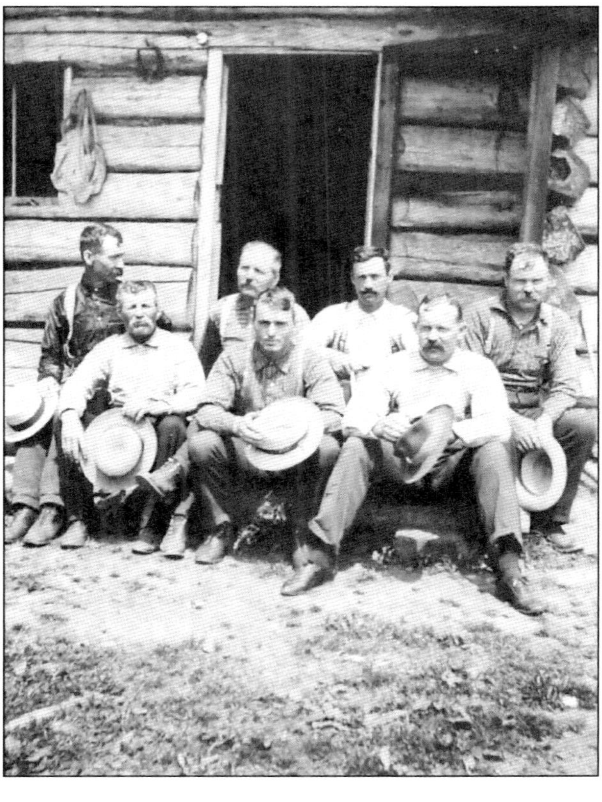

The guides at Marr's Camps, July 1900. From left to right are Will Forsythe, Joe Richards, Bub Durgin, Will Durgin, Billie McKay, Charles Hunnewell, and Walter Durgin. Guiding "sports," though not often a full-time livelihood, was an important source of income for many local families.

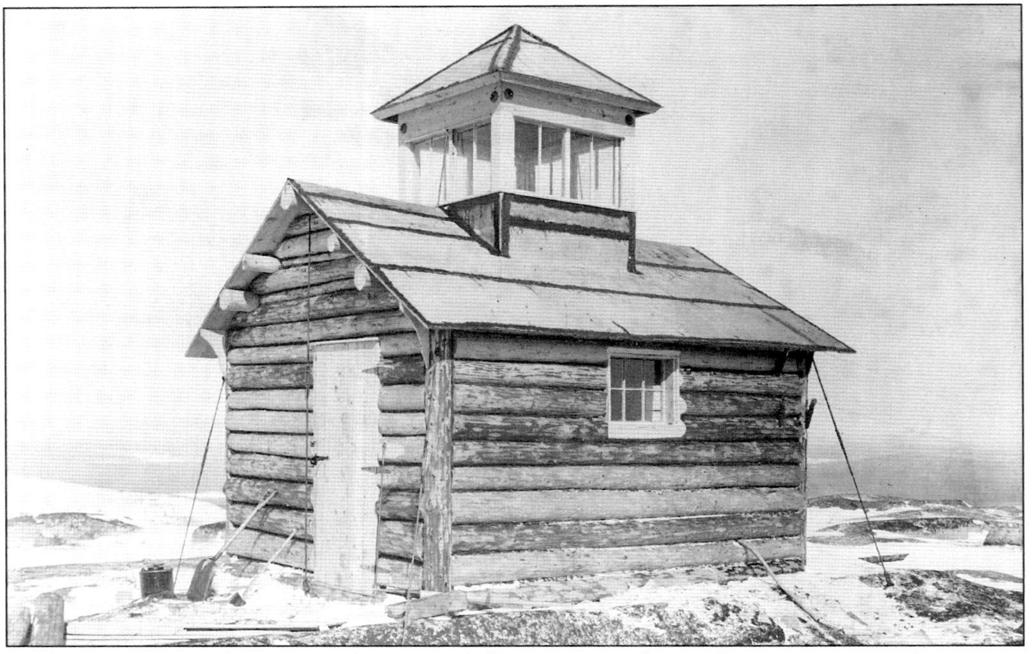

Bald Mountain Lookout near the turn of the century. This early mountaintop observation building was part of the fire lookout network for the North Woods. Even though made of logs, it still has to be cabled to the rock. The wires at the back of the building are for the telephone line.

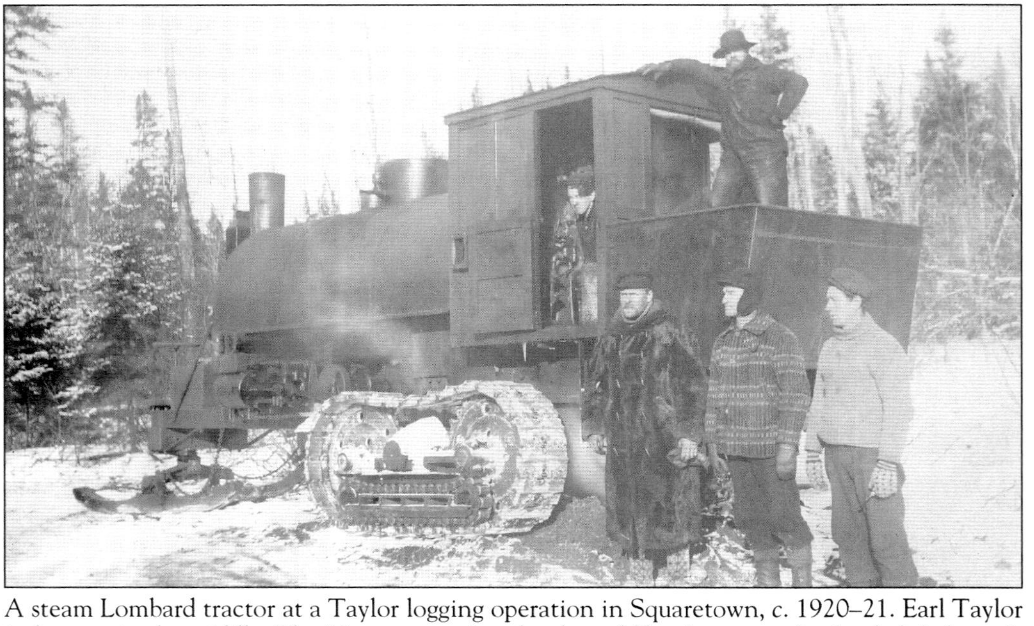

A steam Lombard tractor at a Taylor logging operation in Squaretown, c. 1920–21. Earl Taylor is the man in the middle. The 20-ton steam Lombards could haul up to twelve loaded sleds, each containing 6,000 board feet. Gasoline Lombards could haul only five sleds. Alvin Lombard of Waterville is credited with inventing the lag tractor tread that led to the development of the World War I military tank.

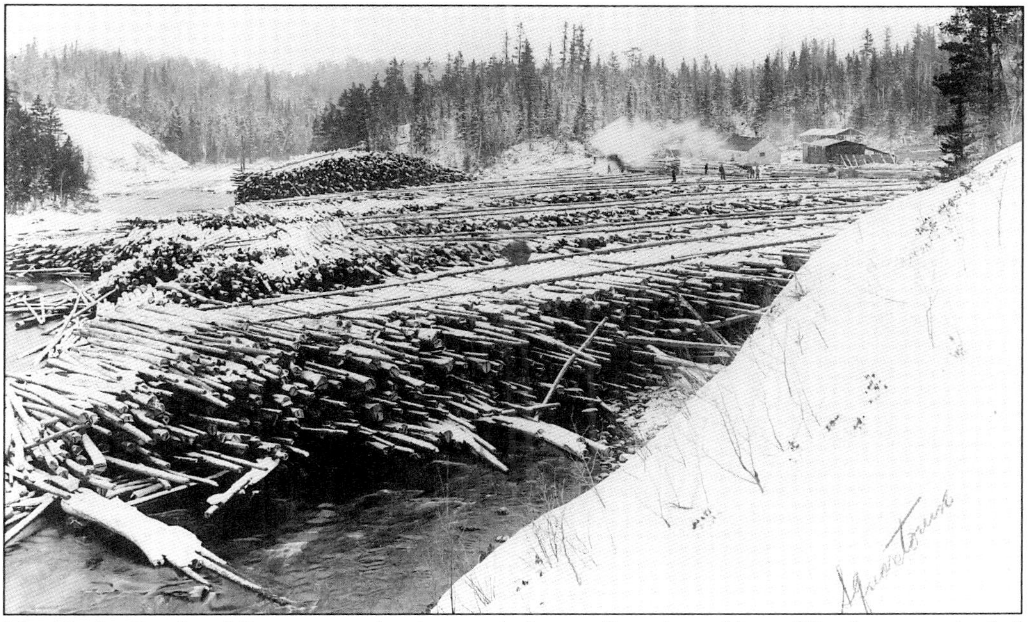

The Taylor Brothers' Squaretown landing with four million feet of logs. Wood was stockpiled through the winter for transport on the spring freshet. Then the very hazardous job of driving the logs down the river began. Maine author Holman Day made much use of the colorful lore of logging in his books and poetry, and loved the local names like Misery Gore, Jerusalem, and Enchanted Townships. A gore is a small piece of land that is a surveyor's adjustment between townships. Most of the filming of Day's *Rider of the King Log* was done in Deadwater and on Lake Moxie .

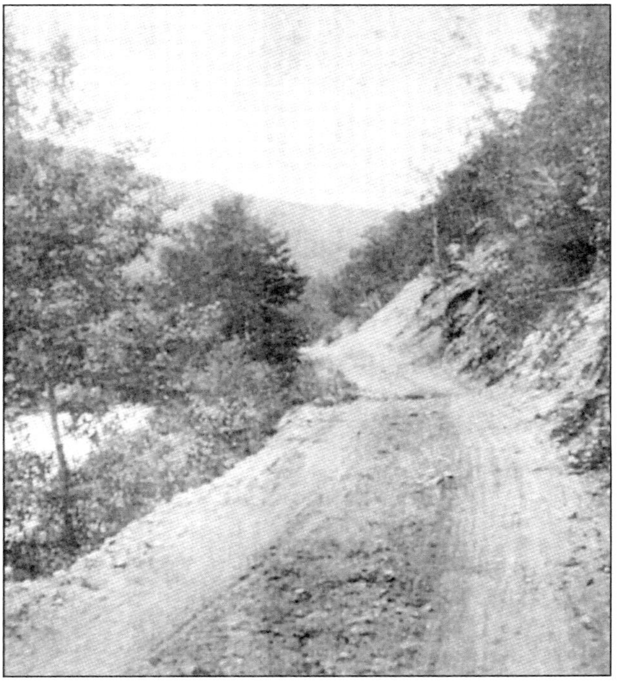

An early stereo photograph of one of the "dugways" on the road north toward The Forks. The roads along the Kennebec were steep, treacherous, and often washed out by floods. A "dugway" was a section of road where the steep river bank had to be dug into to allow passage of the road.

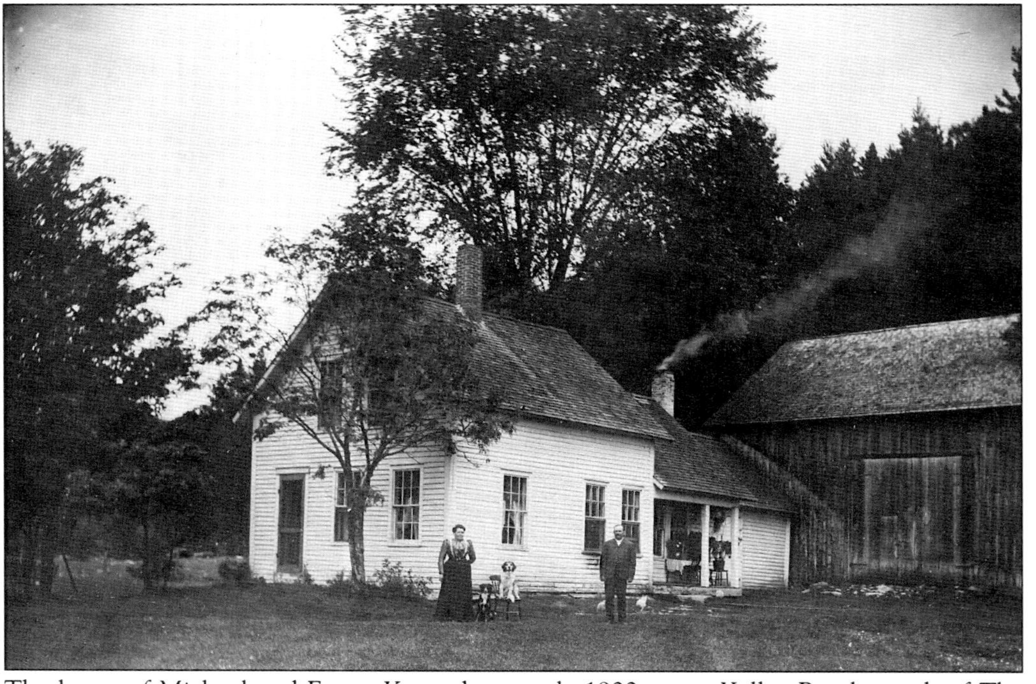

The home of Michael and Fanny Kennedy, *c.* early 1900s, near Kelley Brook, south of The Forks village. The building is now the headquarters of Downeast Whitewater.

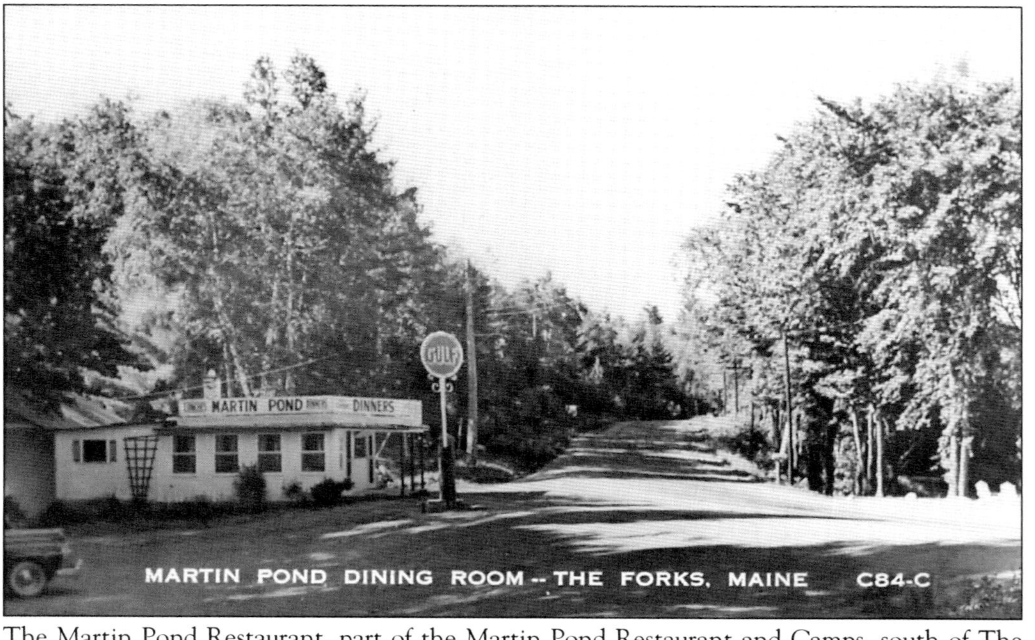

The Martin Pond Restaurant, part of the Martin Pond Restaurant and Camps, south of The Forks on Route 201, *c.* 1950s. This was originally a drive-up food stand owned by Frank and Rose Nadeau. Their daughter Clarisse and her husband, Tom Berry, ran the popular eating place for many years. The building was torn down in the 1970s, and the property is now part of Northern Outdoors rafting.

Two

Caratunk

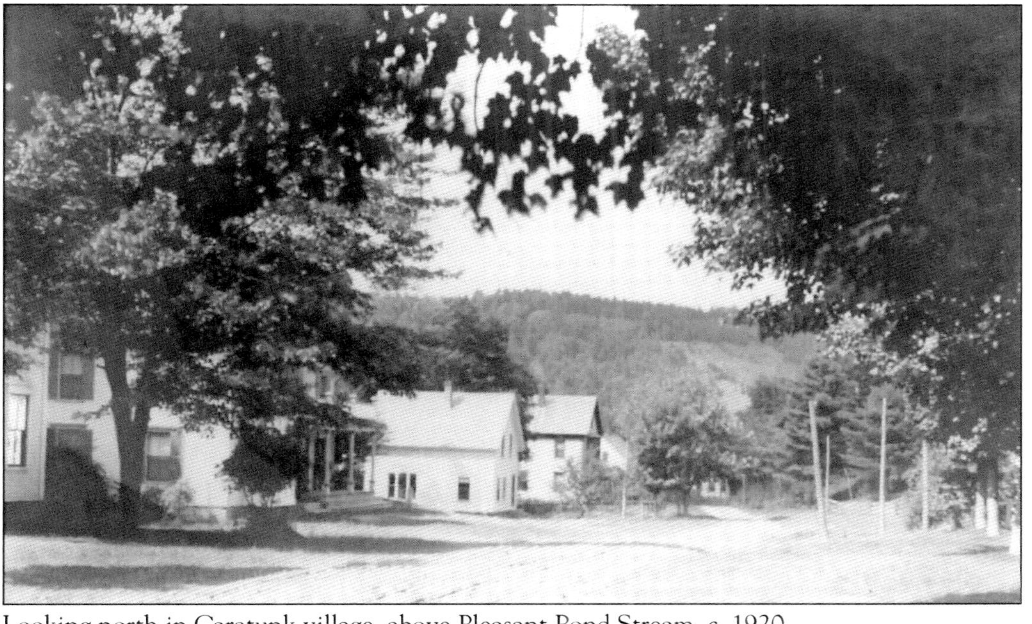

Looking north in Caratunk village, above Pleasant Pond Stream, c. 1920.

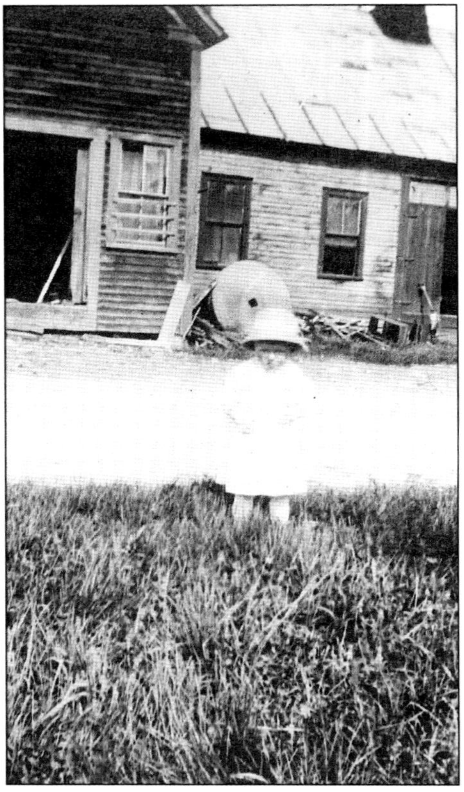

The Witham Axe Factory and Blacksmith Shop, on the east side of Main Street, just south of Pleasant Pond Stream. Ephraim Witham established the factory about 1865, and with the help of his son Gustavus, he manufactured the well-known Witham axe as well as cant dogs and other woods tools. Ephraim manufactured a boot caulk (spike) with a threaded shaft which became the popular model on the market. The factory operated until 1928. The building was torn down in 1938. This *c.* 1918–19 photograph shows the large grindstone which was shipped in by rail, found to be cracked, and never used. The child in front is Howard Mitchell, who still lives across the street.

The Caratunk Store and Post Office (and Boarding House according to the sign), Main Street, looking north, late 1890s. At this time there was also an apartment above the store, in which longtime storekeeper Albert Clark and longtime postmistress Alice Owens Clark lived following their marriage in 1903. Later they moved to the house across the street, the present home of today's storekeeper, Dan Beane. In the photograph, the man third from left is "Bub" Beane.

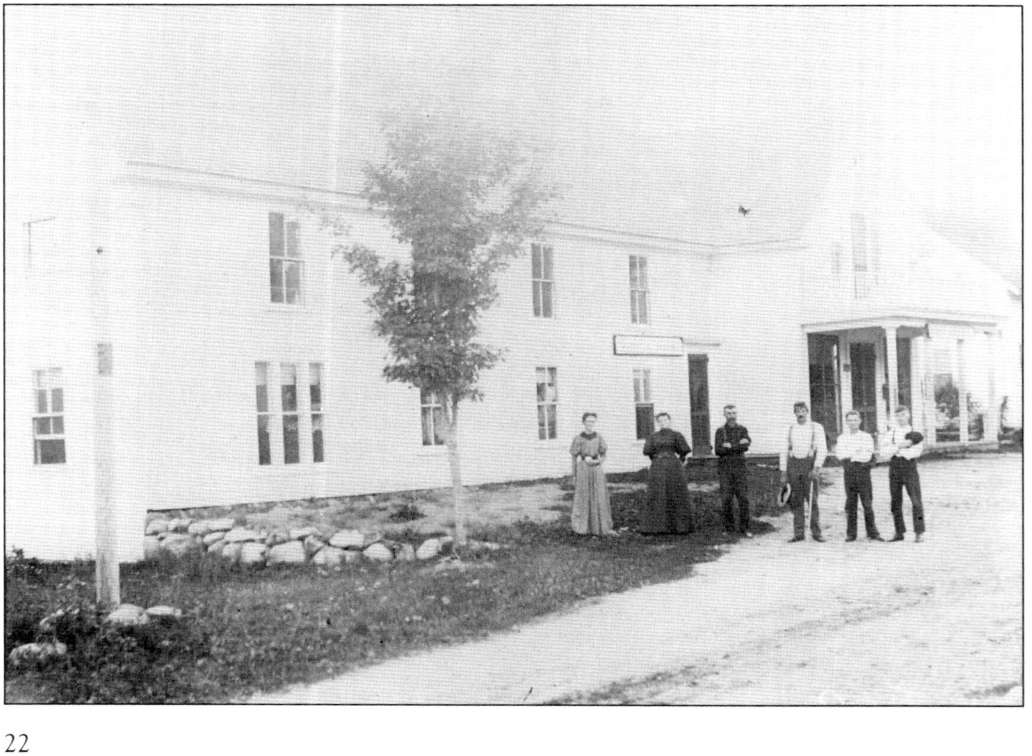

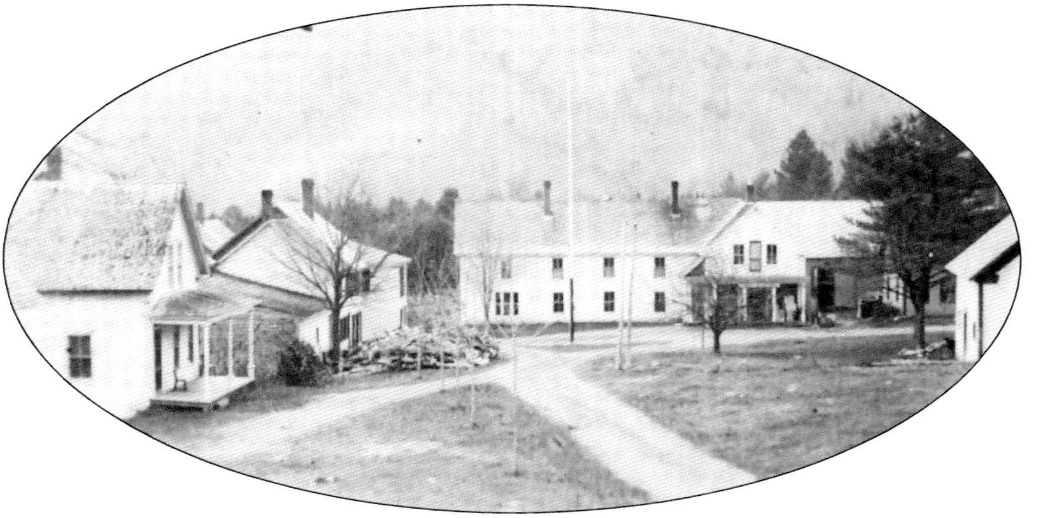

Caratunk from the Pleasant Pond road, *c.* 1905. The store and post office are in the center. A large pile of unstacked wood is beside the Shea house to the left. Much time was spent in those days putting up enough wood for the long winter. Note the large flagpole in the intersection.

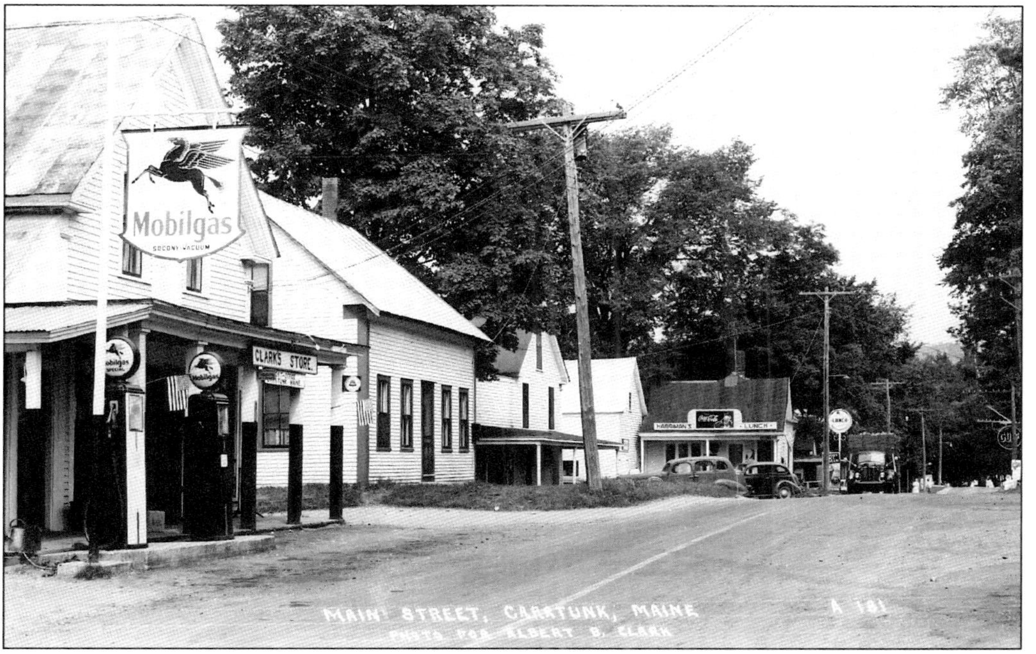

Main Street, Caratunk, looking north from the store/post office, *c.* 1948. The sign now says Clark's Store, and Harriman's Lunch is now the home of Kenneth Hanscom.

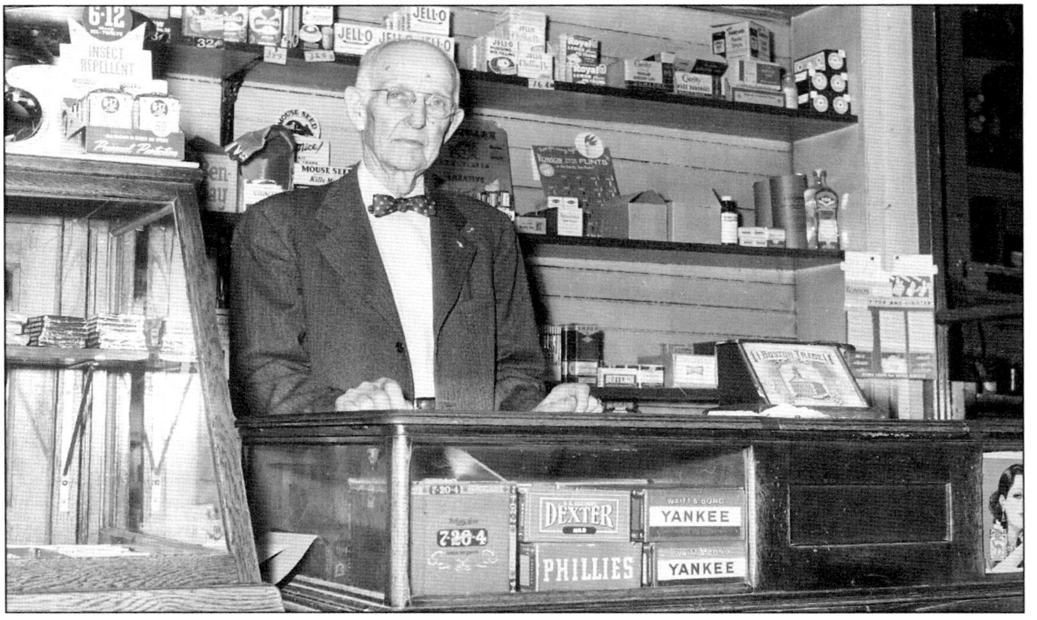

Albert Clark in his store, *c.* 1956. A familiar figure, Mr. Clark ran the store (earlier in partnership with his brother Fred) for over sixty years. He sold the business about this time to his longtime assistant, Howard Mitchell. Albert Clark was known for his ever-present Yankee cigars (boxes can be seen in the case). The slant-front object on the case is a cigar cutter.

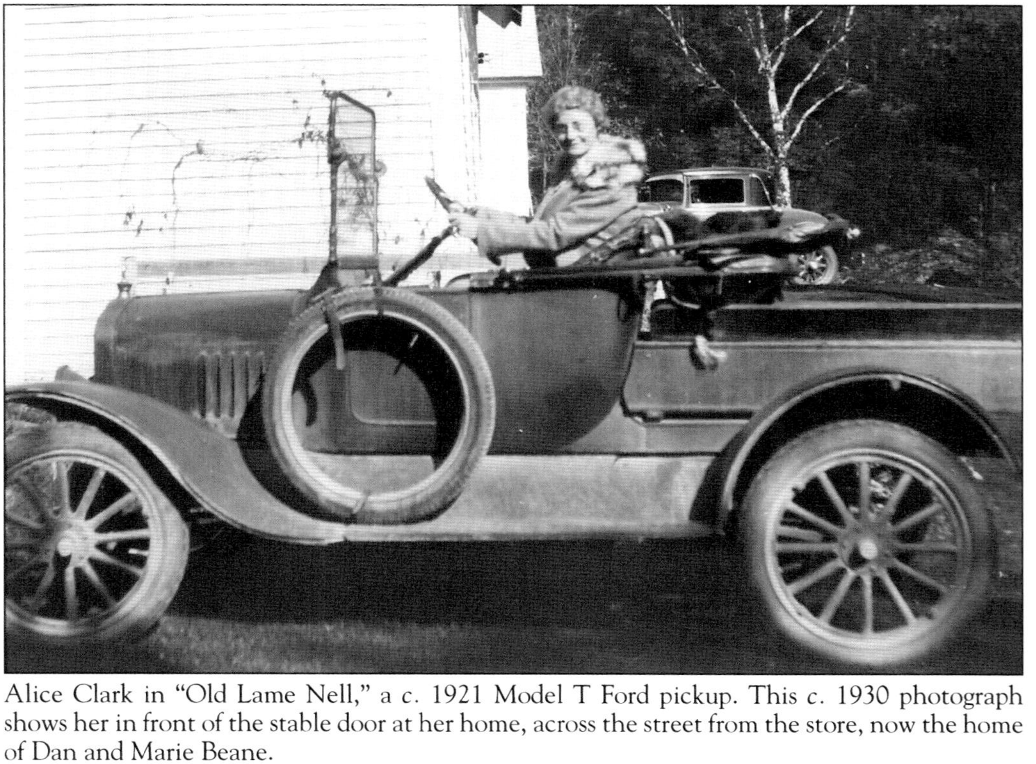

Alice Clark in "Old Lame Nell," a *c.* 1921 Model T Ford pickup. This *c.* 1930 photograph shows her in front of the stable door at her home, across the street from the store, now the home of Dan and Marie Beane.

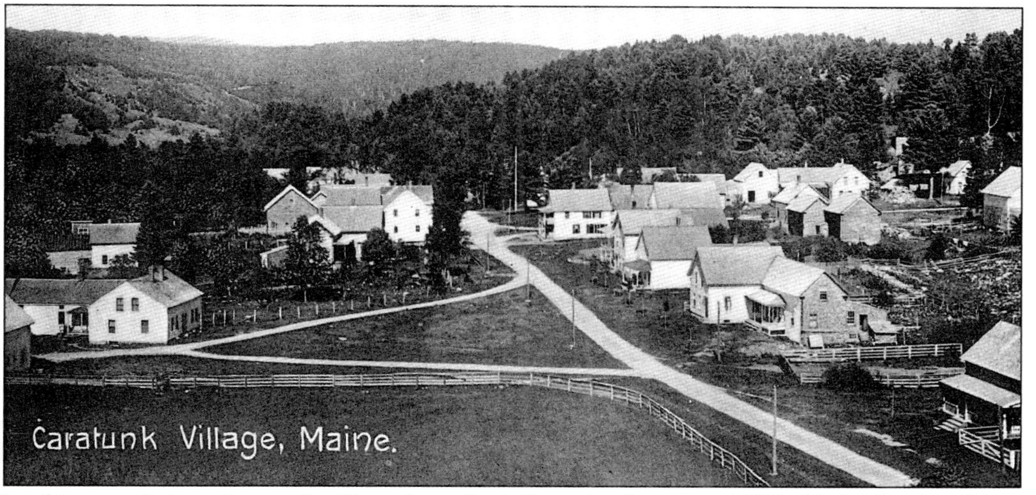

Looking north into Caratunk village from the hill south of town, *c.* 1907–1908. The Spaulding home on the left burned *c.* 1956. The store is in the center distance.

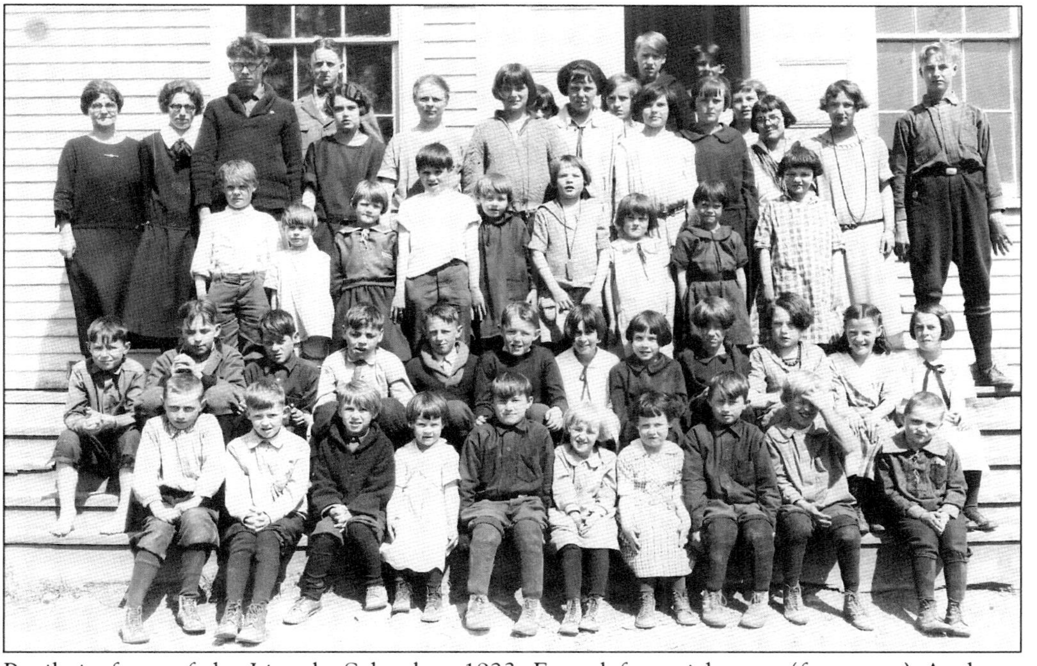

Pupils in front of the Lincoln School, *c.* 1923. From left to right are: (front row) Anthony Comber, Howard Mitchell, Carol Martin, Janet Shea, Dan Shea, Vesta Beane, Agnes Martin, Donald Shea, George Beane, and Hugh Comber; (second row) Howard Spaulding, Charlie Whorff, Eddie Beane, Eldon Spaulding, Douglas Spaulding, Bill Clark, Millicent Martin, Berdena Hunnewell, Ethel Beane, Lena Beane, Irene Pooler, and Gertrude Moore; (third row) Erwin Martin, Minnie Martin, Geraldine Beane, Bernard Martin, unidentified, Gladys Beane, unidentified, Jessie Beane, and Sarah Comber; (back row) teacher Ella Bowler, unidentified, Payson Spaulding, teacher Mr. Snow, Althea Hunnewell, Esther York, Dorothy Beane, Anna Pooler (Berry), Lena Beane, and Wm. Beane (back row) Howard York, Elva Beane, Alta Moore, Mildred Sterling (Smith), Muriel Spaulding, and Clyde Spaulding.

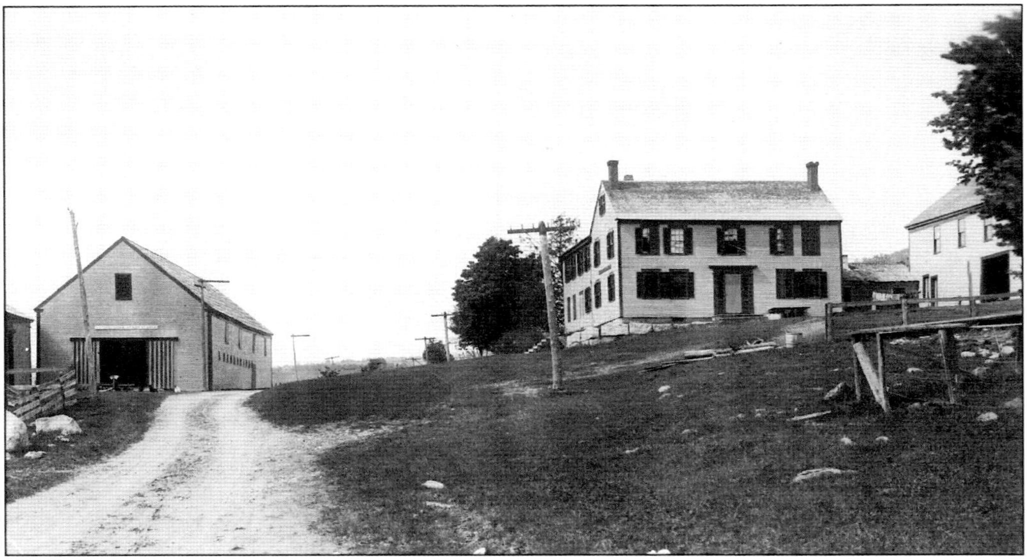

Hotel Sterling, *c.* 1912–13, located south of Caratunk village on Route 201. Built *c.* 1816 by Joseph Spaulding, this building was used as a hotel very early in its history. There is some dispute as to whether this hotel, or the former Bingham Stage House, was built earlier. The hotel has been owned by the Clark, Webster, and Sterling families through most of its life. Even into recent days, it had windowless rooms for children (to protect them from the "poisonous night air"). It was sold to Matt Polstein in 1988, and is the oldest building currently standing in Caratunk.

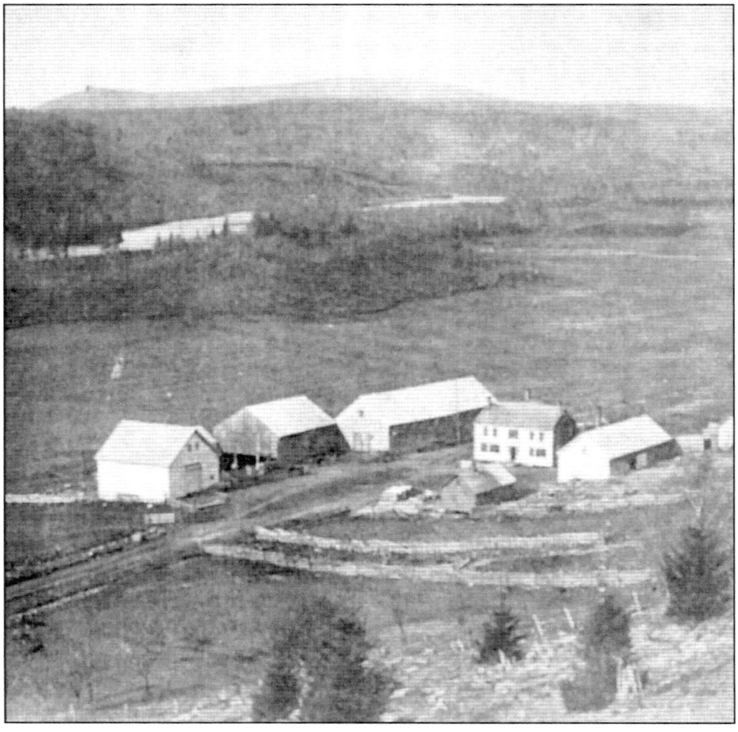

An early view of the Sterling Hotel (then Clark's Hotel), *c.* 1875. This stereo photograph shows the large amount of cleared land around the site. From here, Joseph Clark Jr. left to build the Forks Hotel. At this time Omar Clark, son of Joseph, and his family, including son Albert, were living here.

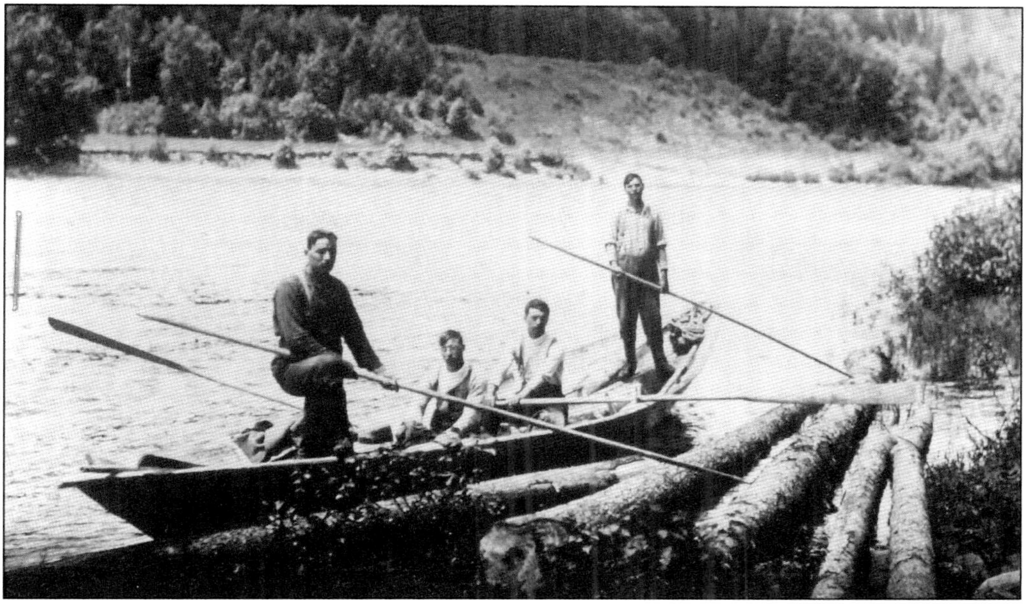

Kennebec river drivers at Caratunk, *c.* 1890. They hold their pick poles in the traditional double-ended bateau. The Kennebec Log Driving Company was started in 1834, and in 1835 was granted a charter by the legislature giving it ". . . the right to drive all logs and other timber belonging to said company or any members thereof that may be in the Kennebec River for that purpose, below The Forks to such places of destination as may be designated . . . such places not to be below the town of Gardiner." They continued to do so until the drive was discontinued in 1976. Shown in the bateau are Mark Merrill, Jock Martin, John Kennedy, and Dave Pooler.

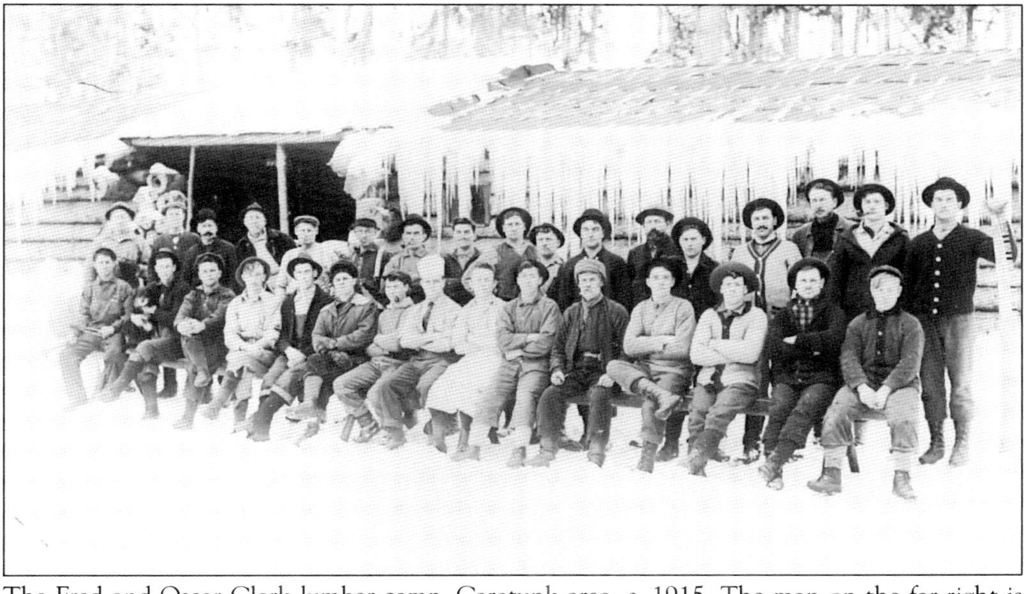

The Fred and Oscar Clark lumber camp, Caratunk area, *c.* 1915. The man on the far right is holding a two-man crosscut saw, a forerunner of today's chainsaw but more labor intensive. Dick Paige is in the front row in the apron; in the back row on the far left are Charles Mitchell and Fred Clark.

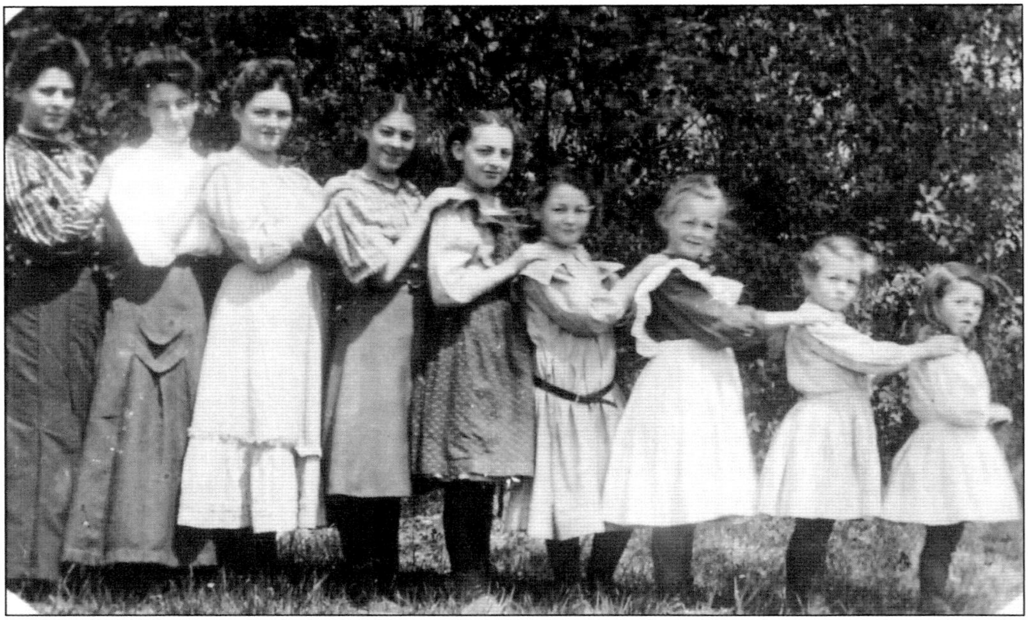

The daughters of Frank and Esther Sterling, photographed in Caratunk, c. 1906–1908. There were sixteen children in the family, eleven of which were girls (including one who died young). From left to right are Kathleen, Frances, Bessie, Marion, Gladys, Esther, Helen, Alice, and Marjorie (Imogene, the youngest daughter, is not shown).

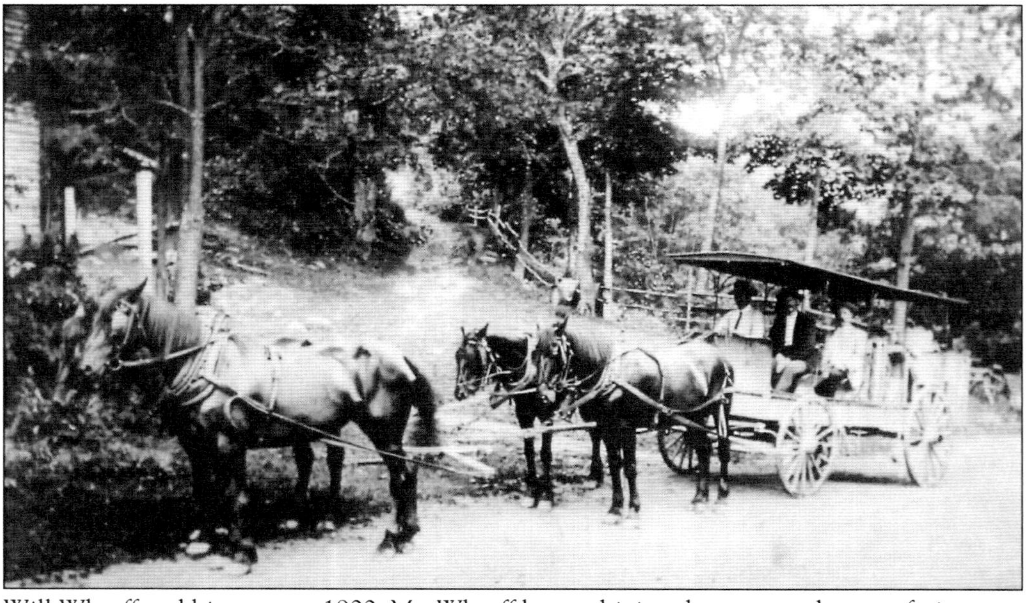

Will Whorff and his stage, c. 1900. Mr. Whorff began driving the stage at the age of nineteen, c. 1893, and retired in 1943. There were usually two changes of horses on his route from The Forks to Bingham: one at the Sterling Hotel, the other at the George Gordon place in Moscow. Mr. Whorff himself owned twenty-five horses, most stagers weighing 1100–1200 pounds. The horses were replaced by a Buick truck in 1912. Photos from the 1930s show a canopied Brockway truck.

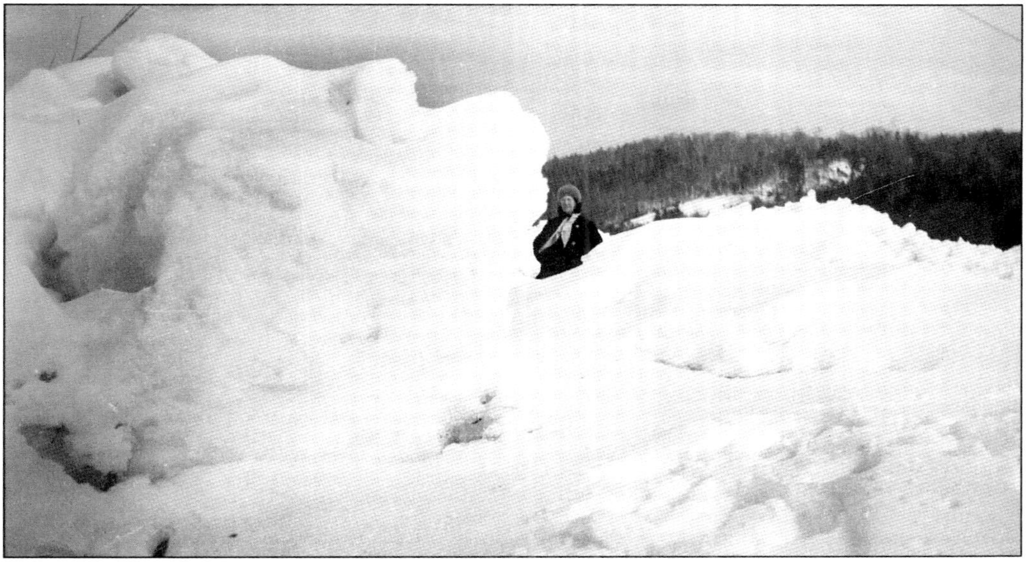

Longtime local photographer and reporter, Eva Bachelder, on a jam of ice, *c*. February 1932. Ice jams, even without logs, were a problem when Route 201 ran close to the river. This jam near Caratunk consisted of nearly 50 million pounds of ice, nearly a mile long and 5 to 12 feet high.

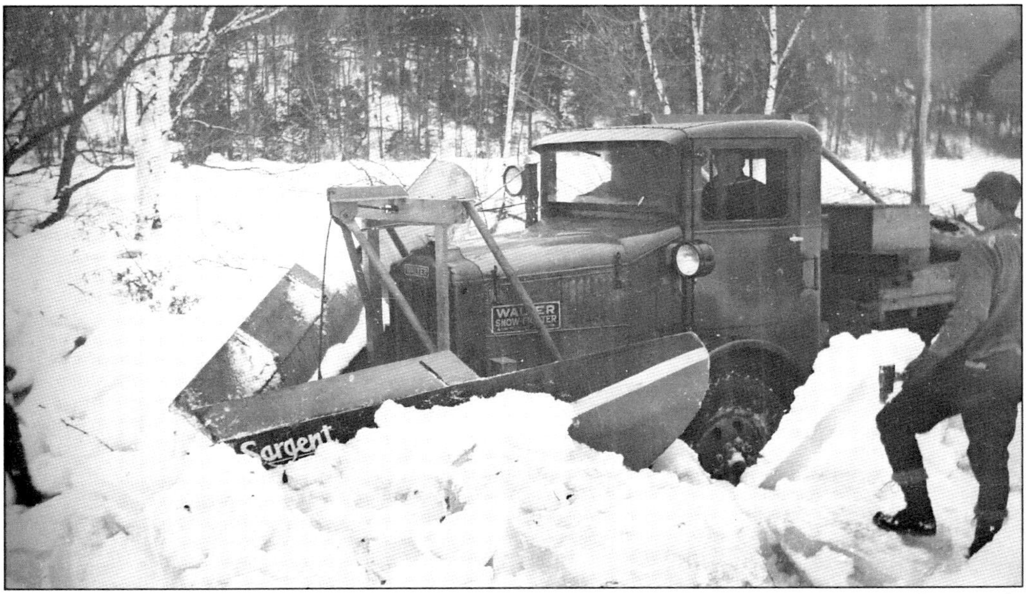

A new Walter chain-drive truck, with a Sargent V-plow. Expectations were that this truck, owned by Hill and Taylor of Bingham, might be able to plow away enough of the ice to allow steam shovels to get at the rest. In the truck are driver Leo Hill and John Hunnewell. Howard Spaulding is the man with the axe. Dynamite was used to crack up the thickest layers, and after five days of continuous bucking and plowing, the job was done entirely by the rugged truck, much to the amazement of members of the highway department. Mr. Hill, who had bucked the jam days and done his town plowing at night (it had continued to snow), was eventually able to get some sleep. The Walter truck is still in usable condition and has been owned for many years by William Lancaster of Embden.

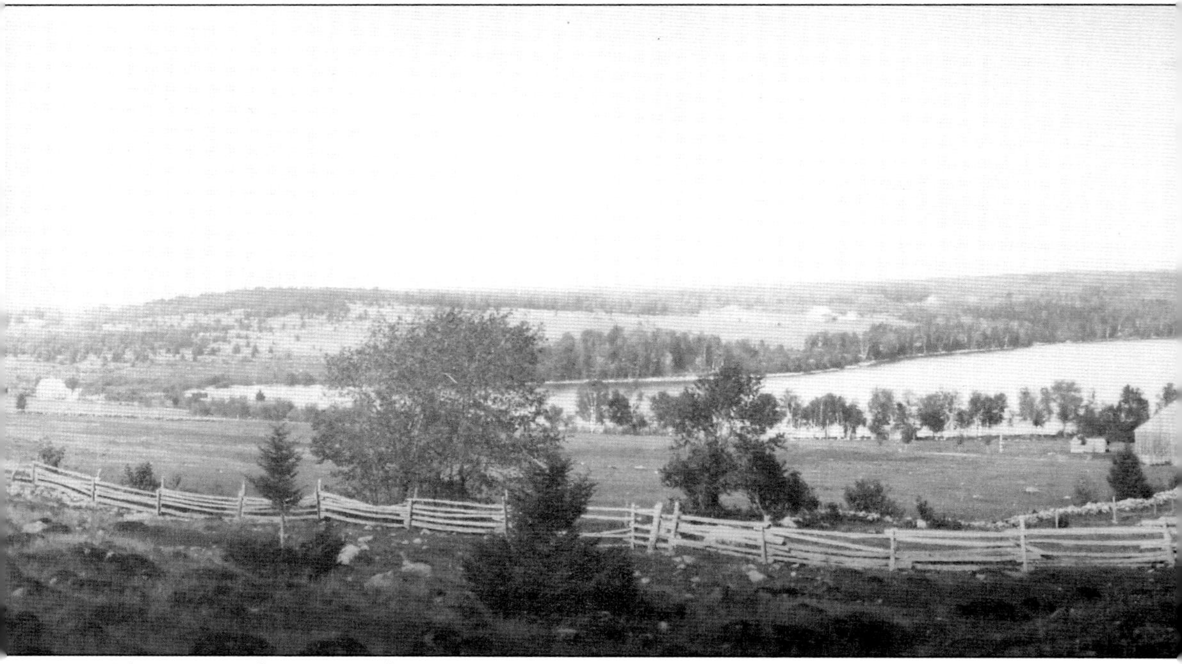

Pleasant Pond, *c.* 1912. This panoramic view shows the Pleasant Pond Inn (center, with barns) from the back side. Also visible is the section of shoreline known as "The Grove" (to the right

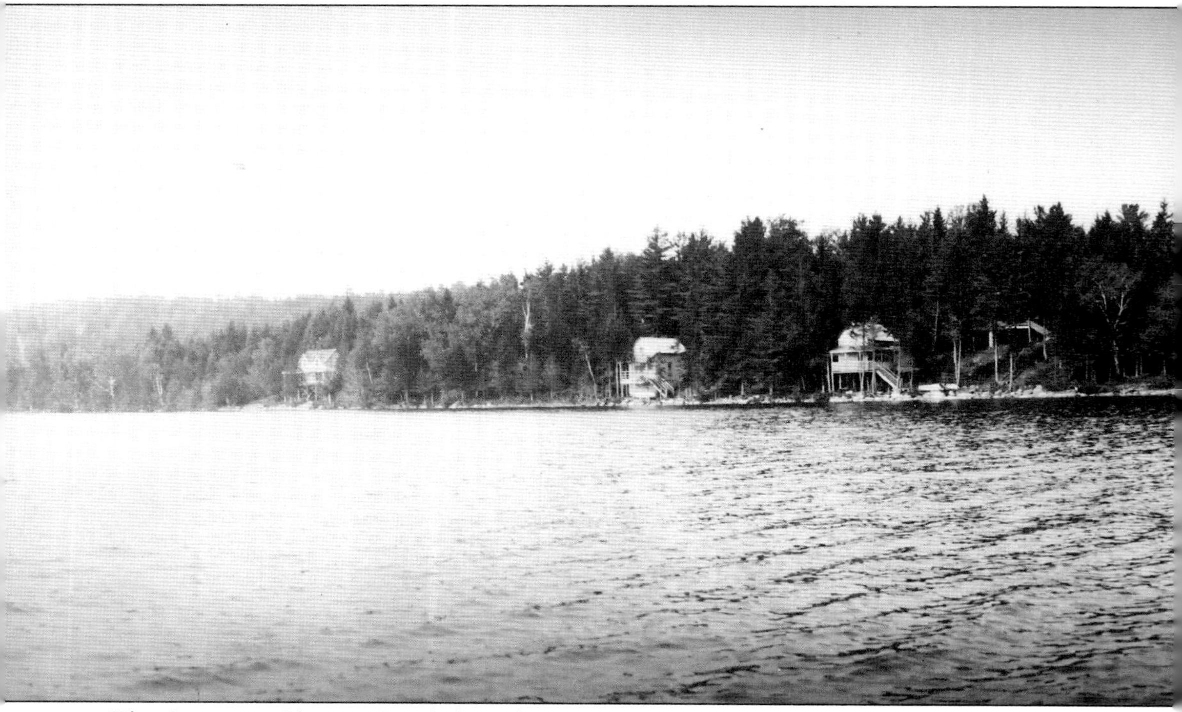

The Grove, on Pleasant Pond, from the water, *c.* 1912. This area was one of the first built up, and many of these cottages still exist today. This strip of shoreline offered a large public space,

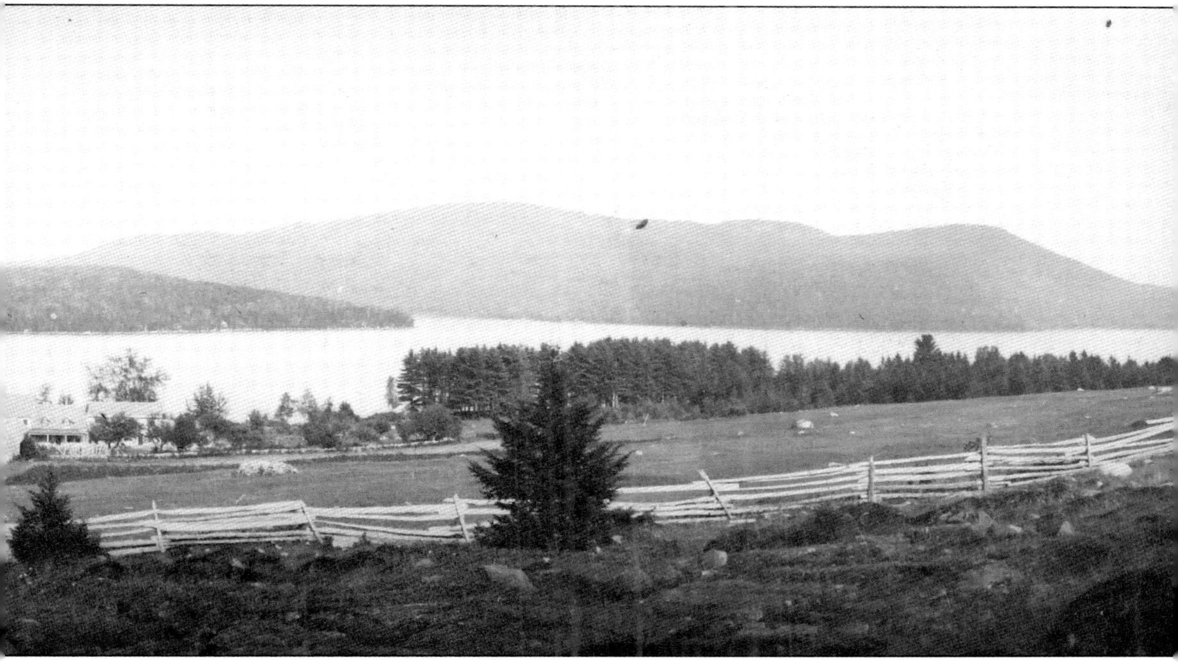

with the tall pines), and the farm owned by Fred and Maud Clark (upper center, slightly to the left). A few cottages had been built by this time, but much of the shore remained undeveloped.

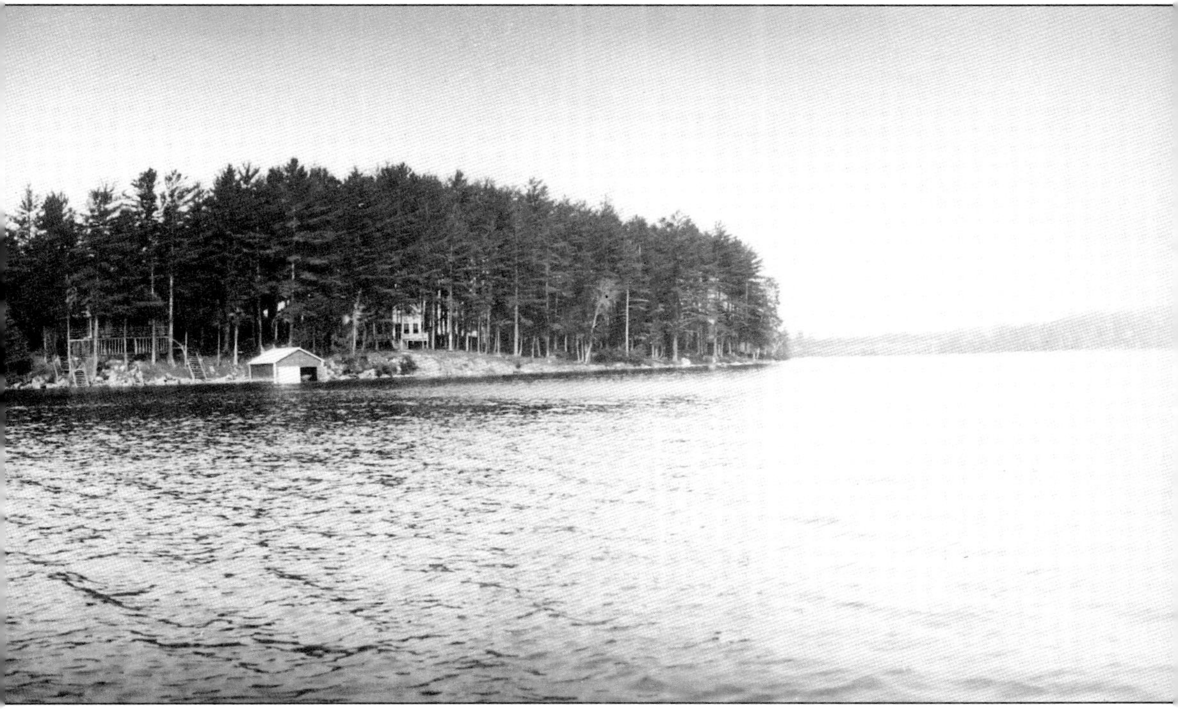

near the camps of the Bushey and Williams families, which was often used for dances, picnics, and church services.

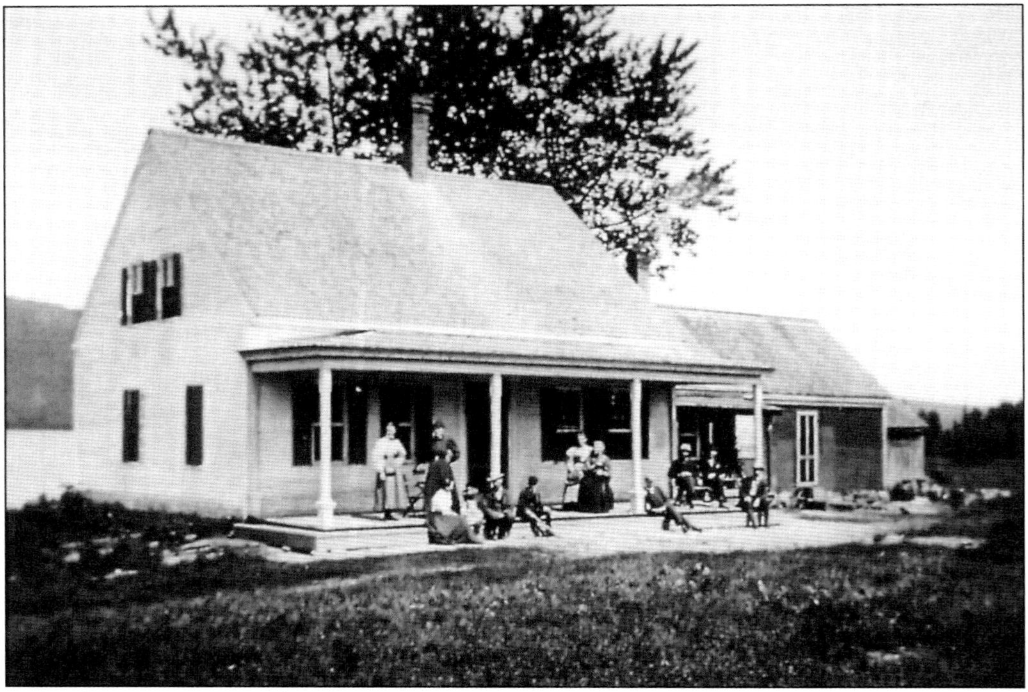

A farmhouse, c. 1890s. This farmhouse later became the Pleasant Pond Inn. The photograph shows the original building, which already appears to have guests. At the turn of the century, the inn was owned by the Martin family. At that time, it was known for its game dinners. Families would hitch up their fast teams and drive to Pleasant Pond for Sunday dinner (the Blin Page family would come from as far as Skowhegan). The inn was later sold to Aloysius J. Rogan. It closed to the public in the 1930s and the derelict building was torn down c. 1954 by its owner, Arthur Hall.

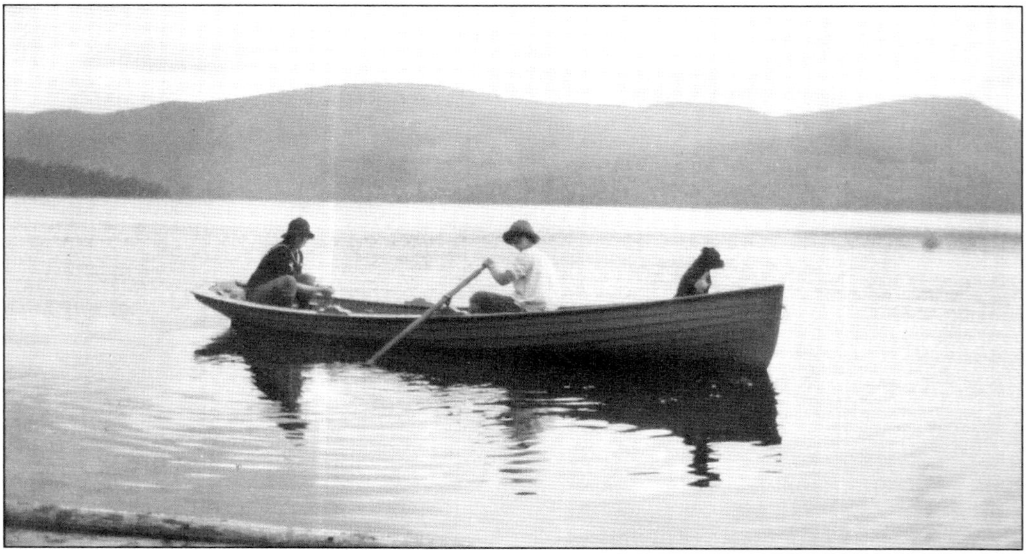

A form of transportation, c. 1920s. Locomotion on the water was largely by hand until the 1930s. Sylvia Reynolds is at the oars, with Gertrude Shoppe in back, and "Mikey" in front.

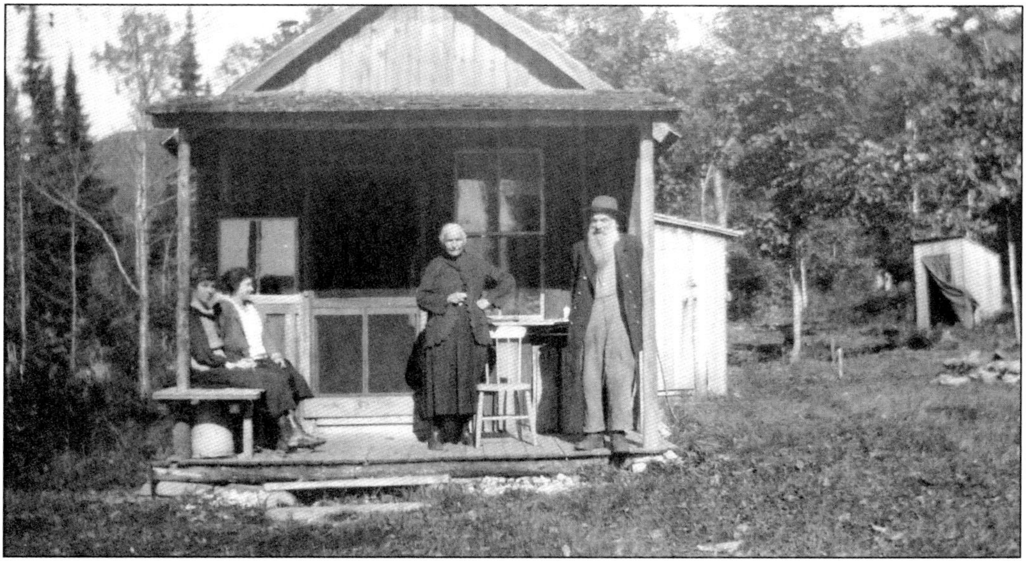

The cottage of Henry and Lisa Collins, near North Beach. This *c.* 1908–1909 view shows Mr. and Mrs. Collins on their porch with two young visitors. Photographs of this period often show two shorelines, since the dam at the outlet seems to have been in intermittent use.

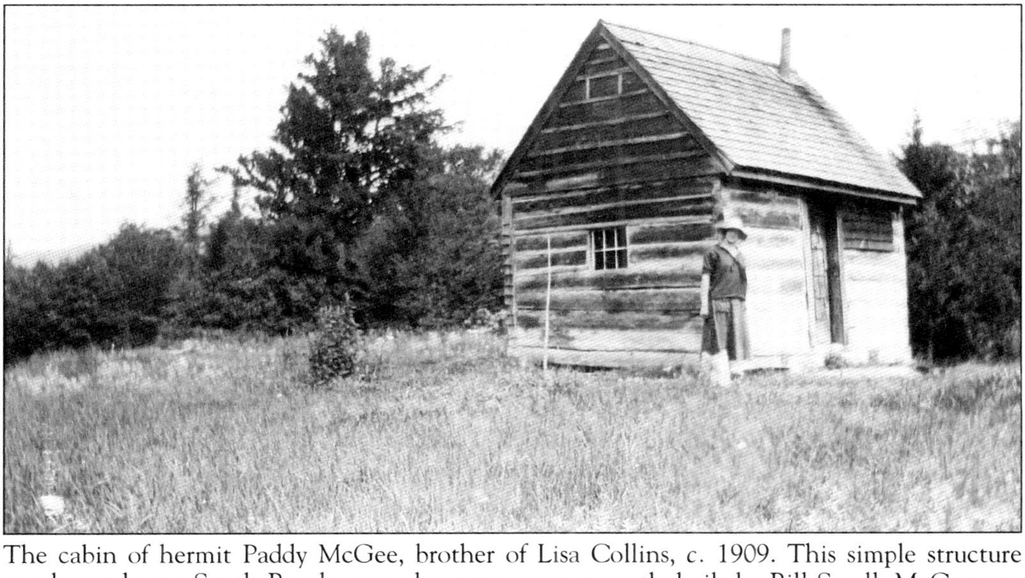

The cabin of hermit Paddy McGee, brother of Lisa Collins, *c.* 1909. This simple structure was located near South Beach, near the camp more recently built by Bill Small. McGee was apparently a fearsome eccentric. Local parents would scare their children with tales of Paddy McGee. Eventually his misanthropy advanced to the point where he would shoot at strangers, and in the 1920s he was taken to an institution. The legend on the back of this photograph reads "he had a double set of teeth which would scare anyone."

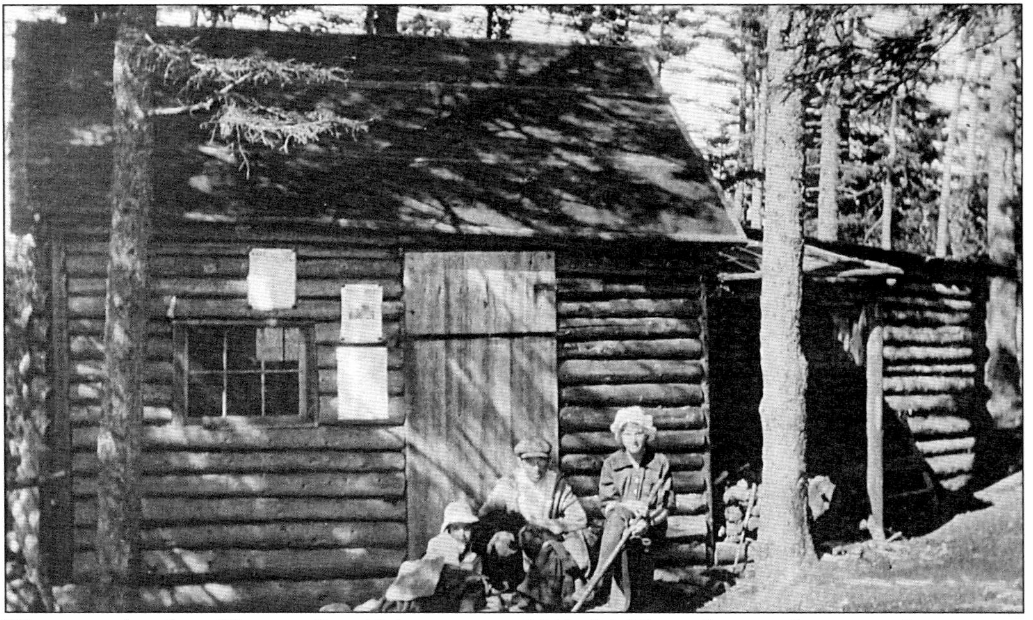

The ranger's cabin, Pleasant Pond Mountain, *c.* 1912–14. The cabin was home to whoever was manning the fire tower at the top of the mountain, and stood a bit below the summit. Remains of the cabin may be seen even now. Rachel S. Knapp is shown here on the right, Carl Purinton is the boy in the center, and the child on the left remains unidentified.

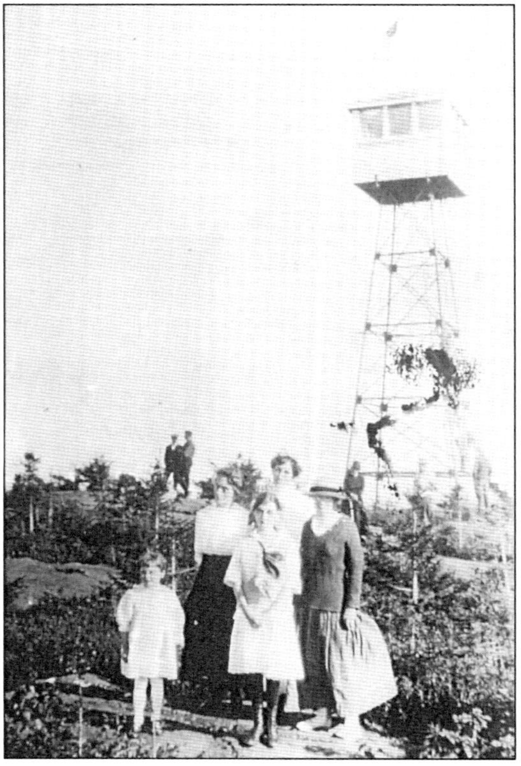

Pleasant Pond Mountain tower, *c.* 1920. The Maine Forestry Service towers were of uniform design, and varied only in the height of the steel structure. This was one of the taller ones at 35 feet. It was removed in the 1940s.

On the steps of a camp in the "Bates Colony," c. 1912. From left to right are: (bottom) Esther Knapp; (middle) Herbert Purinton, Francis Purinton, Carrie Knapp, Fred Knapp, Carl Purinton, and Arthur Purinton; (top) Carrie Purinton, Edwin Purinton, and Fred Pomeroy. These were all family members of Bates College professors.

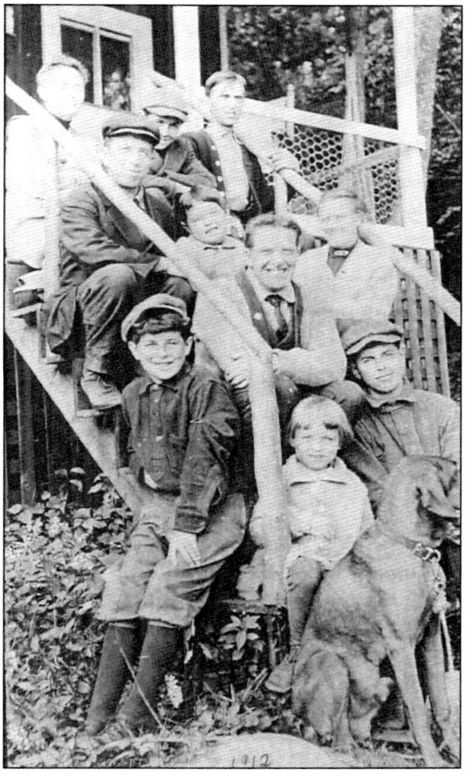

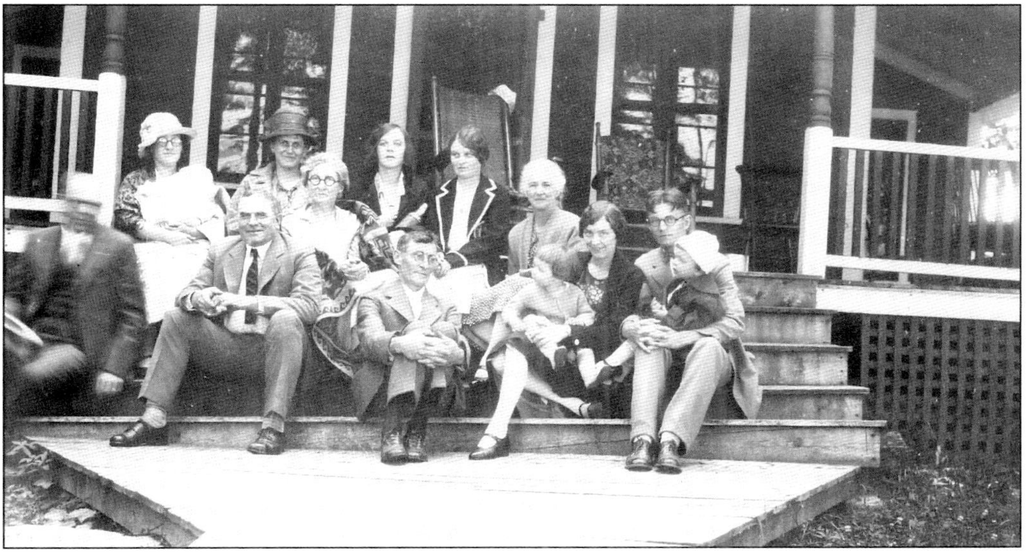

On the front steps of Alice Clark's "Seldom Inn" cottage, on the West Cove, July 1927. This group of people from the Bingham Congregational Church has just been to the annual service in the Grove, with Reverend Arthur Macdougall preaching. From left to right are: (front row) Arthur Tupper, Walter Robinson, Jack Owens, Ruby Robinson holding Jean Macdougall, and Allan Robinson holding Leah Macdougall; (back row) Leah Macdougall holding one-month-old Nellie, Nellie Robinson, Florence Owens, Alice Owens, Esther Owens, and May Tupper.

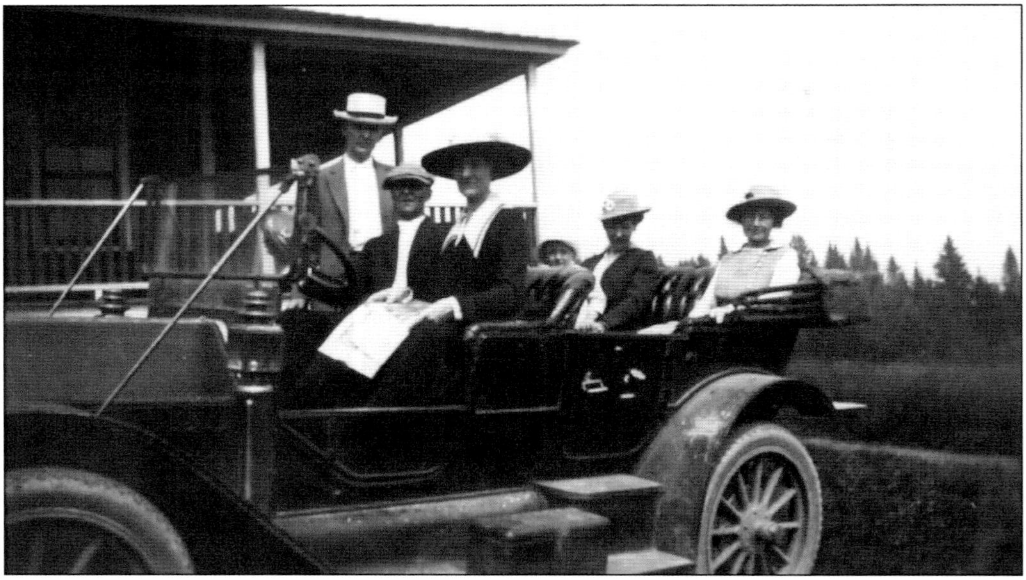

A 1911 Buick. This was the first automobile owned in Caratunk. It is shown *c.* 1915 at the Pleasant Pond farmhouse of owners Fred and Maud Clark. From left to right are: (front row) Albert Clark, Fred Clark, and Belle Clark; (back row) Albert Piper, Mary Piper, and Alice Clark. The car had a four-chime "Jericho Horn" which Fred Clark would blow, coming down the hill into Caratunk village.

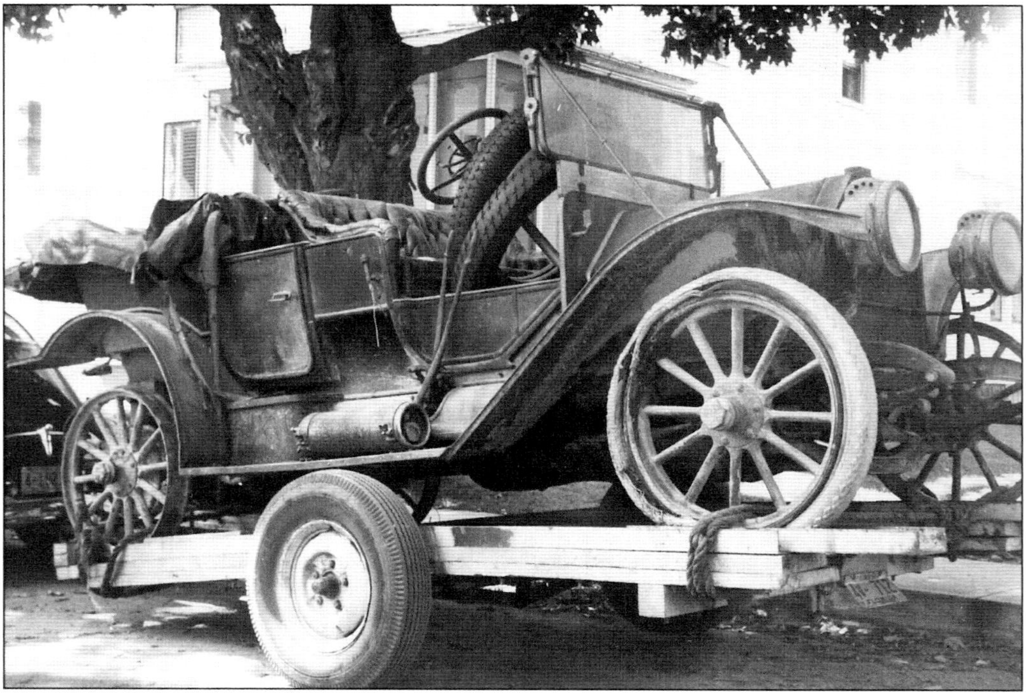

The same 1911 Buick. Long kept by Maud Clark, it was sold in the early 1950s, and is shown here on its way south, passing through Bingham. The Buick was subsequently restored by Maynard Leighton of Winthrop.

Three

Moscow and the Surrounding Area

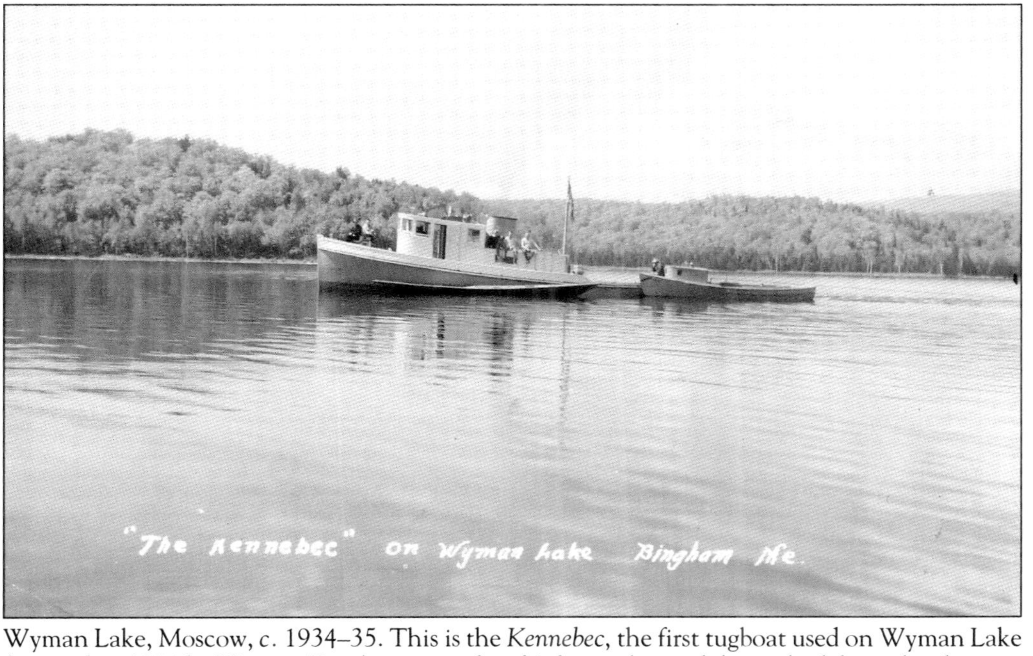

Wyman Lake, Moscow, *c.* 1934–35. This is the *Kennebec*, the first tugboat used on Wyman Lake (created in 1931 by Wyman Dam) to tow rafts of 4-foot pulpwood down the lake tothe sluice at Wyman Dam. The boat crew, from left to right, are John Hunnewell, Elon Hill, Charles Frith, and Floyd Rollins. Shown alongside is an old-style bateau and a smaller powerboat.

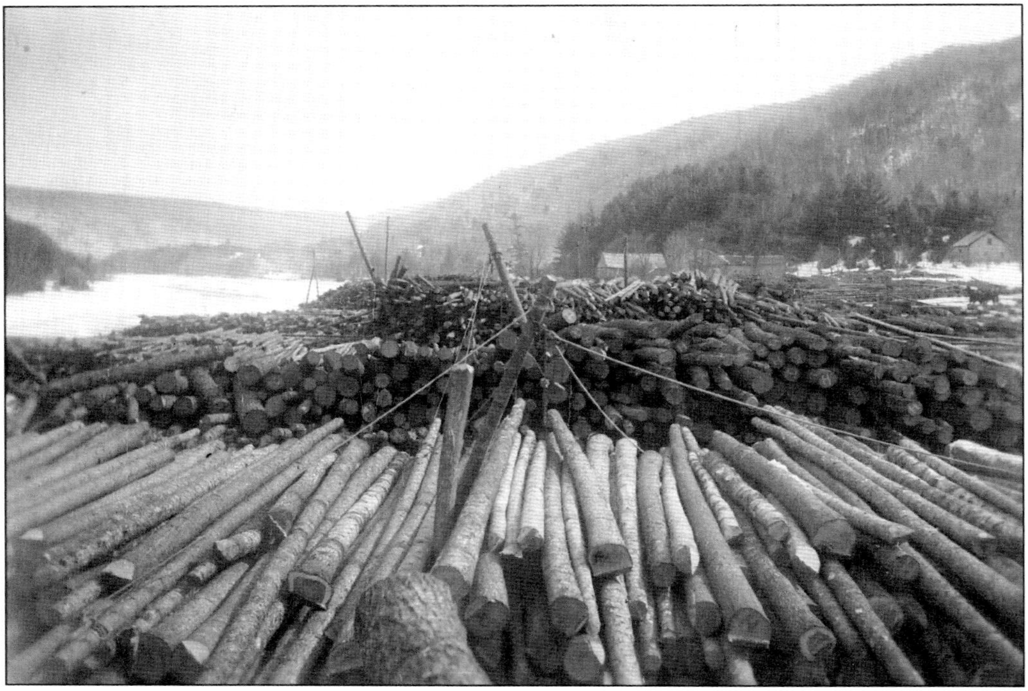

Full-length logs at Briggs' landing on the Kennebec, early 1900s. This is near the spot where Benedict Arnold's 1775 expedition to Quebec crossed the river. The house at the right was the John Williams farm. This area is now covered by Wyman Lake.

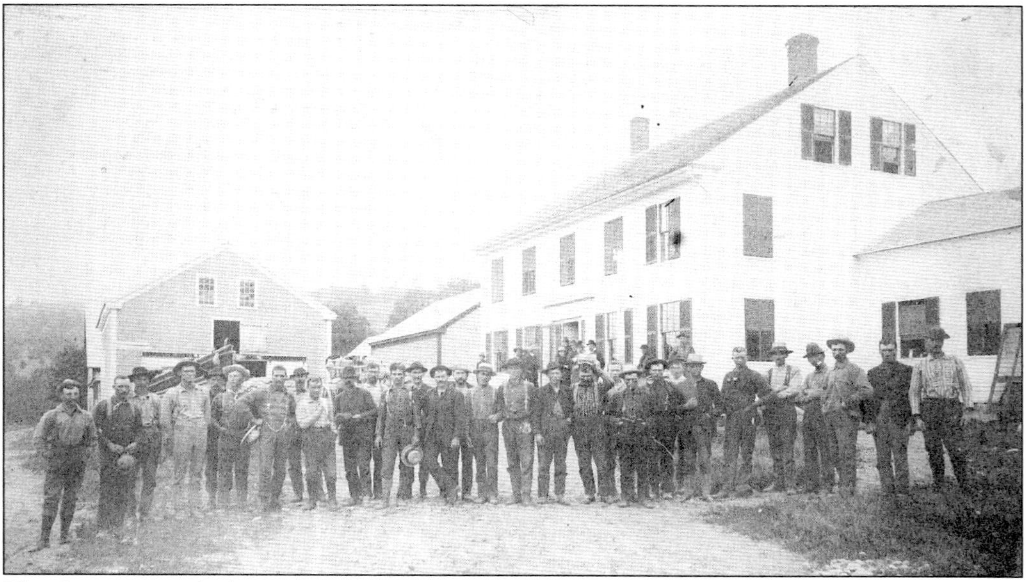

The Carney Hotel, above Carney Brook, Moscow. This building burned in 1888, but Ed Berry eventually built another hotel here. This group of river drivers, some wearing the shortened trousers typical of their trade, stayed at the hotel. Most river drivers of this era never earned more than a dollar a day.

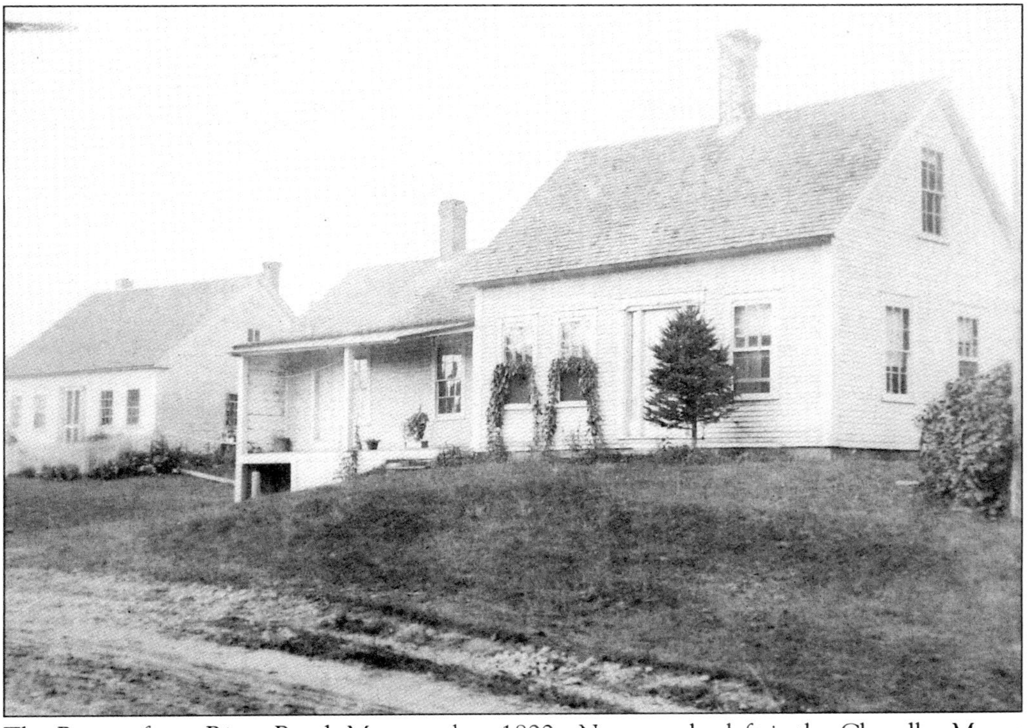

The Bassett farm, River Road, Moscow, late 1800s. Next on the left is the Chandler Moore home, later the home of Addie Moore Cates. Addie was the daughter of Chandler and Cleo Bassett Moore.

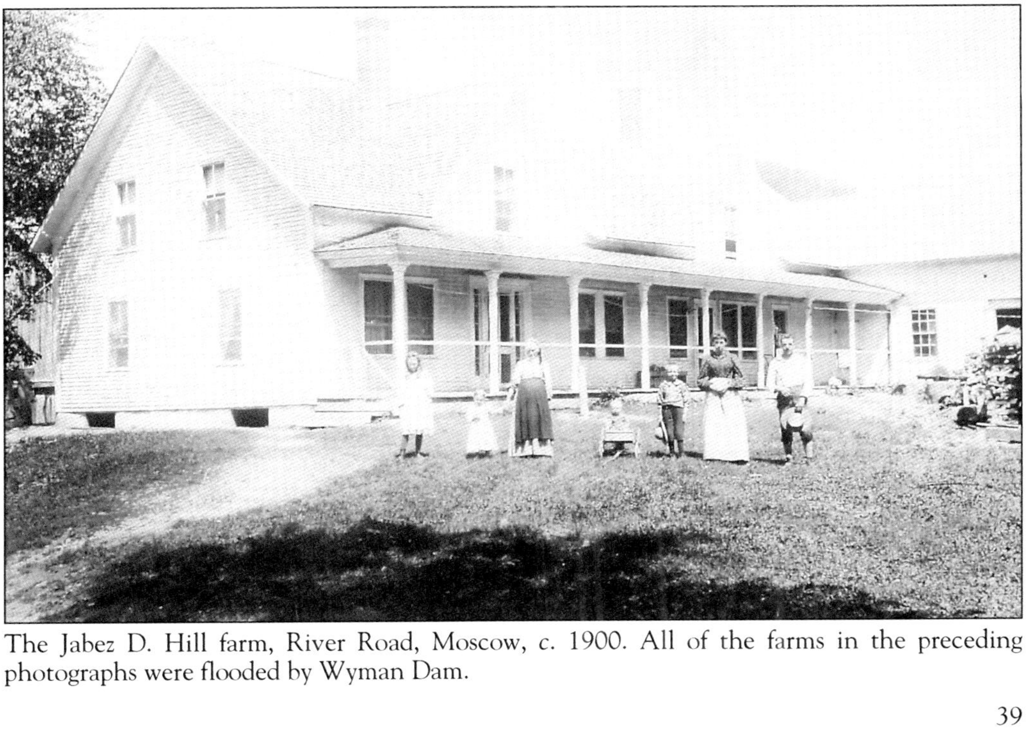

The Jabez D. Hill farm, River Road, Moscow, *c.* 1900. All of the farms in the preceding photographs were flooded by Wyman Dam.

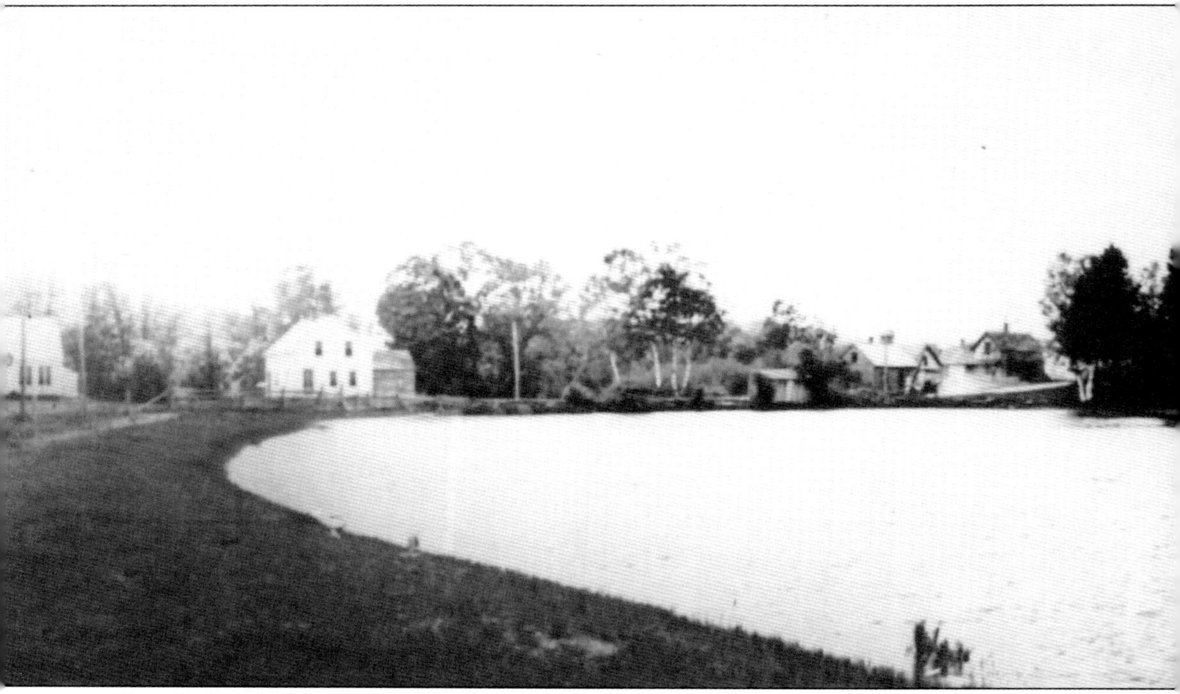

Temple Pond, Moscow, c. 1912. Located near the river, this pond was destroyed by the construction of Wyman Dam. From left to right are the Fred Temple house, the Clyde Dunton house, the "dam house" (built over the outlet), the Frank Hunnewell house, and the Charles

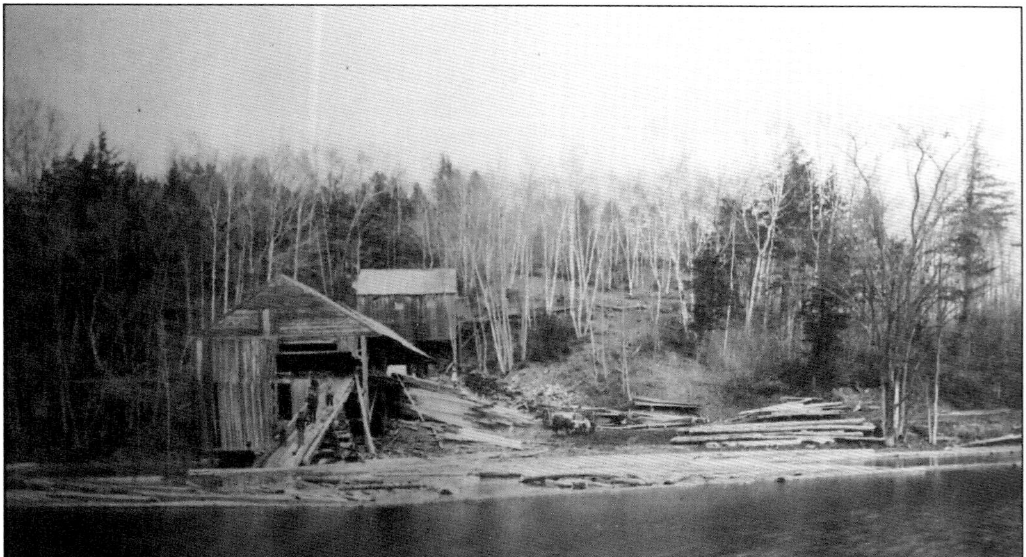

Temple Mill, Kennebec River, Moscow, c. 1890. Run by the outflow from Temple Pond (regulated at the "dam house" in the previous photograph), this sawmill was also displaced by the lake.

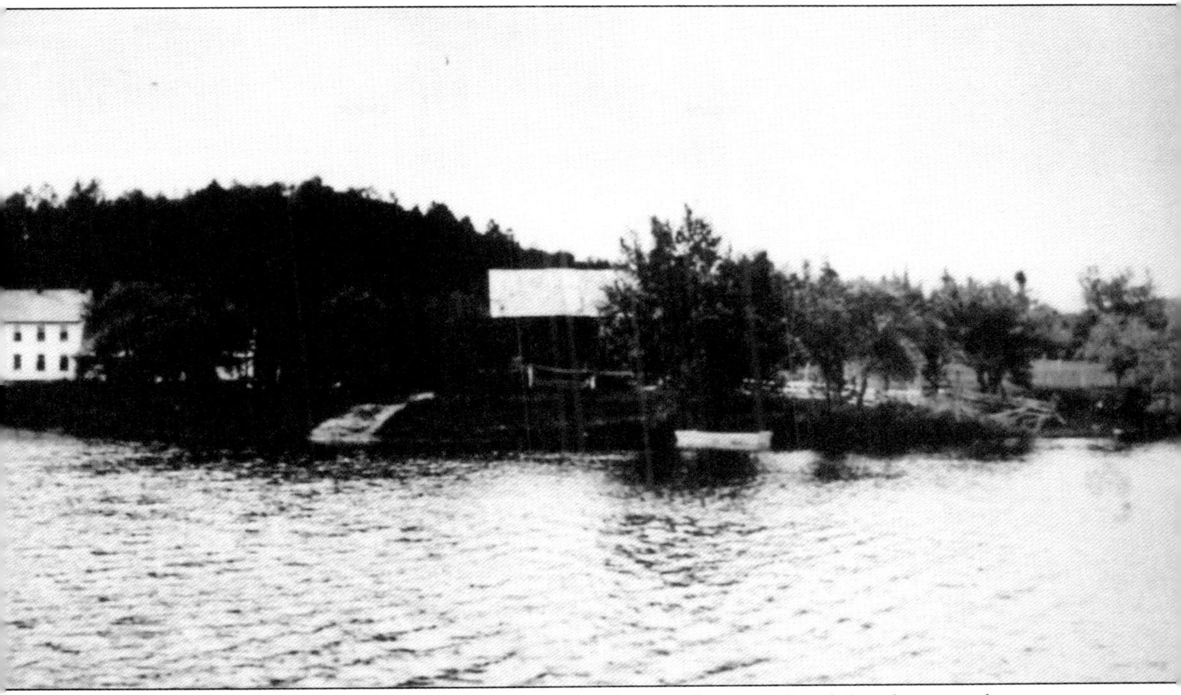

Collins farm (center). Baker Mountain is in the background. Many local families got their ice from Charles Collins, who cut it here.

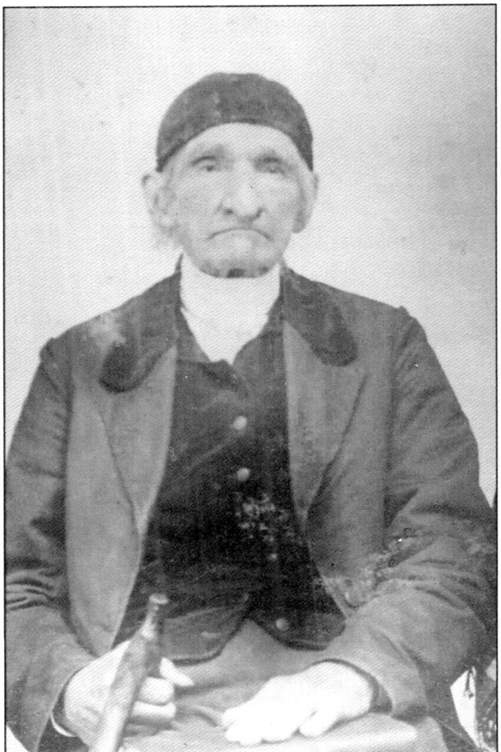

Dr. Jonah Spaulding, 1778–1871, the first physician in the area. Dr. Spaulding came to the Moscow area about 1812 and settled on a farm on the River Road. He healed several generations of local citizens, and practiced at an advanced age, as shown in this *c.* 1865–70 photograph, where he proudly holds a book (a Bible or a medical text?) and what appears to be a cane. He was known for his long black coat and broad-brimmed hat (the latter is not apparent here).

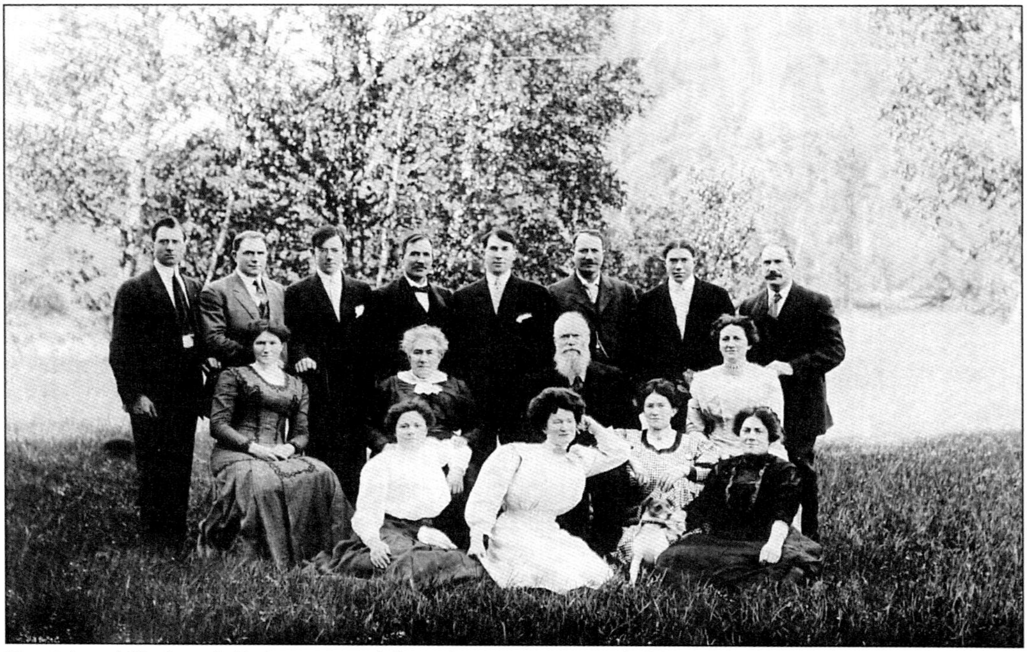

Daniel and Hadassah Robinson and their fourteen grown children, c. 1918. From left to right are: (on ground) Grace, Josephine, Effie, and Angeline; (middle row) Lena, Hadassah, Daniel, and Carrie; (back row) Leon, Walter, Alton, Coney, Olon, Perley, Robie, and Will. The Robinson farm was located on the west side of the Kennebec, very near the site of Wyman Dam.

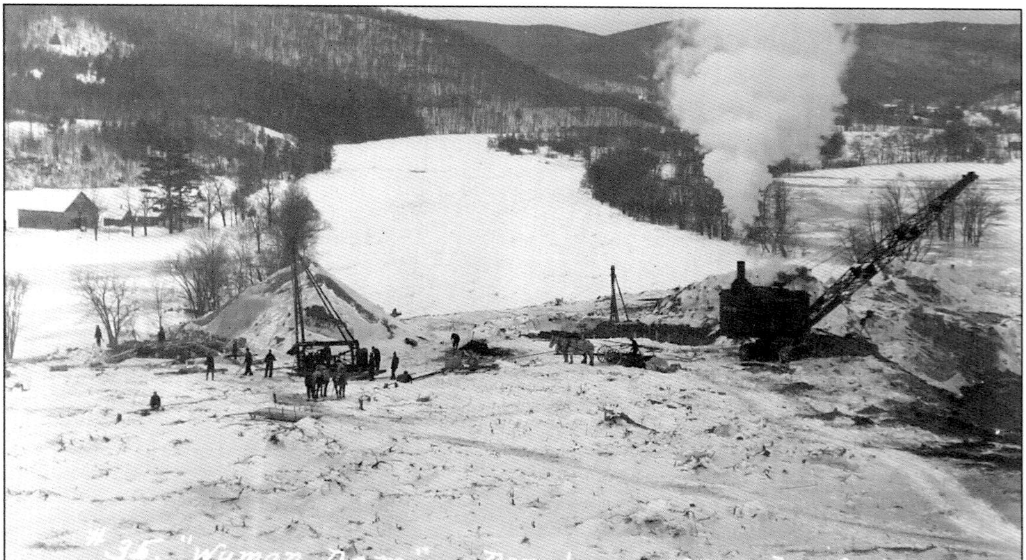

Early construction on Wyman Dam, January 3, 1929. The Robinson farm can be seen on the left. The dam replaced a natural course of rapids 140 feet high. Construction was started in October 1928, and the first unit was operated December 24, 1930.

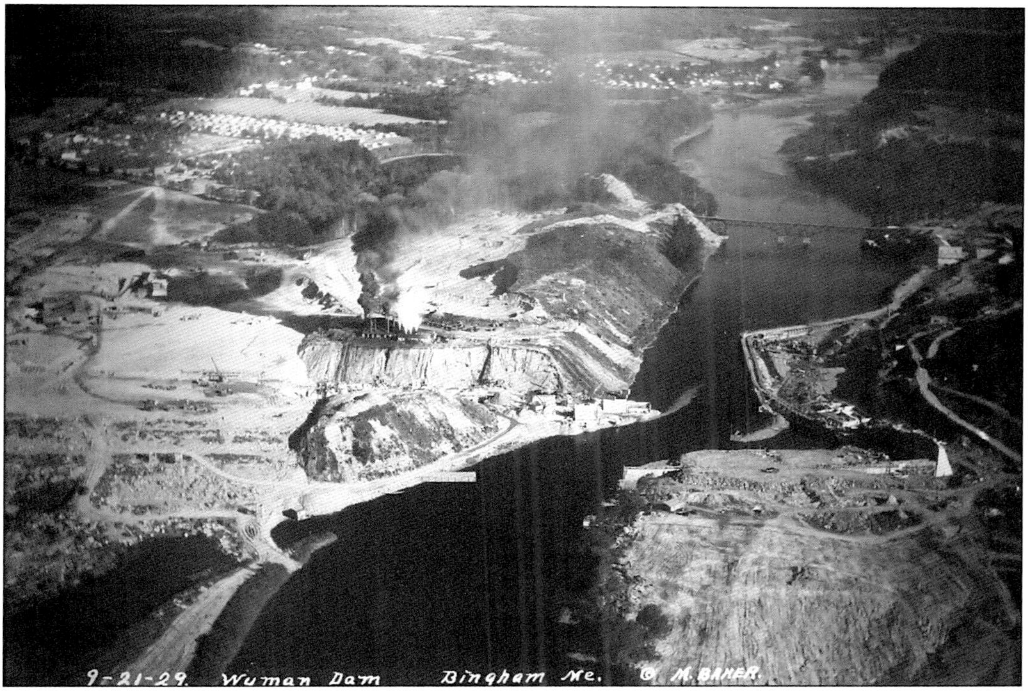

An aerial view taken on September 9, 1929. This view, looking toward Bingham, shows the dam construction. The railroad bridge below the dam was used only during construction.

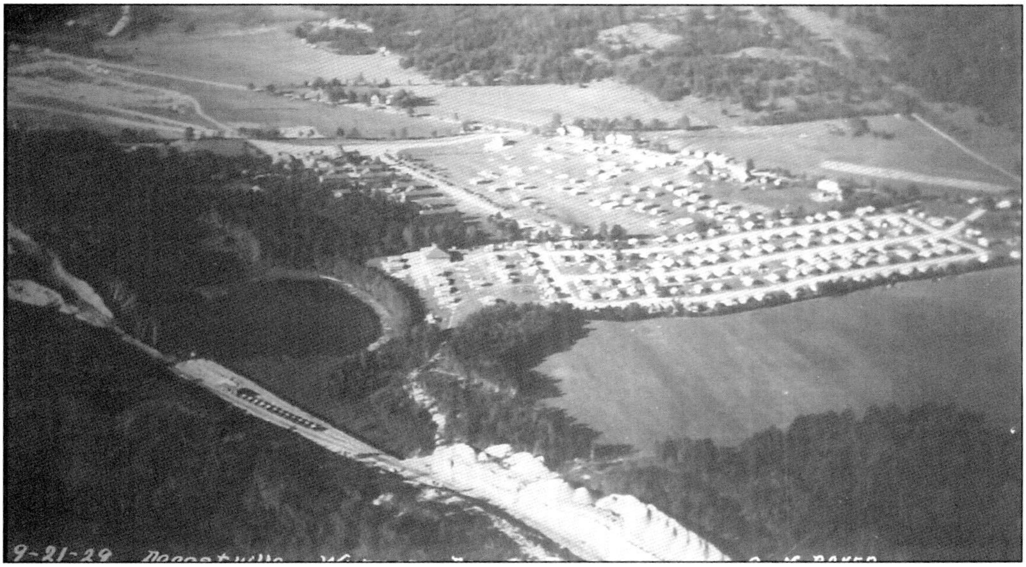
An aerial shot of "Daggetville." This settlement was erected to house construction workers and their families, and came complete with a hip-roofed schoolhouse. Nearly 300 homes and dormitories were constructed to help house the labor force of 2,400 men and their families. It was named for Mr. Daggett, who laid out the settlement.

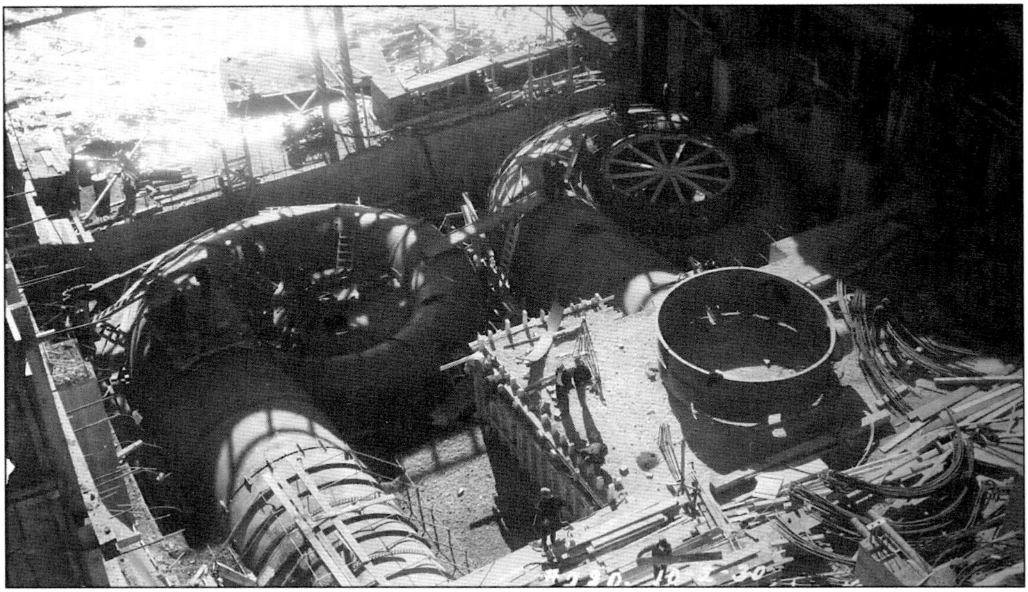

Powerhouse turbines in the process of completion, September 20, 1930. The top of the dam is 3,000 feet long, its crest is 150 feet above the water on the downstream side, and the powerhouse is 155 feet long. The cost of the dam and two transmission lines was $15 million. Wyman Lake is 12 miles long and its upper end is near the Hotel Sterling in Caratunk. Approximately 160,000 cords of pulpwood were sluiced through the dam in 1966.

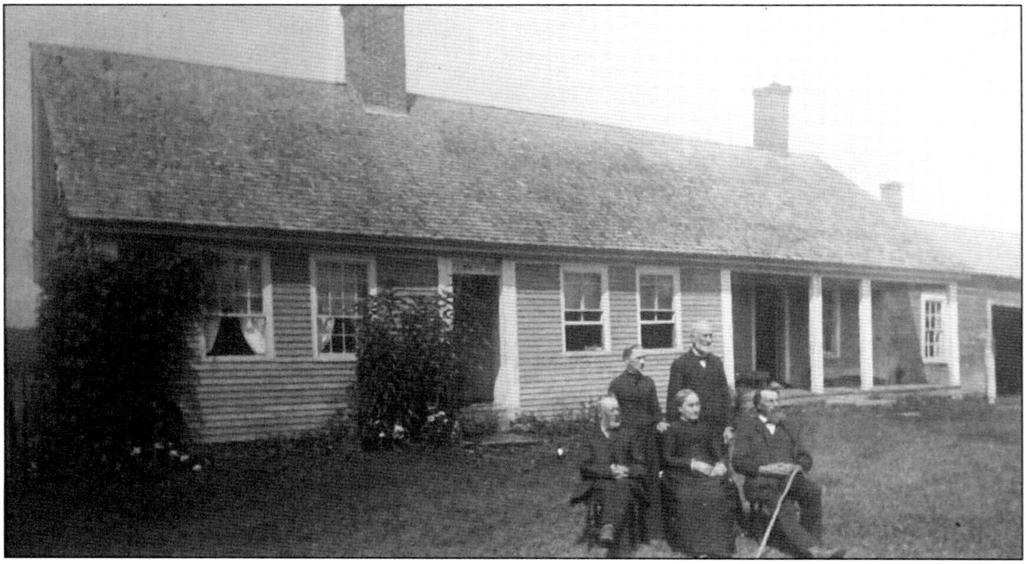

The Baker farm in the Sugartown section of Moscow (up Route 16 from Bingham), c. 1885–90. Twins Reuben and Abner Baker came from Litchfield with their wives and settled in Sugartown in the early 1800s. This farm was the home of Reuben and Sarah Smith Baker, and was more recently the home of Elmer and Nettie Baker, after which it was sold to Edson Carpenter. The seated man with the cane is H. Bardwell Baker, who was injured in the Civil War. The others are Ephraim R. Baker, Mehitable D. Baker, Lucyann Baker Goodrich, and Reverend Lewis Goodrich.

Sarah Smith Baker (1777–1867), wife of Reuben Baker, one of the early settlers of Moscow. Sarah was the mother of twelve children. She and her husband owned the Baker farm, shown on the previous page.

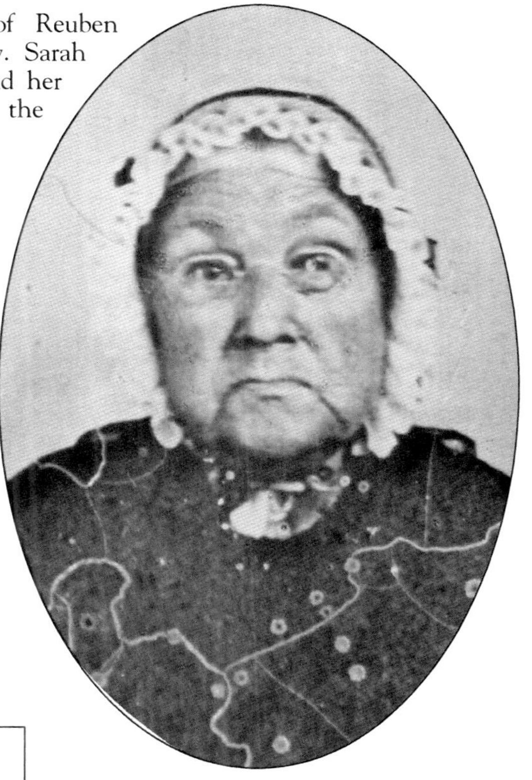

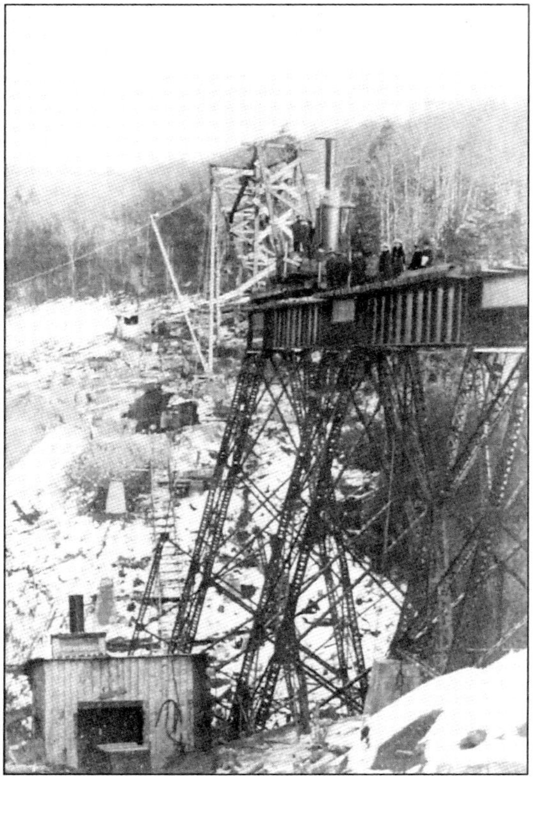

The Gulf Stream trestle of the Somerset Railroad, part of the 51-mile section of the railroad between Bingham and Moosehead Lake. The change of 900 feet in elevation from Bingham to Deadwater presented an engineering problem. The trestle was 700 feet long and 125 feet high. The Boston Bridge Company began construction in 1904. By 1933, woods operations had decreased and the train was no longer needed above Bingham. The rails were scrapped in 1936 and the trestle became part of the road for pulp trucks. Eventually it was bypassed by a road and was scrapped in the 1970s.

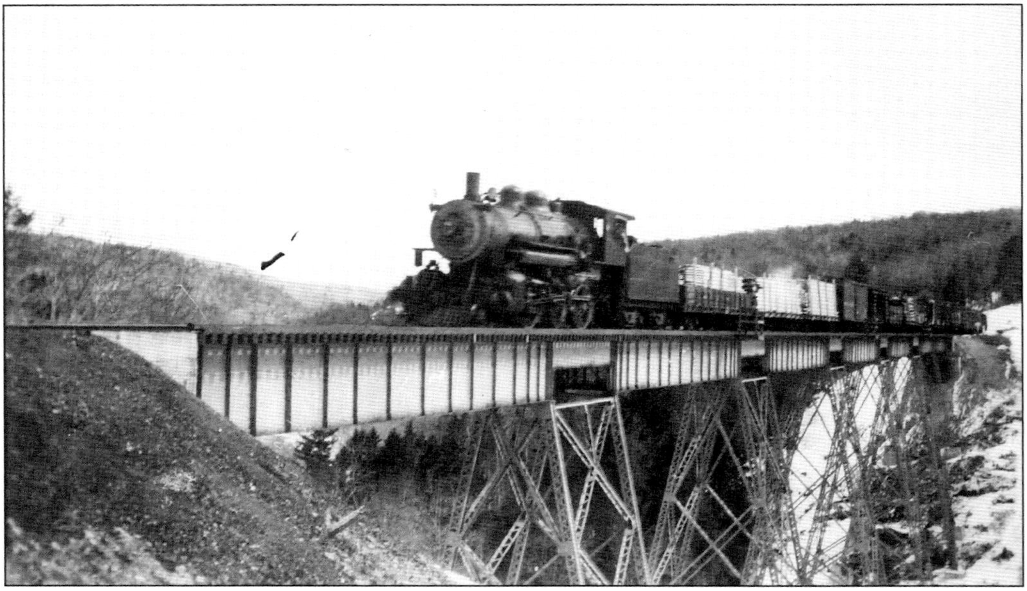

A lumber train crossing the Gulf Stream trestle, *c.* 1910–20. Because of the downgrade of 900 feet going into Bingham, the brakes on heavily loaded log cars had to be set leaving Deadwater (only the old engines had airbrakes), or the train would be going much too fast for safety.

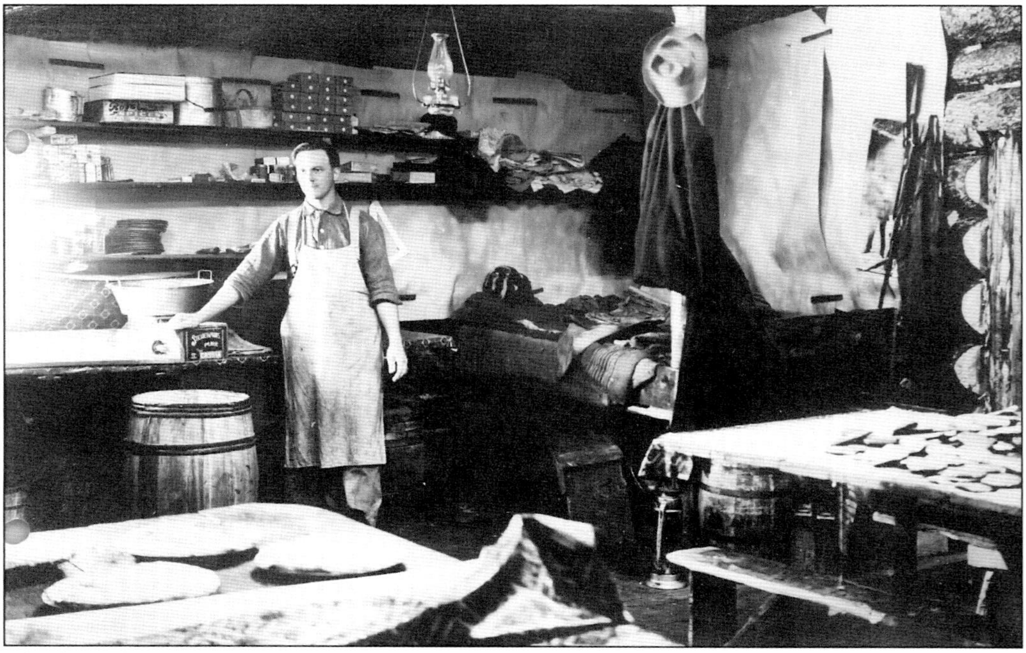

Charlie Baker, cook, at a lumbering camp in Deadwater north of the trestle, *c.* 1915. Note the good-sized pies on the table. Mr. Baker has his hand on a very large box of cassia (cinnamon). Mrs. Donohue, who cooked for Walter Robinson's crews in this area, used up a barrel of flour a week.

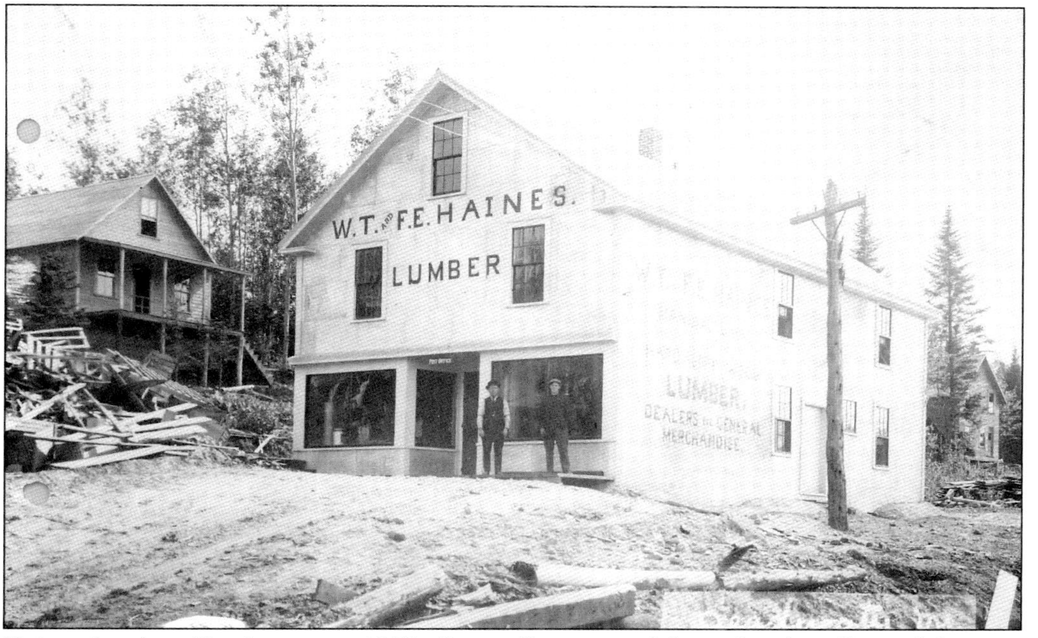

Haines Lumber, Deadwater, *c.* 1915. Originally sustained by railroad traffic and logging, Deadwater and other places like it are now gone.

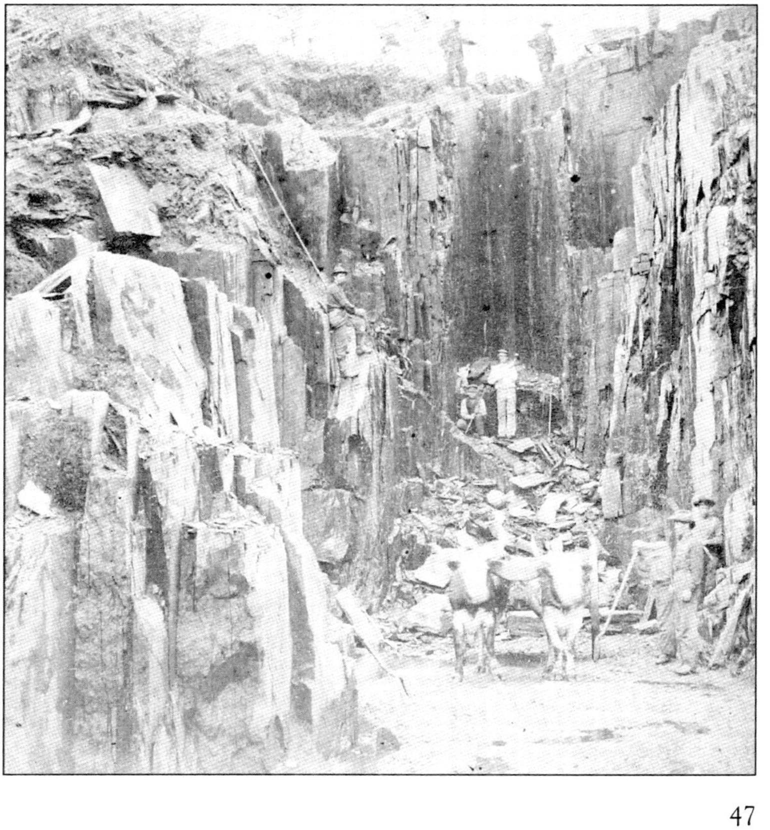

The old slate quarry, Mayfield. This stereo photograph from 1875–80 shows a team of oxen at work along with the quarrymen.

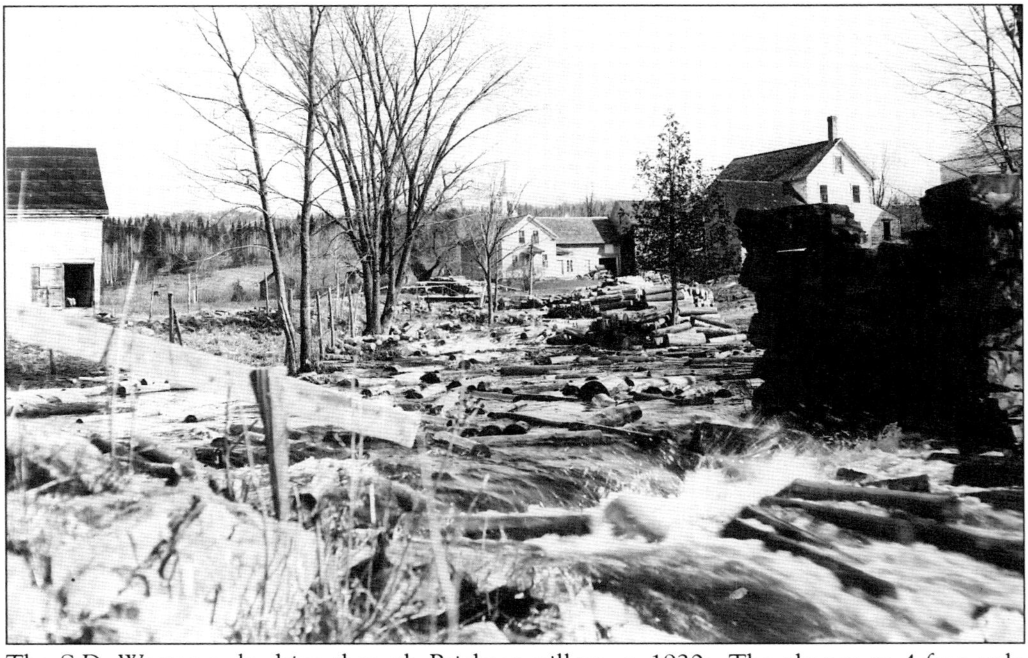

The S.D. Warren pulp drive through Brighton village, *c.* 1920s. The change to 4-foot pulp reflected ease of transport by truck, rail, and water, and developments in mill machinery. On the far right is the Donigan Store branch, run at this time by Orrin Hill; next is the Guy Hamlin home. Warren owned two dams above Brighton, with which they could control the flow.

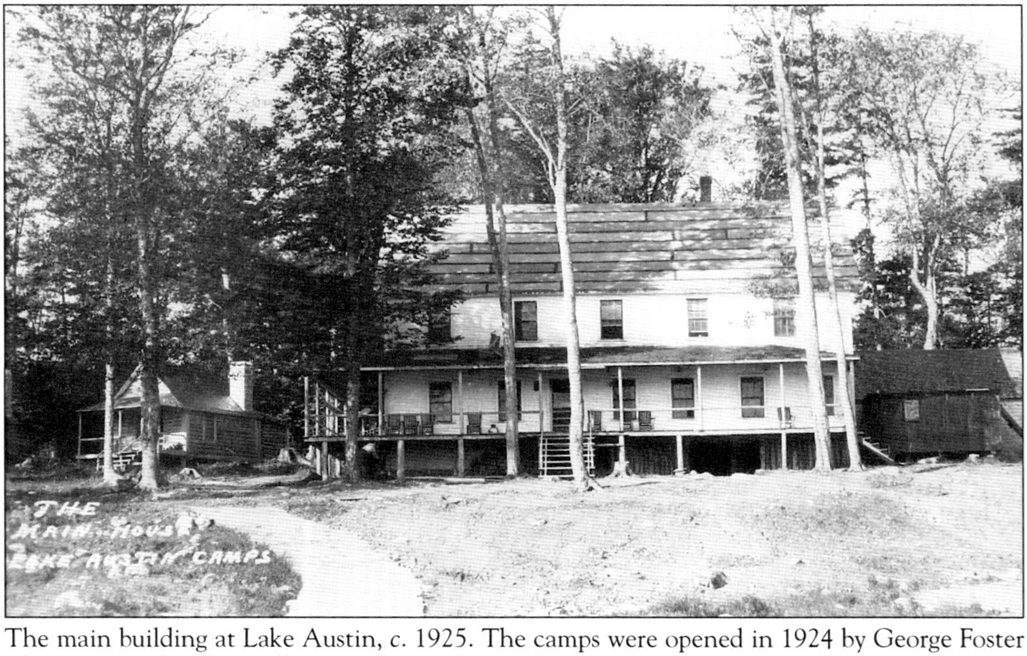

The main building at Lake Austin, *c.* 1925. The camps were opened in 1924 by George Foster of Moscow. After the Hollingsworth & Whitney logging was done, the main logging camp was remodeled for a sporting camp. Mr. Foster transported his clientele in a Model T Ford jitney.

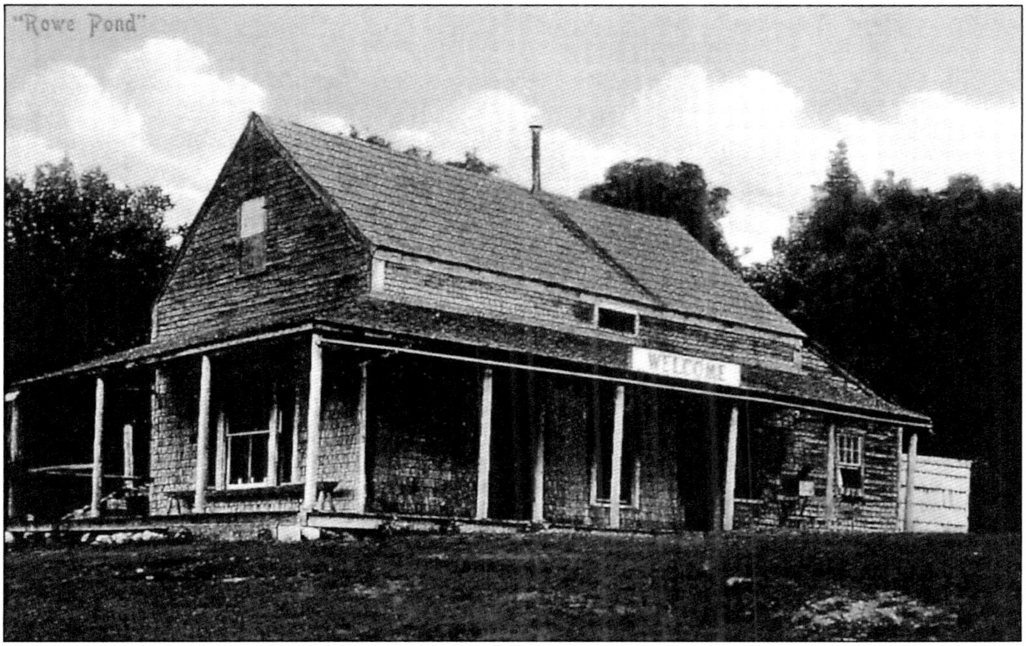

The main building at Rowe Pond, c. 1906. This rustic, shingled building is typical of the central buildings of early sporting camps. Note the "deacon's bench" made from a half-log (on the porch).

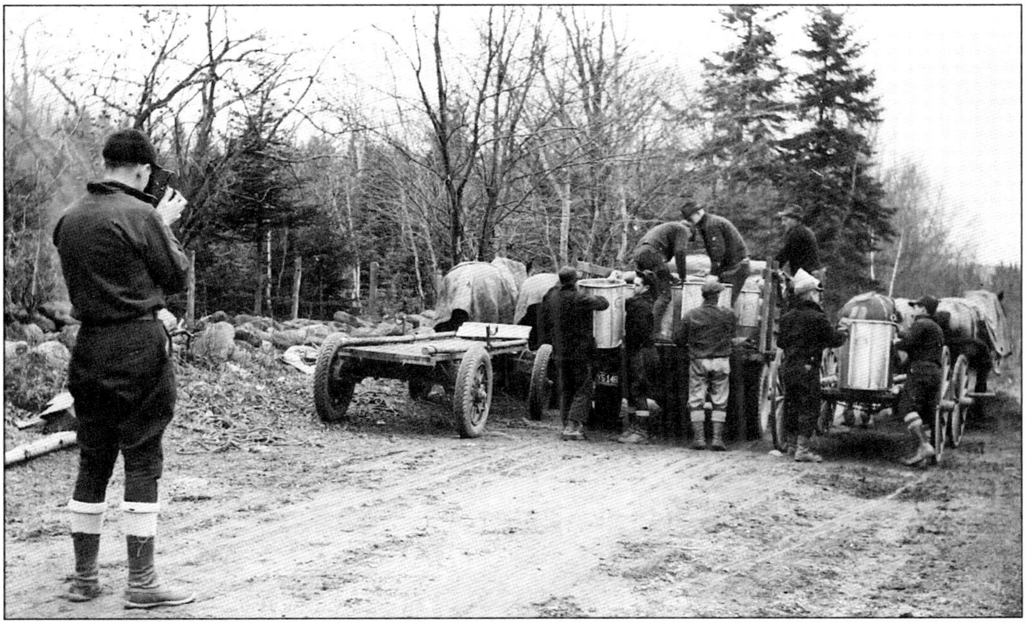

Transporting fish for stocking, c. 1937. The men are unloading containers of fish from a truck which has transported them from a hatchery. They will take them from here by buckboard to Rowe Pond. Most of the reasonably accessible small ponds were being stocked for sport fishermen. From left to right are Elon Hill, Orrin J. Hill, Avery Rollins, Evander Andrews, Percy Steward, Stanton Beane, and Merle Andrews.

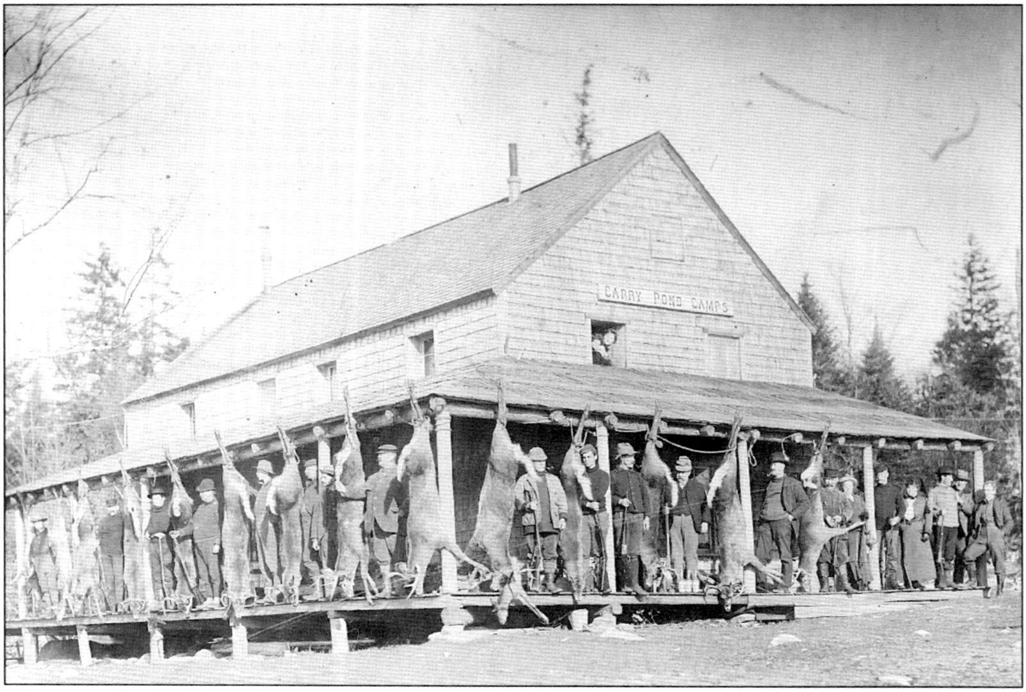

The main building at Carry Pond Camps, c. 1905. The porch is lined with "sports" and their trophies. This photograph shows some of the female help at the upstairs window and includes several local guides, who appear to be at the far right. They include Charlie Jones, Henry Lane, John Owens, Harry Givens, and Evander Andrews.

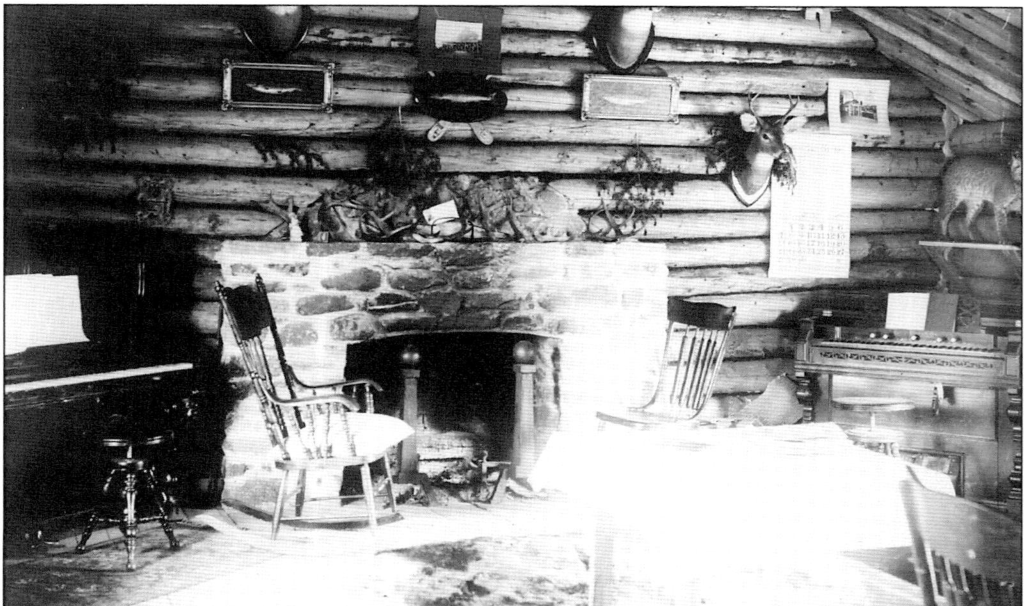

the interior of a guest cabin at Carry Pond, c. 1920. The style may be rustic, but the choice of either a piano or an organ isn't, and the fireplace is impressive.

Four

Bingham

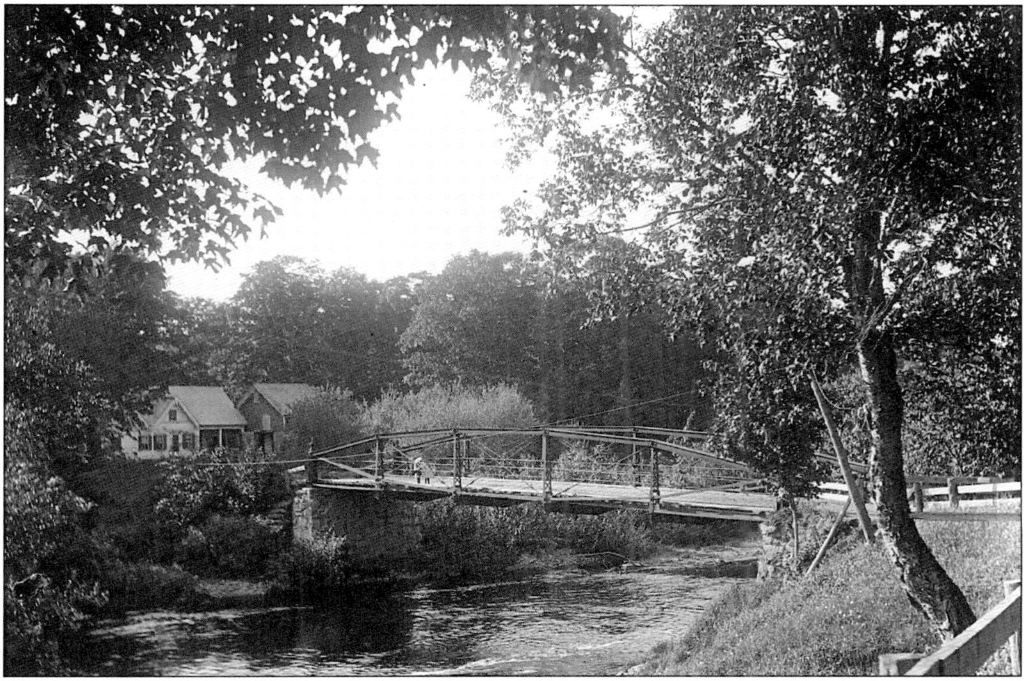

The iron bridge over Austin Stream, *c.* 1900. This bridge was located up old Route 16 from the present bridge on Route 201. The home of Will Robinson can be seen across the stream in the distance.

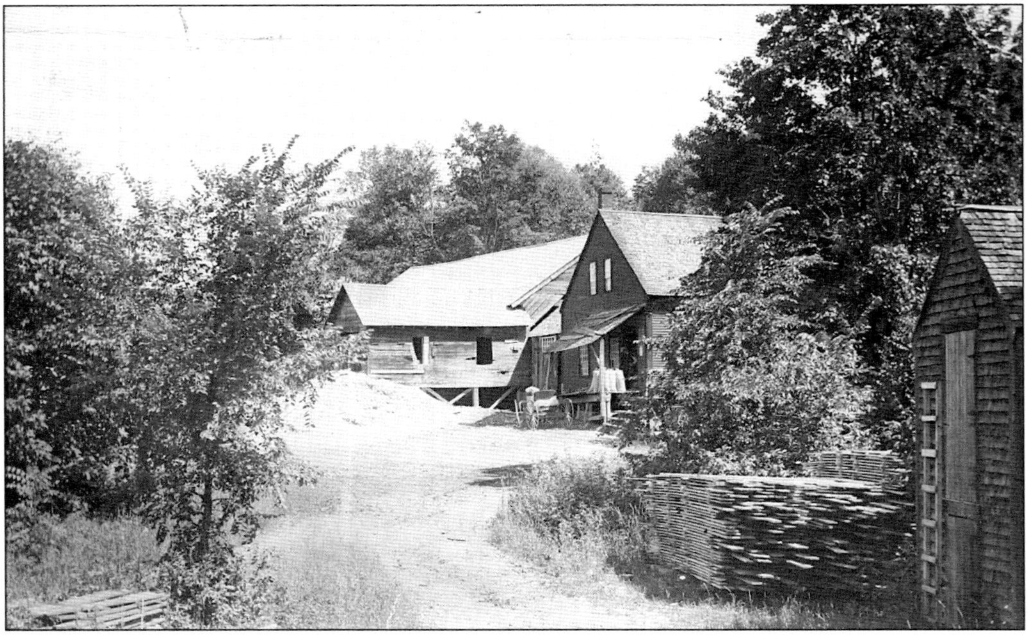

The Old Mill on Austin Stream, from the side toward Route 16. A mill was built on this site c. 1820, and it was there that Ephraim Heald ran an up-and-down saw, a shingle machine, a clapboard machine, a lath machine, and ground all kinds of grain. The mill was later owned by Allen Heald and Ed Gray, Pickard and Seth Goodrich, Seth Goodrich and John Baker, John Baker and George Miller, Brackett and Andrews, and finally W.E. and E.E. Andrews. It ceased operation in 1954 and was deliberately burned in the 1960s.

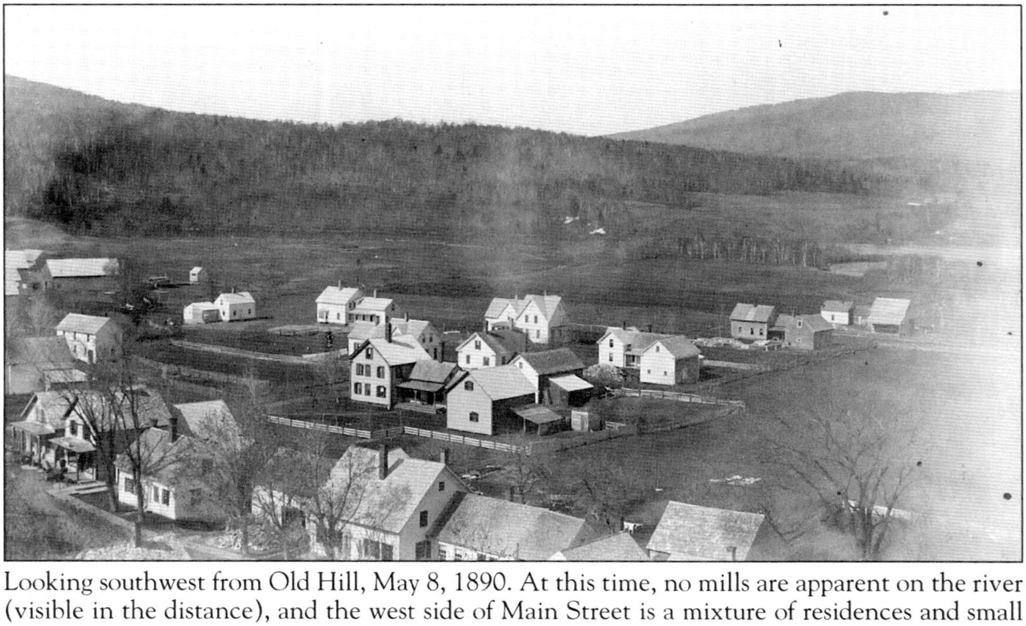

Looking southwest from Old Hill, May 8, 1890. At this time, no mills are apparent on the river (visible in the distance), and the west side of Main Street is a mixture of residences and small stores. Preble Street has started to develop, and there are several houses on Baker Street.

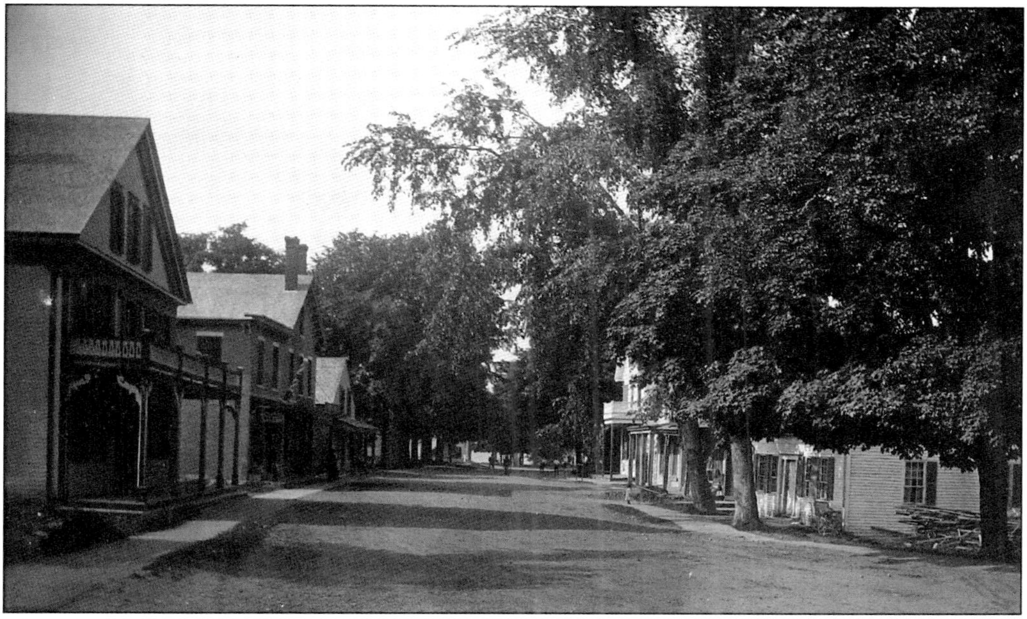

Main Street, looking south, *c.* 1900–1905. Ervin Moore bought the brick building shown here from Joel Colby, his father-in-law. At this time, he and John J. Lander shared the store. Later, F.S. Hunnewell had a grocery store in part of the building. It was destroyed in 1911, along with the Old Bingham Hotel (on the left) and the small building beyond the drugstore, in a fire that seems to have started in the Old Bingham.

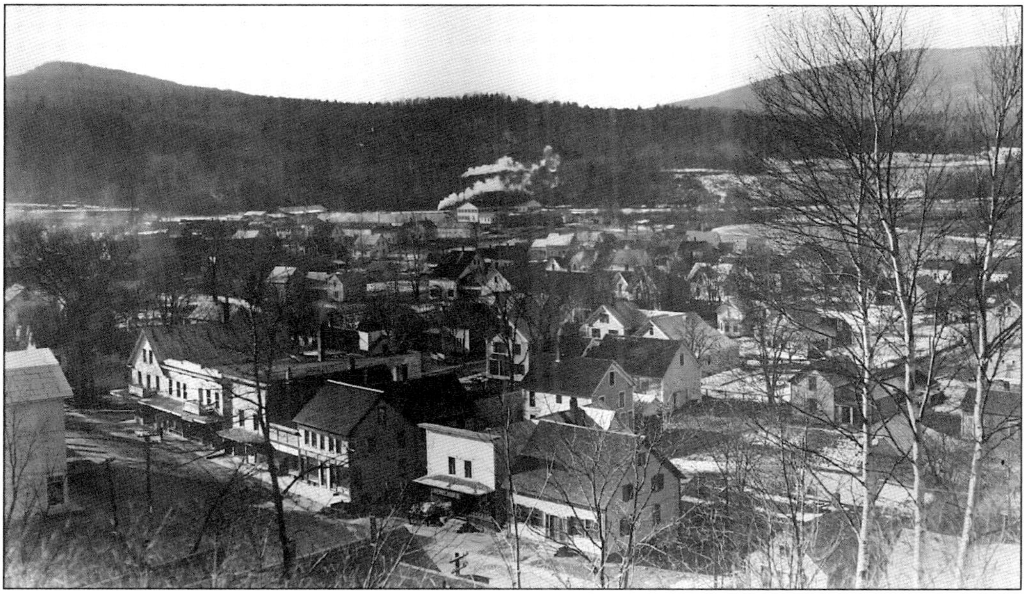

Looking southwest from Old Hill, *c.* 1920. As can be seen in this photograph, development in the village progressed significantly. The Donigan Block has been built (center left facing east), the fire of 1911 has removed the Old Bingham Hotel and the brick drugstore, and the tall Hunnewell block (far left) has been built. The residences on Main Street in the 1890 photograph have vanished, and in the distance smoke rises from the mills on the river.

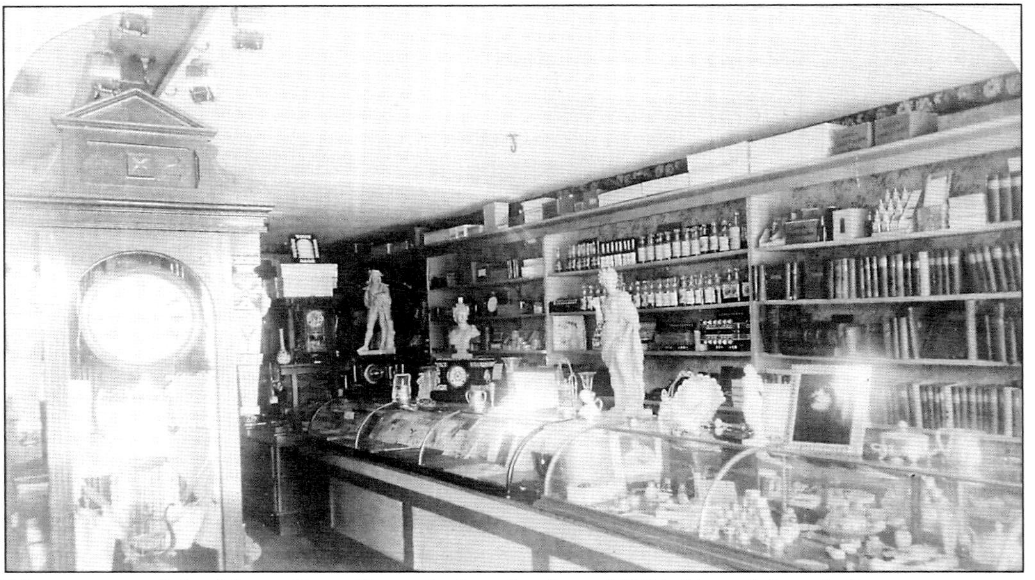

The interior of the Moore Drug Store, before the fire of 1911. Ervin Moore's first store, across the street, was a jewelry store. The mixture of clocks and jewelry with drugs and medicines attests to the developing nature of Mr. Moore's business. When fire broke out on August 5, 1911, several valued objects were saved: the large clock, a nickel-plated cash register, and the Tufts Soda Fountain (the latter never reinstalled, but now in the Waterville Historical Society's Apothecary Museum).

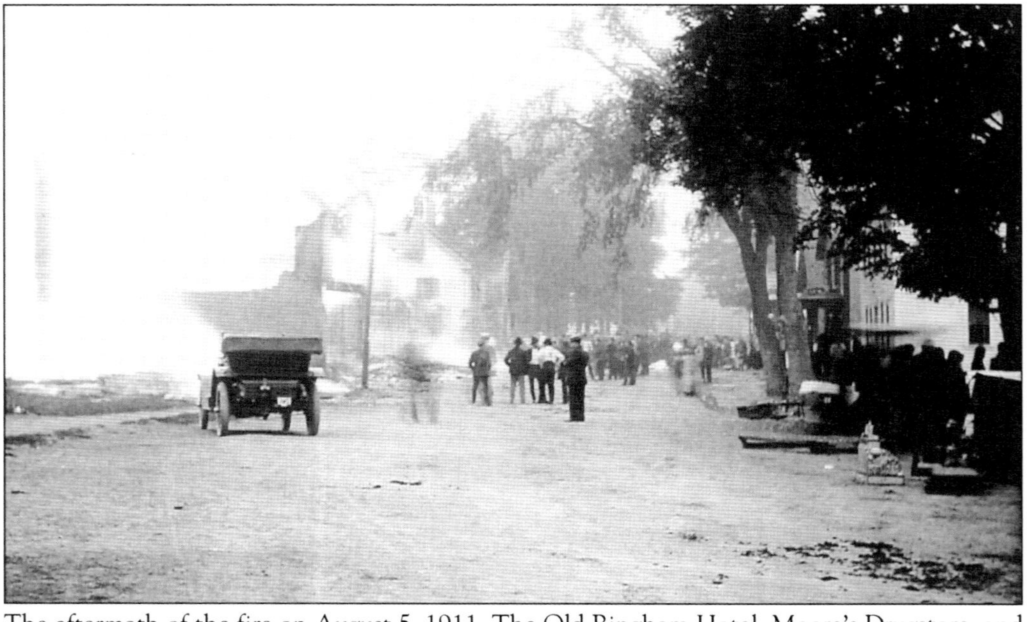

The aftermath of the fire on August 5, 1911. The Old Bingham Hotel, Moore's Drugstore, and F.S. Hunnewell's Grocery Store all burned to the ground. There appears to have been damage to Ervin Moore's home just beyond, judging from the ladder on the roof and smoke damage to the attic window. The cash register salvaged from the drugstore is still sitting at the edge of the street on the right.

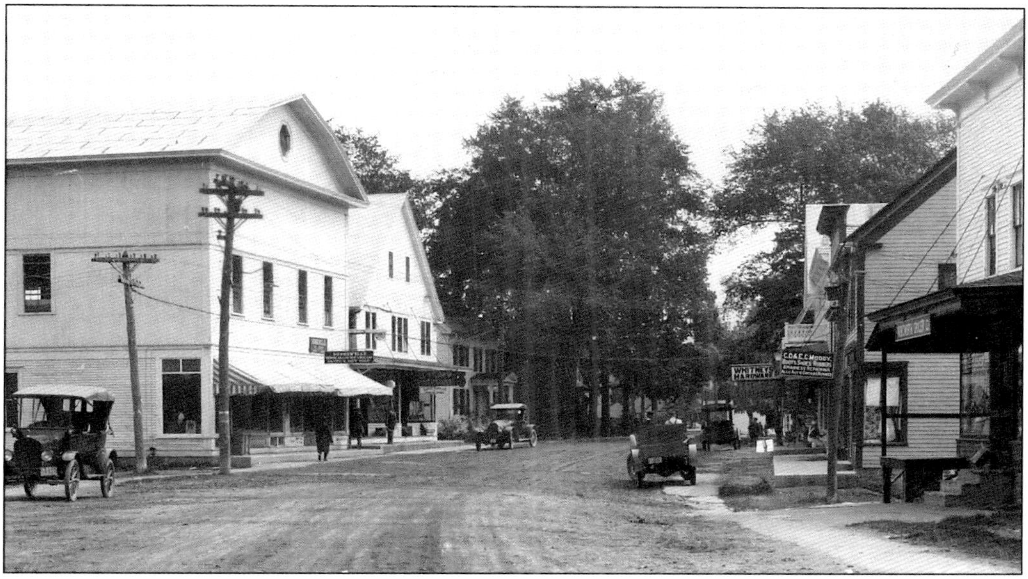

Main Street looking south, *c.* 1920. The tall Hunnewell block (F.S. Hunnewell's store and restaurant) was lowered after a fire in 1937. A barn from behind the Moore house has been moved to the street to become the drugstore, sharing the building with Earl Folsom's Hardware. On the right is Wentworth's Grocery, which later became (in succession) Whitman's and Lidstone's. Beyond are C.O. and E.C. Moody Boots Shoes and Rubbers, Price's Clothing, Whitney's Hardware, and Donigan's Furniture and Men's Clothing.

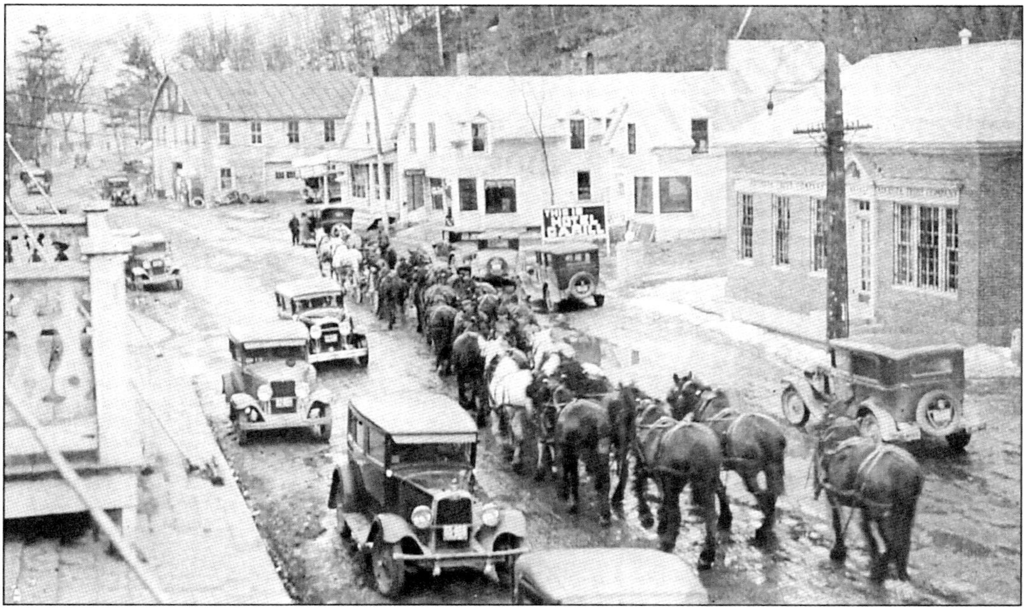

Walter Robinsin's horses, used in his woods operations, heading north up Main Street, *c.* 1931. This shot was taken from the porch roof of the Donigan Block. The sign for Hotel Cahill points to the hotel, which is set back from the road. The brick Augusta Trust Bank is in the foreground; beyond it are the Keep Sweet Kandy Shop of Beecher Vincent and Robie Howes' Garage.

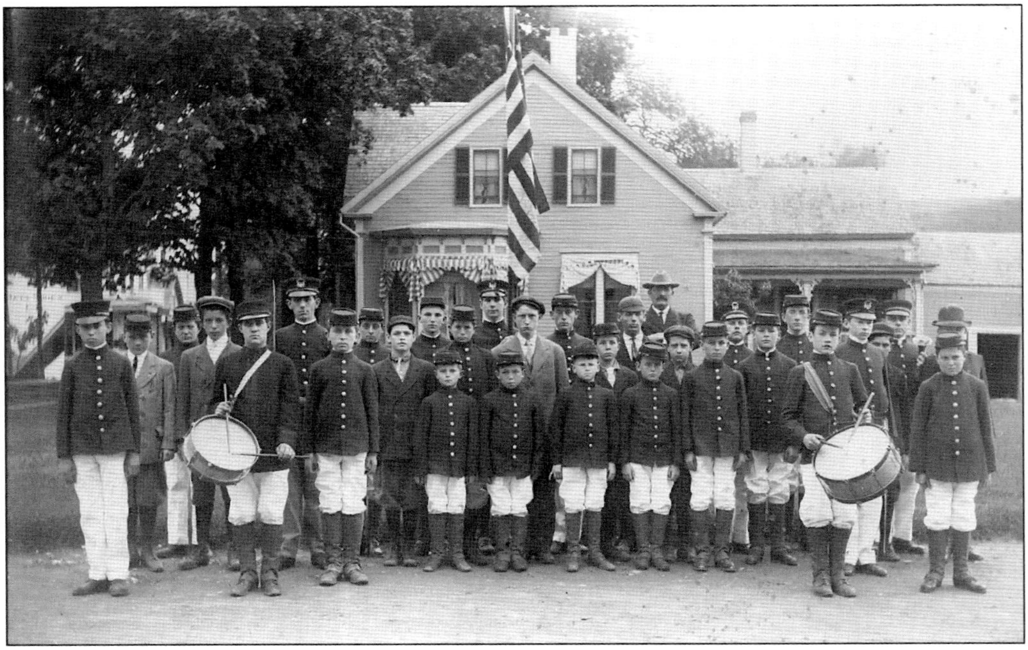

The Bingham Boys' Brigade on Murray Street near the corner of Main just before the Fourth of July parade in 1910. The following members have been identified: on the left in the front row is Errold Hilton; the small boys in the middle are Allan Robinson and Colby Robinson; to the left of the drummer boy is John Gordon; to the right of the drummer is Robert Moore. A.F. Donigan is at the rear. Mr. Donigan took a keen interest in the youth of Bingham, and outings and trips of the "Donigan Boys" went on for many years.

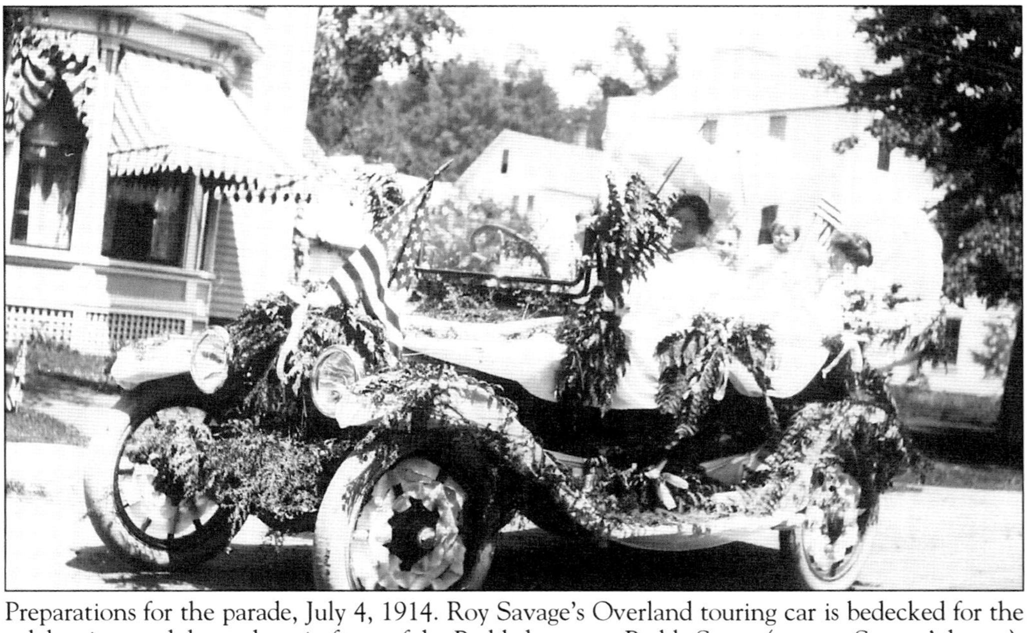

Preparations for the parade, July 4, 1914. Roy Savage's Overland touring car is bedecked for the celebration, and shown here in front of the Preble house on Preble Street (next to Savage's home). One year the car backfired and the bunting caught fire. Fortunately, no one was injured.

The interior of the Bingham Post Office, c. 1900, "behind the desk." The post office was located where the Valley View Market is presently. Shown here in this posed-for-fun photograph are postmistress Sara Belle Clark, Lephe Dinsmore, and Marita Houghton Savage. Note the fashionable bird on Mrs. Savage's hat.

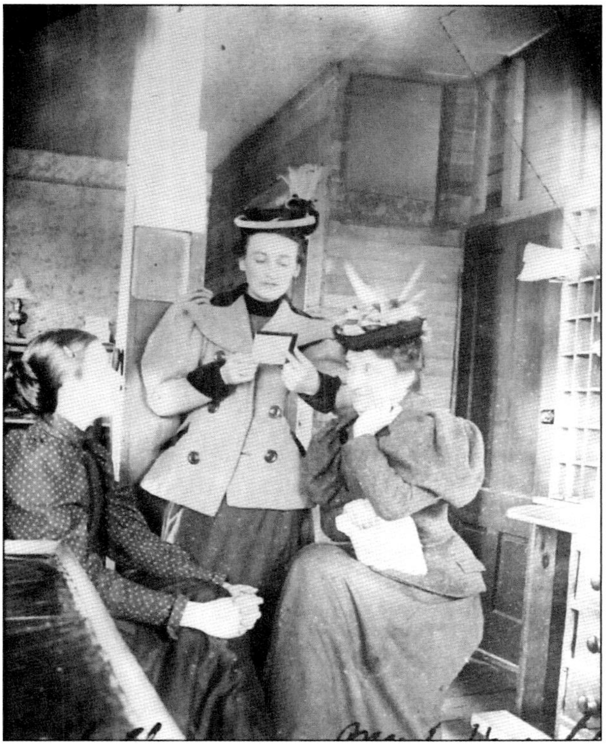

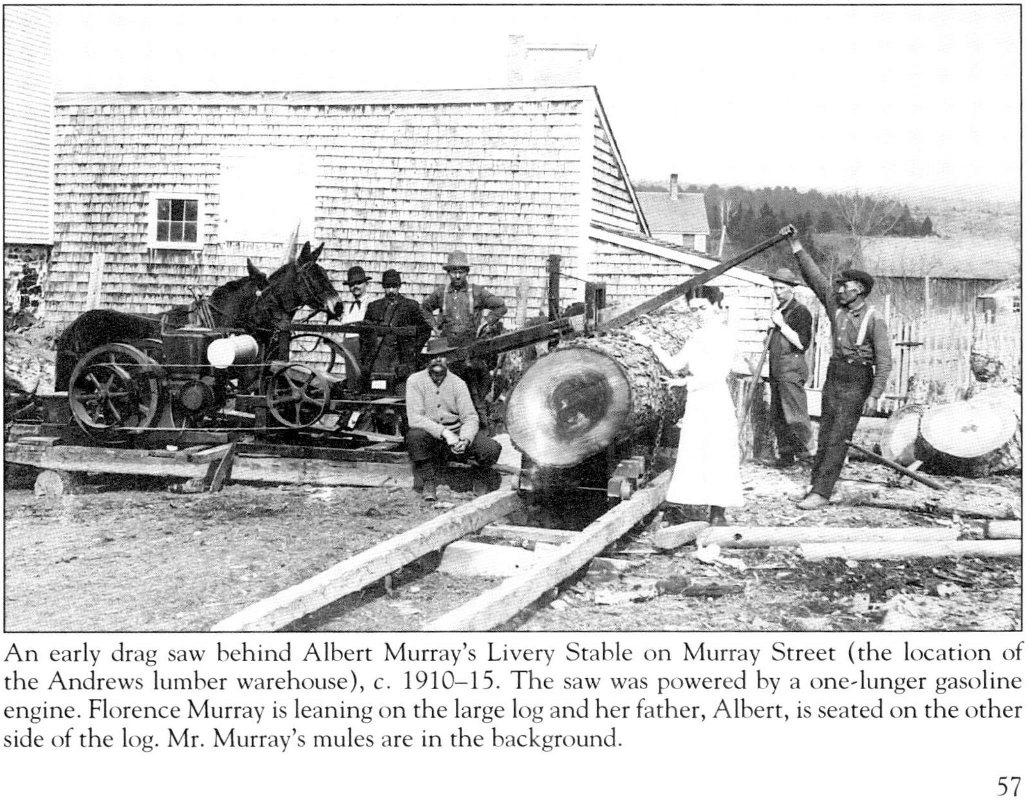

An early drag saw behind Albert Murray's Livery Stable on Murray Street (the location of the Andrews lumber warehouse), c. 1910–15. The saw was powered by a one-lunger gasoline engine. Florence Murray is leaning on the large log and her father, Albert, is seated on the other side of the log. Mr. Murray's mules are in the background.

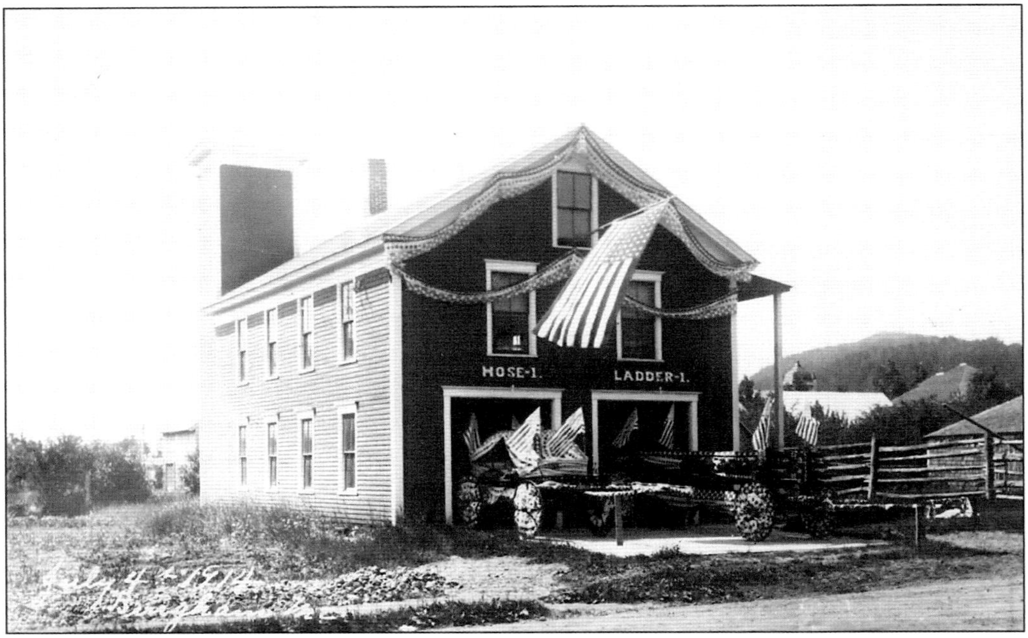

The Bingham Fire Station, July 4, 1914. The fire apparatus is decorated for the parade. As a result of the fire of 1911, a volunteer fire department was organized in 1912, and this building was erected in that same year. In 1914, the board of trade raised $1,000 for materials to finish Firemen's Hall on the second floor. Wet hose was dried in the tower at the back by the aid of a large woodstove.

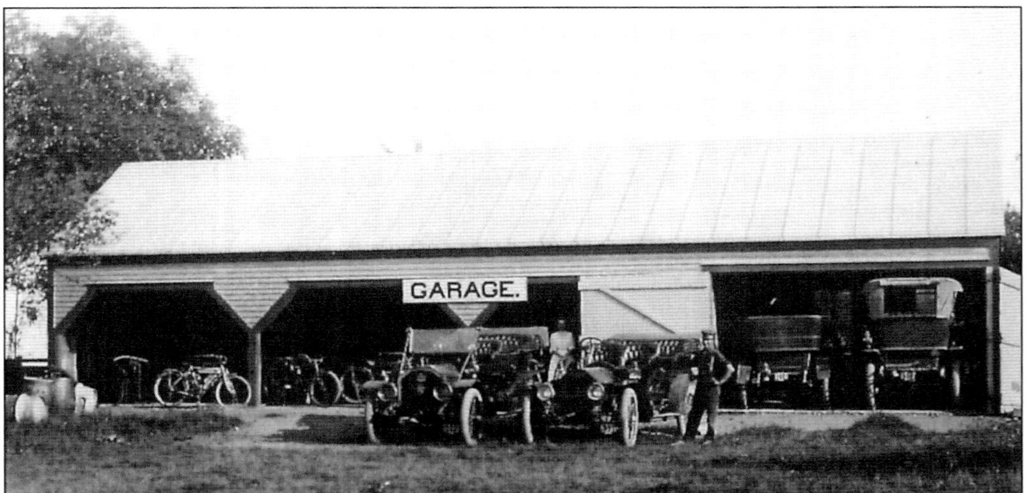

John Briggs' Garage, Murray Street, across from the fire station, *c.* 1908–10. Local interest in transportation technology shows in the nice array of early cars and motorcycles. The first car owned in Bingham was a 1905 one-cylinder Cadillac belonging to Roy Savage and Dr. Nevers.

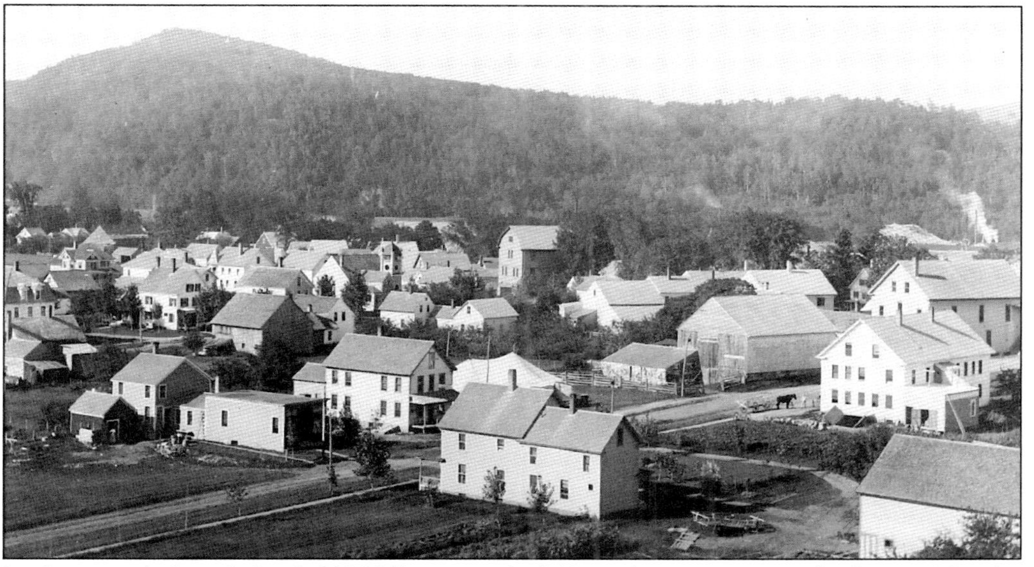

Looking south from behind Old Hill, postmarked 1911. A tent occupies the lot used for the 1912 fire station. Murray's Livery Stable, to the right of the tent, was later replaced by Colby Robinson's Colby Theater, now W.E. and E.E. Andrews' lumber warehouse. In the distance, the top of the 1904 Fraternity Hall can be seen in the center.

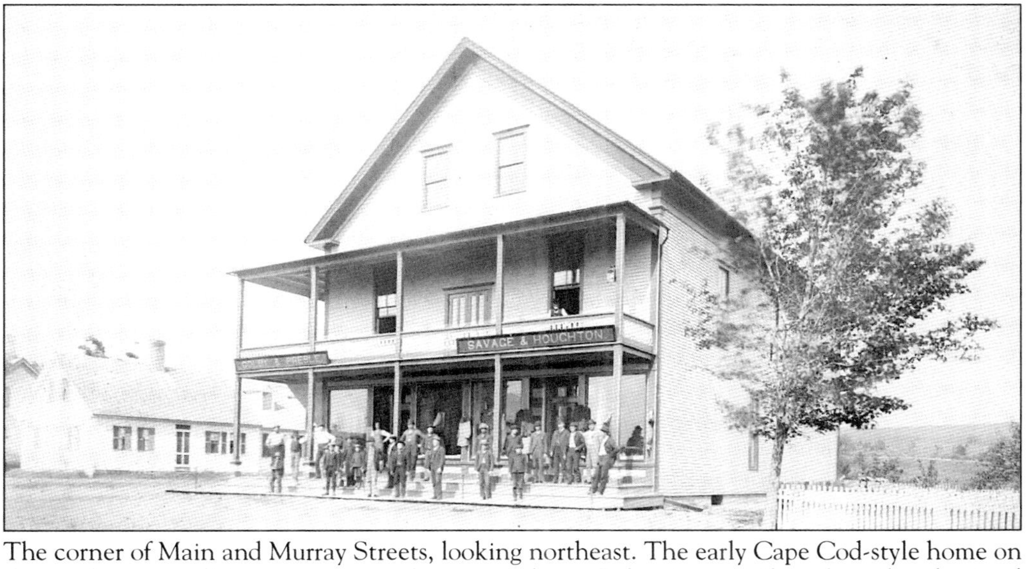

The corner of Main and Murray Streets, looking northeast. The early Cape Cod-style home on the north corner of Murray Street was later moved onto Baker Street. When the railroad arrived in Bingham in 1890, several new stores were built. Colby & Preble was owned by Warren Colby and Fred Preble (father of Nellie Preble Robinson). Savage and Houghton was owned by Mark Savage (father of Roy Savage), who later married Marita Houghton. Colby & Preble became Preble & Robinson, and was run for many years by Allan and Ruby Robinson. Savage & Houghton became Mark Savage & Co., and was run for many years by Roy Savage and John Owens. Preble & Robinson eventually occupied the entire first floor. Kennebec Hall, on the second floor, was long used for town meetings, dances, and silent films. The second floor was removed by the present owner, Wesley Baker, about 1966–67.

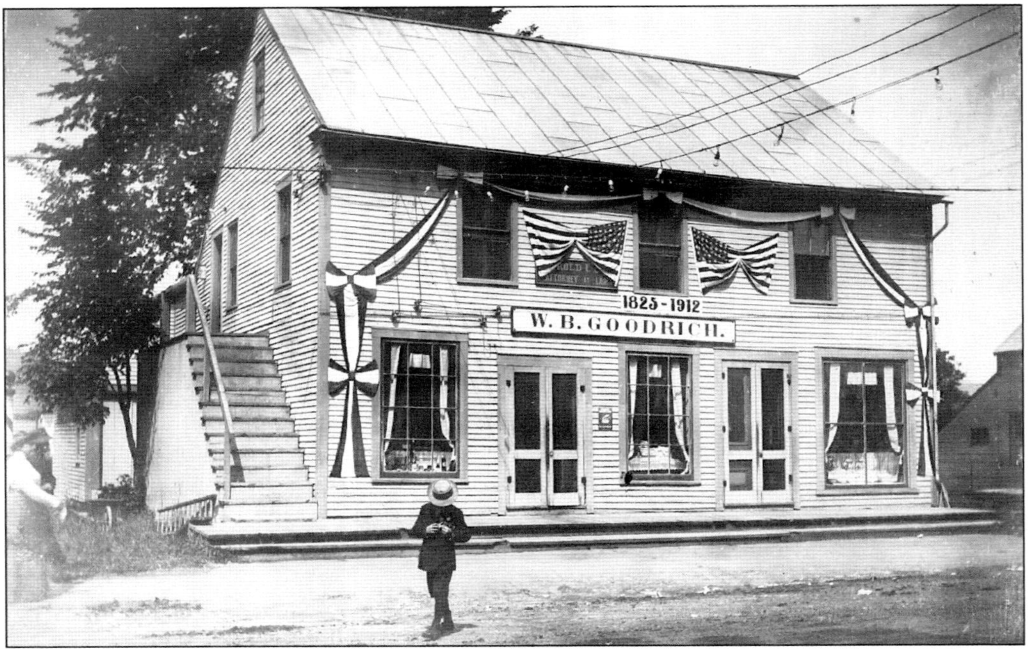

Will Goodrich's store, decorated for the Bingham centennial in 1912. The dates on the front indicate that this is Bingham's oldest store building. It was built by Levi Fletcher, who sold groceries, building materials, dry goods, and rum. In the early 1850s the store passed to Simeon Goodrich, Fletcher's son-in-law. Later it passed to Will. More recently the store was W.E. & E.E. Andrews Hardware, and it is now Jacques Auto Parts. The flag nearly covers the sign for the upstairs law office of Harold I. Goss.

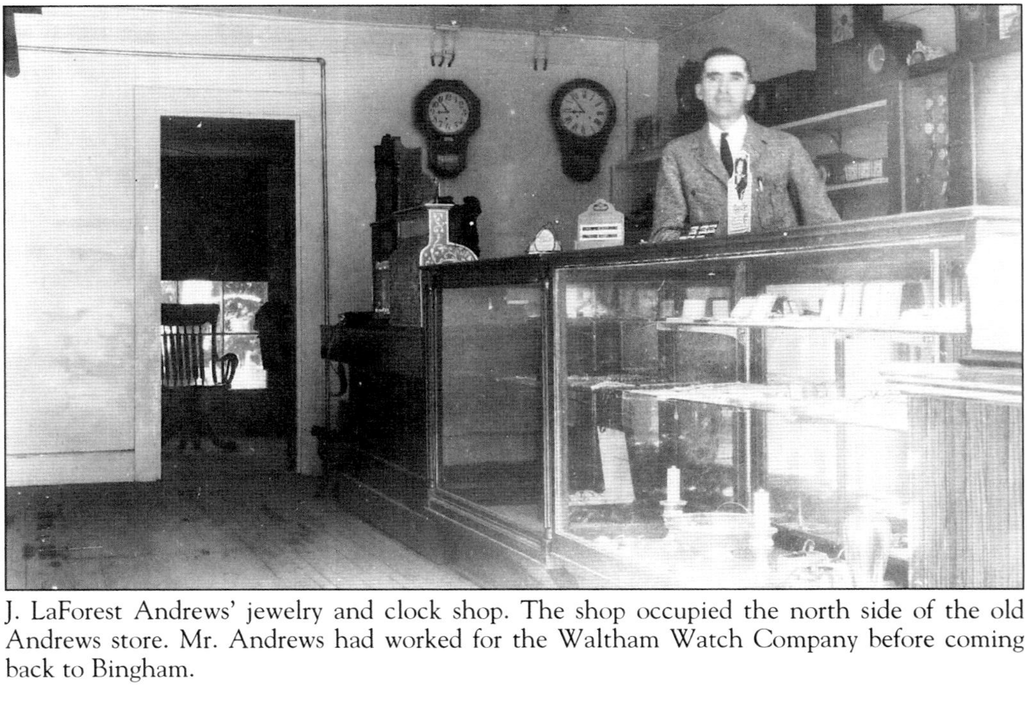

J. LaForest Andrews' jewelry and clock shop. The shop occupied the north side of the old Andrews store. Mr. Andrews had worked for the Waltham Watch Company before coming back to Bingham.

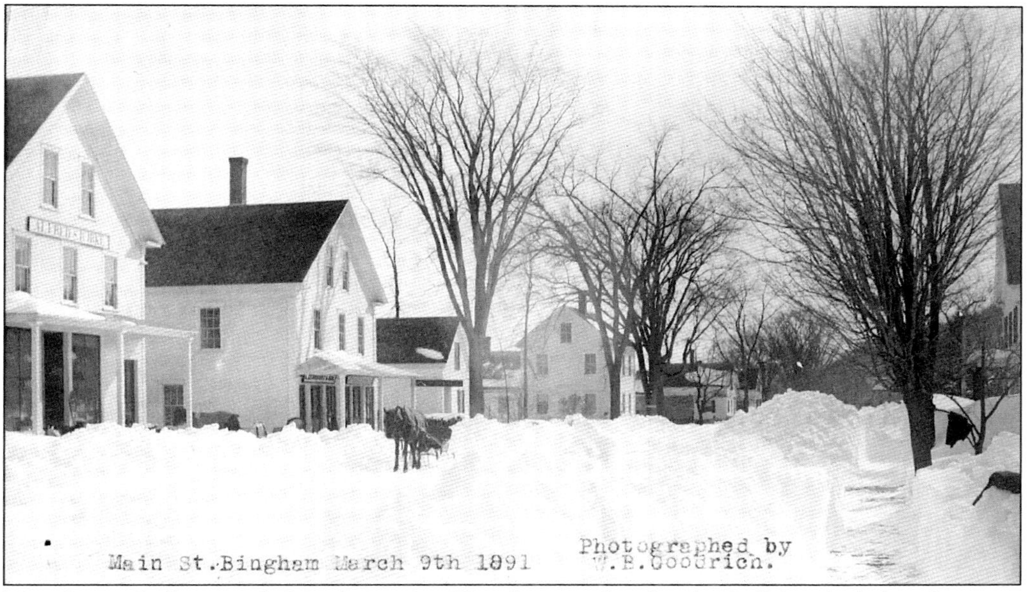

Main Street, looking south, March 9, 1891. This photograph, taken by Will Goodrich from his store, shows the Burke Store (the present location of the Andrews Hardware) and the Dinsmore Shoe Shop, started by Abner Dinsmore. Son Arthur eventually came into the business, as did grandson Arlie. Arthur and Arlie Dinsmore were also the local undertakers. At this time, snow on the roads was rolled and not plowed. It compacted all winter, making for memorable "mud seasons."

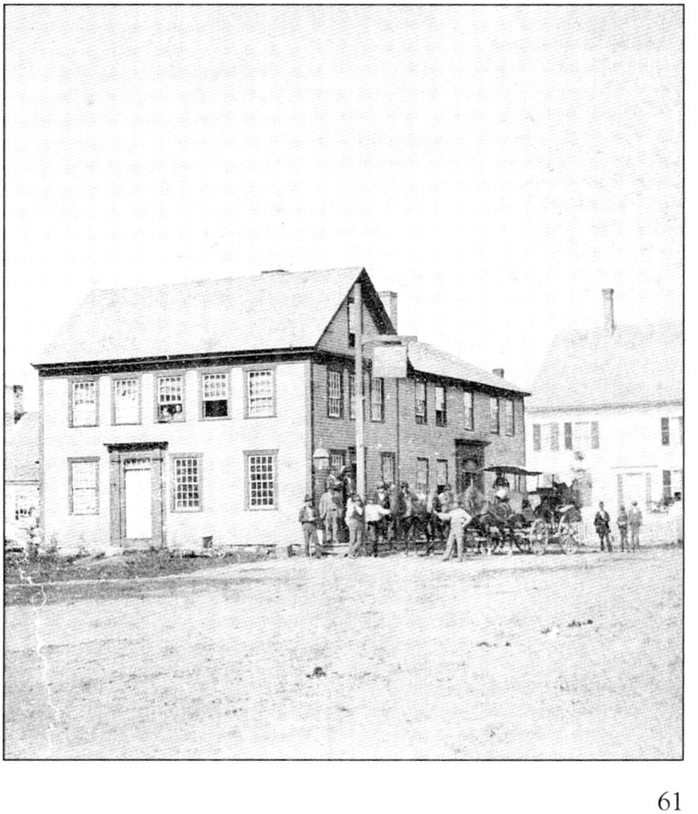

The Bingham Stage House, from a c. 1870 stereo photograph. The stage house was built by Levi Goodrich, c. 1820–22, when the first road came up this side of the valley. It was run by Levi and his wife, Polly Jewett Goodrich, and is said to have been the first stage house and tavern above Caratunk Falls (Solon). In 1835, meals for stage passengers cost 17¢. Levi's son Pickard sold the business to Winthrop Eldridge and Nate Adams and moved across the street in the early 1840s.

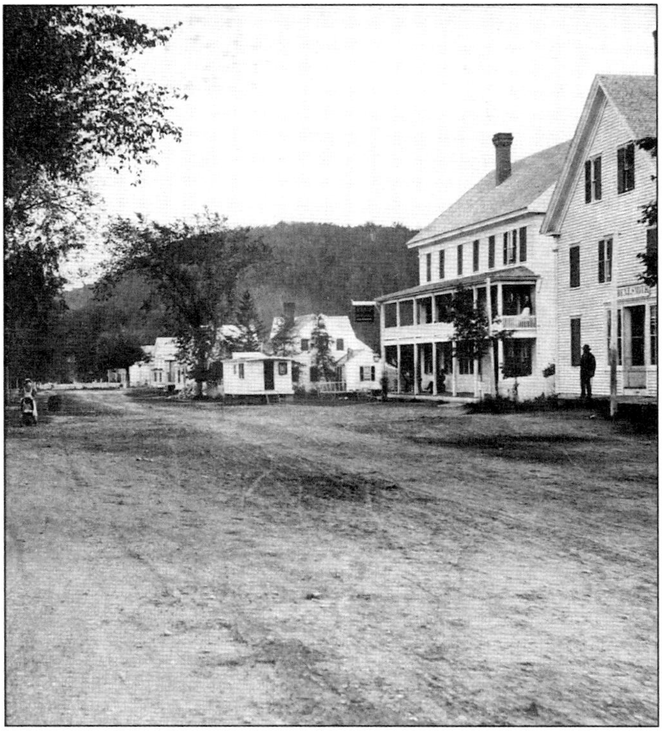

Another stereo view of the stage house as remodeled by Sewell Dinsmore and George Savage, *c.* 1875. Later owners were Mr. Lander, Alonzo Adams, and Henry Fletcher. The Washburn family sold it to Clarence Dutton in 1918. In 1920 the hotel stables held forty driving horses for hire. This view shows the Benjamin Smith store building, later annexed to the hotel. The stereo photographer's portable darkroom wagon can be seen beyond the hotel. Beyond the wagon is the "doctor's house," which has been the home of many area physicians. It eventually became Robie Howes' Garage.

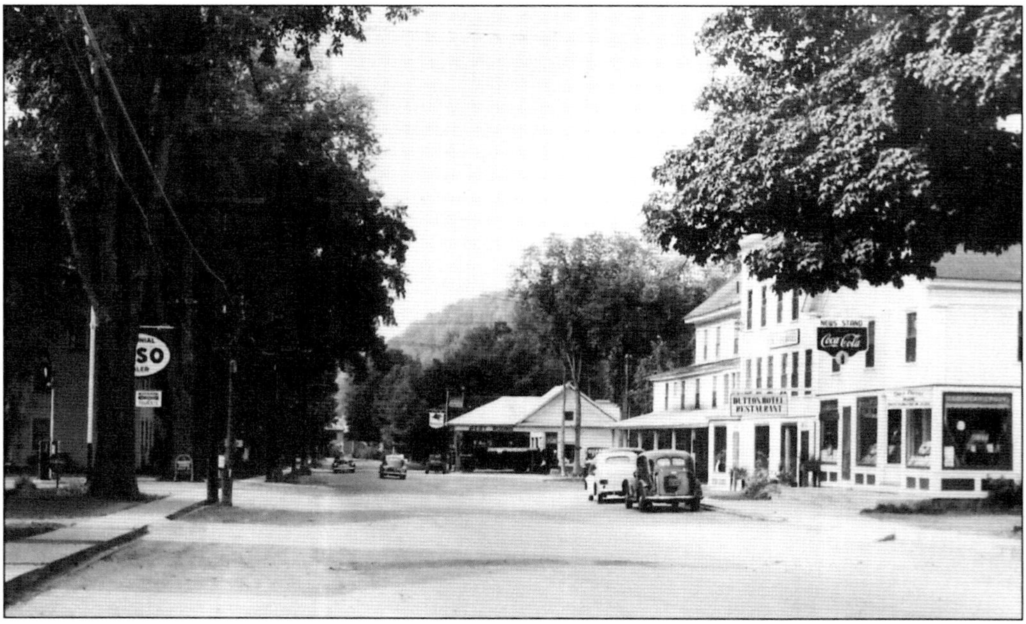

Main Street looking south, *c.* 1948. At the time of this photograph, the massive elms were still standing, and the hotel had incorporated the Smith Store and the Holt house (which houses Eva Bachelder's newsstand and soda fountain). Robie Howes' Garage can be seen beyond the hotel. At one time Mr. Howes had garages both here and at the north end of Main Street.

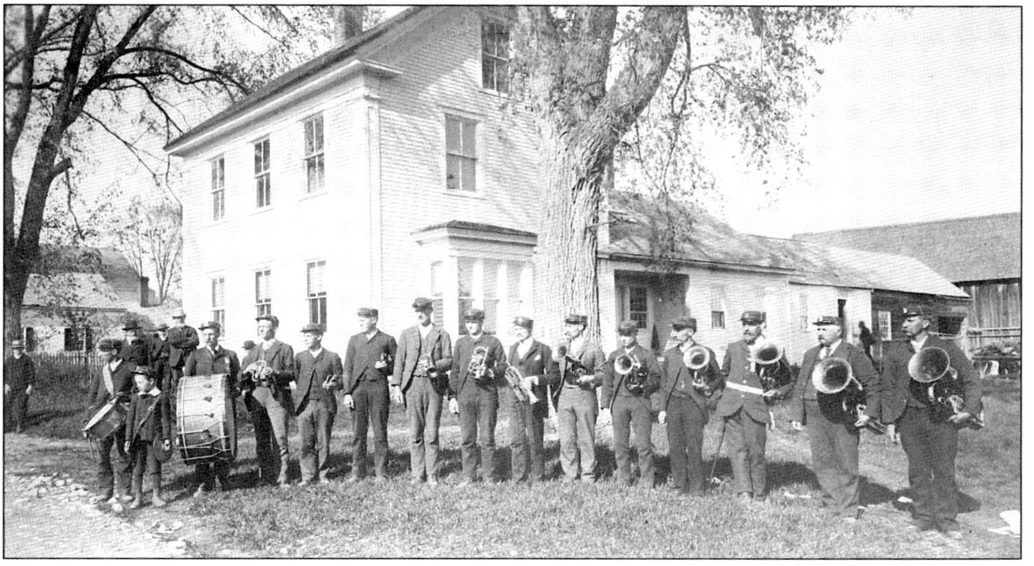

The Bingham Cornet Band in front of the Goodrich house, *c.* 1890. Milford Goodrich greatly expanded the family home after 1880, moving the original back from its foundation to become the ell facing Meadow Street. Band members are, from left to right: George Dyer, small drum; Arlie Dinsmore, cymbals; Sam Smith, bass drum; George Dyer and Elmer Baker, e-flat cornets; Forrest Colby, Albert Cassidy, H.H.Patten, b-flat cornets; Ervin Moore, solo e-flat alto; Fred Preble, e-flat alto; Guy Baker, b-flat tenor; Arthur Dinsmore, b-flat baritone; Bardwell Baker, b-flat bass; and Byram Smith and Oscar Lander, e-flat basses. Behind Sam Smith, at the corner of the house, is Ephraim Baker; behind George Dyer is Hiram Smith.

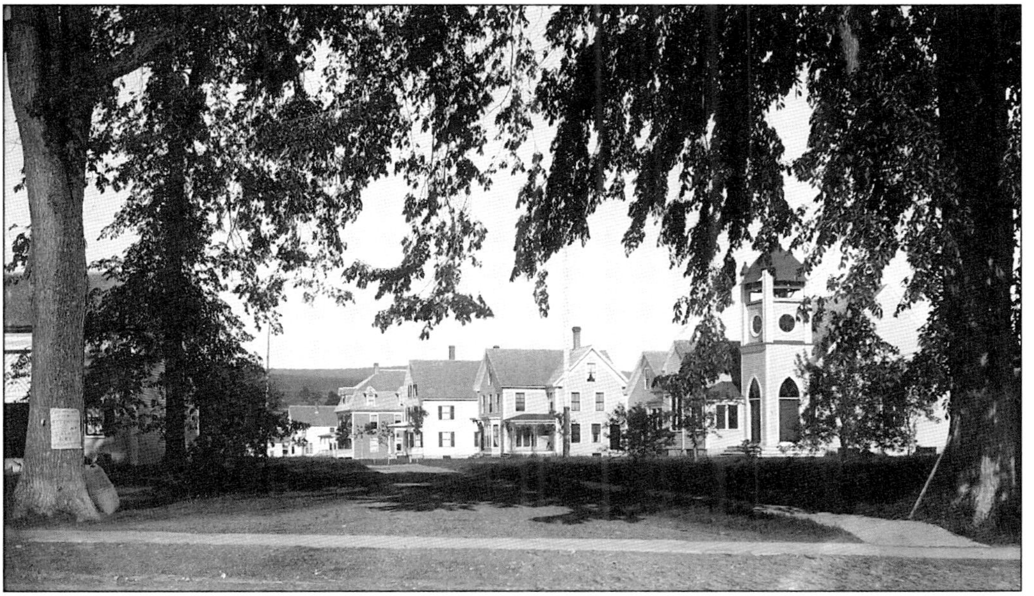

Meadow Street looking east, *c.* 1905. Most of these houses had been built recently, the trees were still small, and the 1909 parsonage had yet to appear beside the 1895 Congregational church. The home of Dr. Piper, later the home of Walter and Nellie Robinson and of Allan and Ruby Robinson, shows its old porch, later changed after a 1939 fire.

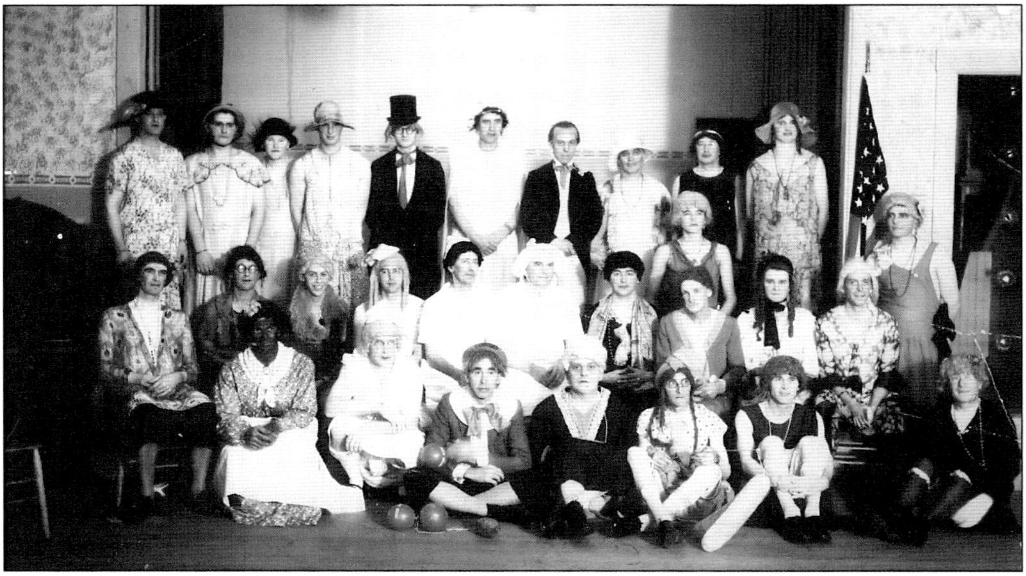

The *Womanless Wedding*, a production featuring the men of Bingham, c. 1930. The cast, photographed in the Congregational church parish house, included, from left to right: (front row) Milford Baker, Orville Forsythe, J. LaForest Andrews, Beecher Vincent, John Owens, Freeman Curtis (or Tony Passerini), and Fred Preble; (second row) Mont Miller, John Hardy, Martin Hastings, Forest Gilman, Arlie Dinsmore, Walter Robinson, John Gordon, Elmer Baker, Allen Hunnewell, and Arthur Macdougall; (third row) Bruce Coleman and Harold Coleman; (back row) Kenneth Russell, Bernard Andrews, John Pooler, Bernard Russell, Allan Robinson, Harry Cummings, Orrin Hill, Jack Shoppe (or Amos Hunnewell), Howard Bowen, and Clayton Andrews.

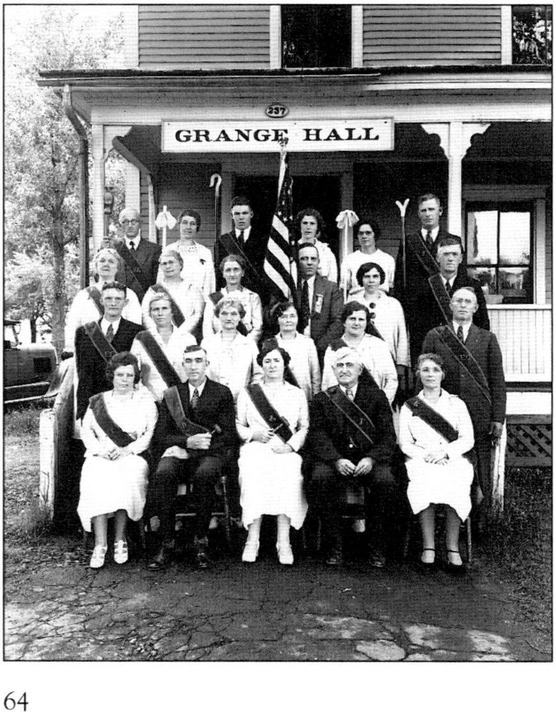

The Bingham Grange in front of their 1902 Grange Hall on Meadow Street, c. 1935–36. From left to right are: (front row) Etta Doyle (lecturer), Walter Hughes (overseer), Ethel Savage (master), Perley Foss (treasurer), and Emma Giberson; (second row) Reuben Crombie (ex. comm.), Floy Robinson, Winnie Henderson (pianist), Jennie Robinson, Edith Rollins, and Eugene Webster (ex.comm.); (third row) Lucy Crombie, Lula Gilman, Anna Savage (secretary), Donald Goff, Olivia Sterling, and George Gilman (ex. comm.); (back row) Arthur Jordan (gatekeeper), Susie Miller (marshall), Blaine Robinson (assistant steward), Arlene Robinson (lady assistant steward), Florence Collins (marshall), and George Giberson (steward).

"Jim Blaine," c. 1895. Sidney Goodrich's family dog was named after one of Maine's most colorful politicians. This unusual studio portrait was a Christmas gift to the two Goodrich children, Elizabeth (Jordan) and Ralph, from their twin aunts, Sarah (Sae) Milliken and Mary (Mae) Goodrich.

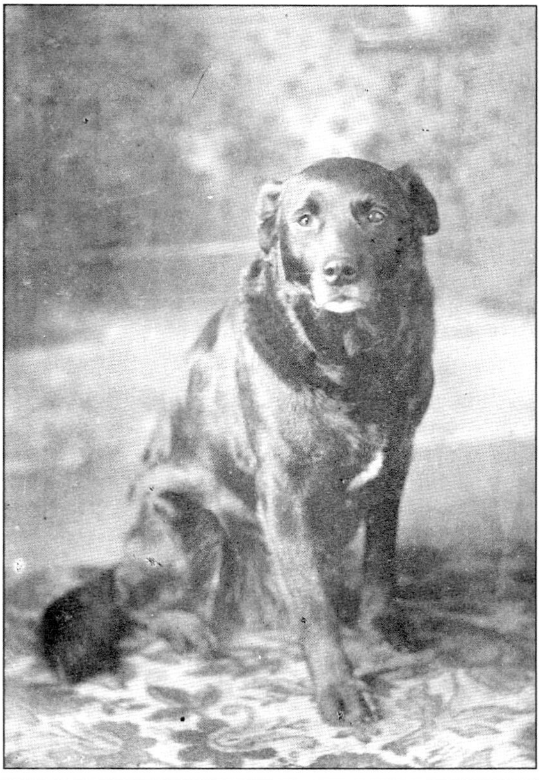

Martha Redmond and pet rooster "Johnie Bob," c. 1918. Martha is the daughter of John and Evie Redmond, who ran a hospital on Meadow Street in what is now the home of Norman and Jean Dionne. The photograph was taken at the Redmond farm east of the village.

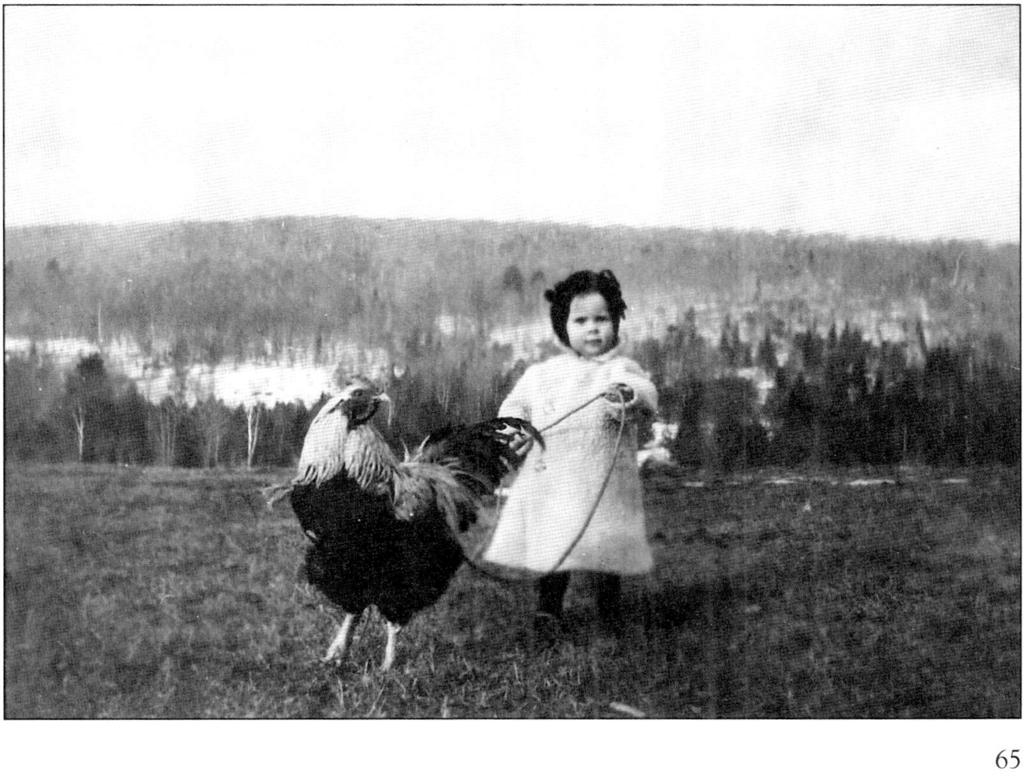

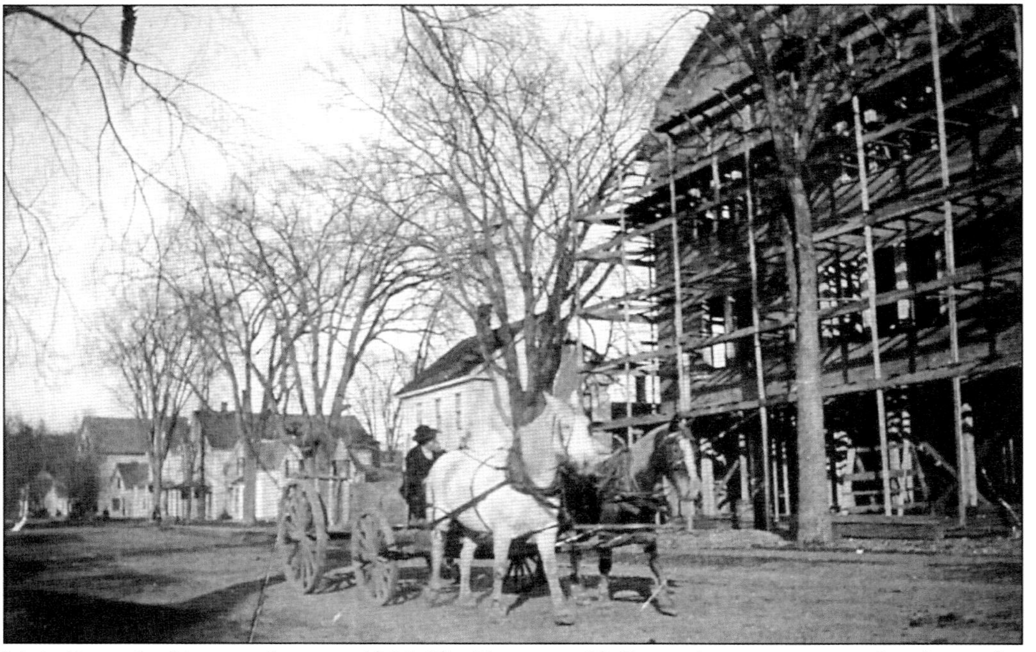

Main Street looking northeast, c. 1904. The Fraternity Hall is under construction. Just beyond is the Goodrich house on the corner of Meadow Street. This hall has been home to Odd Fellows, Rebeckahs, Masons, and the Eastern Star organization for many years, though those groups have fallen on hard times recently. The first floor has banquet facilities, and the upper floors have meeting rooms.

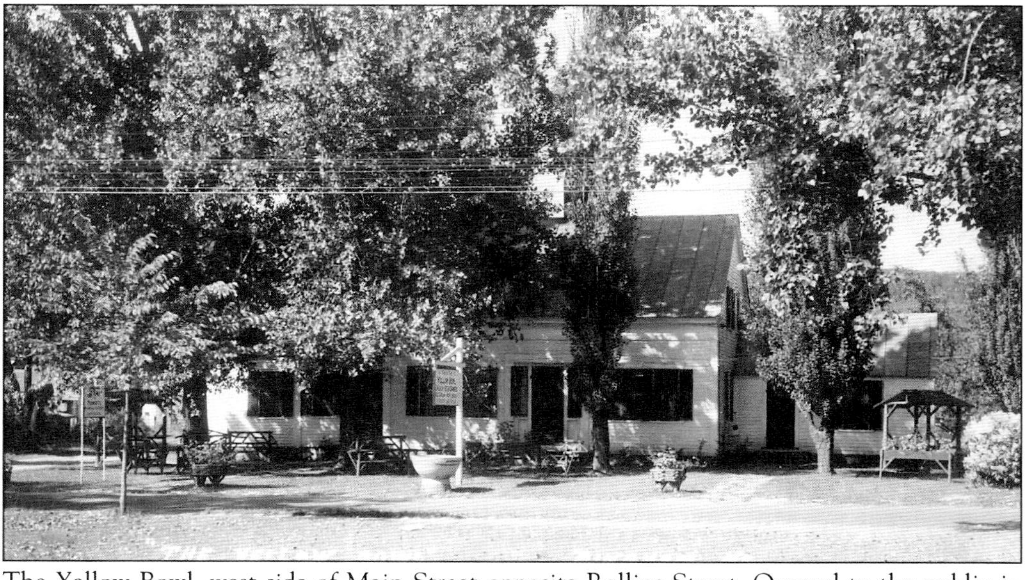

The Yellow Bowl, west side of Main Street opposite Rollins Street. Opened to the public in 1928 by Mrs. Grace Rollins, the lawn bore a large iron potash kettle painted bright yellow. Errold and Harriet Hilton conducted a tea room here for several summers. Grace's daughter Annie ran the business after her mother's death. It was torn down in the early 1970s to make room for the Skowhegan Savings Bank.

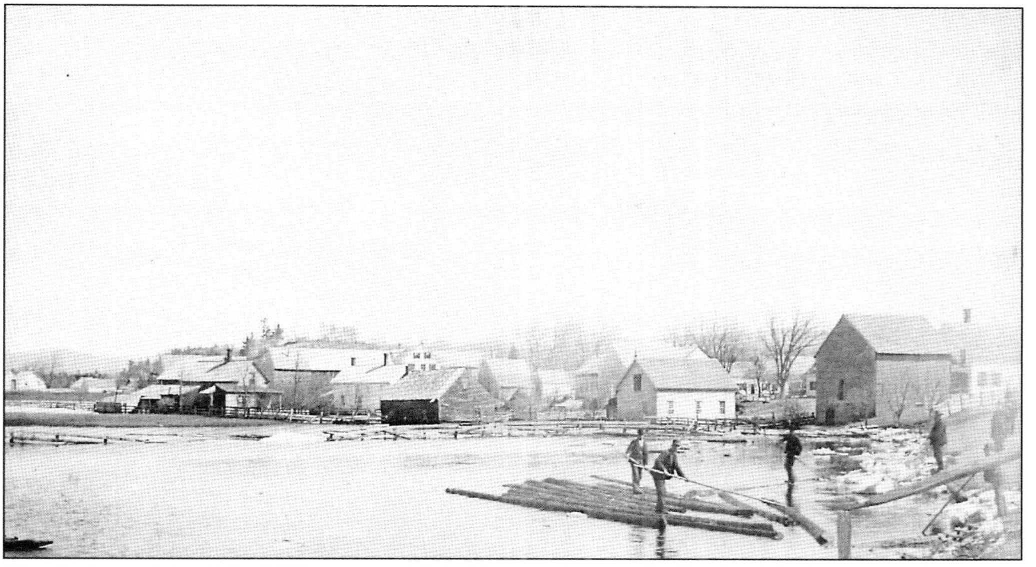

The freshet of April 8, 1892, west of Main Street. Chester Rollins' stable is at the right (more recently the home of his daughter, Elizabeth Cummings—now being opened to the public as a reincarnation of the Yellow Bowl). One doesn't envy the river drivers, who had to manhandle large logs back into the river.

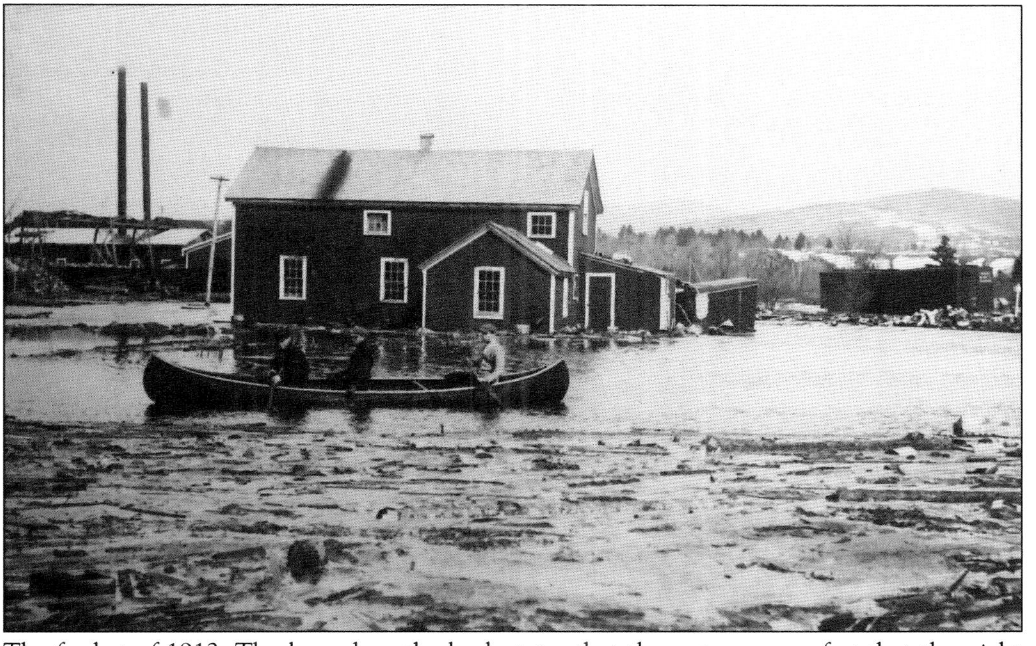

The freshet of 1912. The legend on the back states that the water rose so fast that the night crew at the last block factory had to be taken out by boat. The Bingham last block factory (last blocks were parts of shoes) was organized in 1889, and was originally owned by John J. Lander and S.A. Dinsmore. They later sold to Fitz. Bros. of Durham, Maine. The mill pictured was built by the Tucker-Lovell Company, and was located at the west end of Lander Street. It was the largest plant to make blocks in Maine. It burned in 1923.

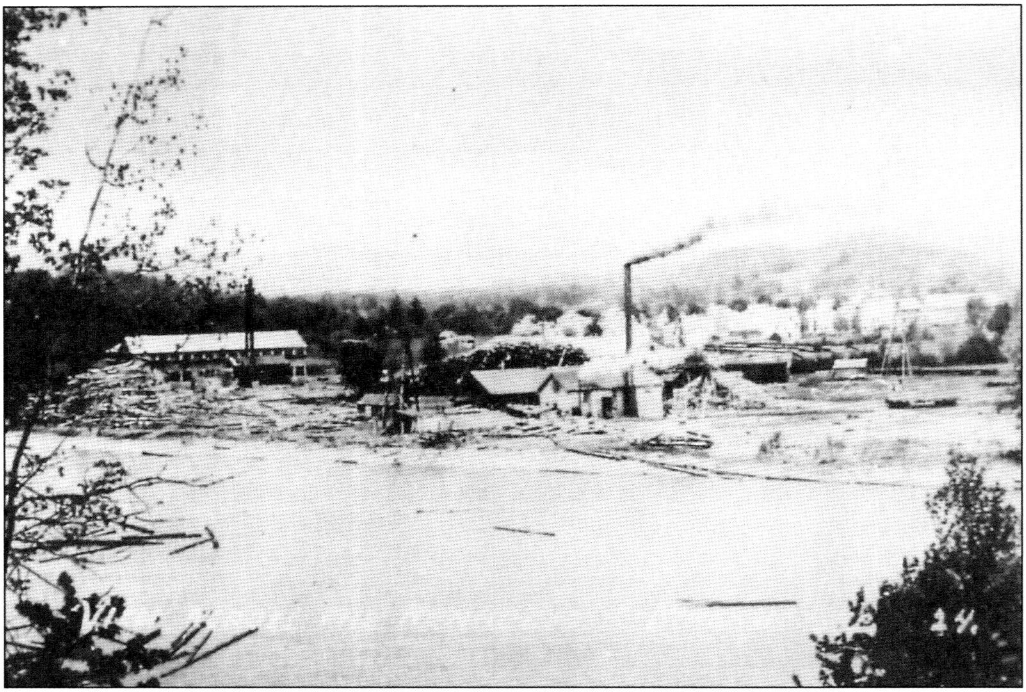

The Kennebec, looking east, *c.* 1920. The shank mill is on the left, with the last block mill in the center. The shank mill machinery was moved to Bingham from North Anson in 1906 and moved into the peg mill formerly owned by the McKay Company. Eventually, as wood supply became a problem, the machinery was moved again, to Savannah, Georgia.

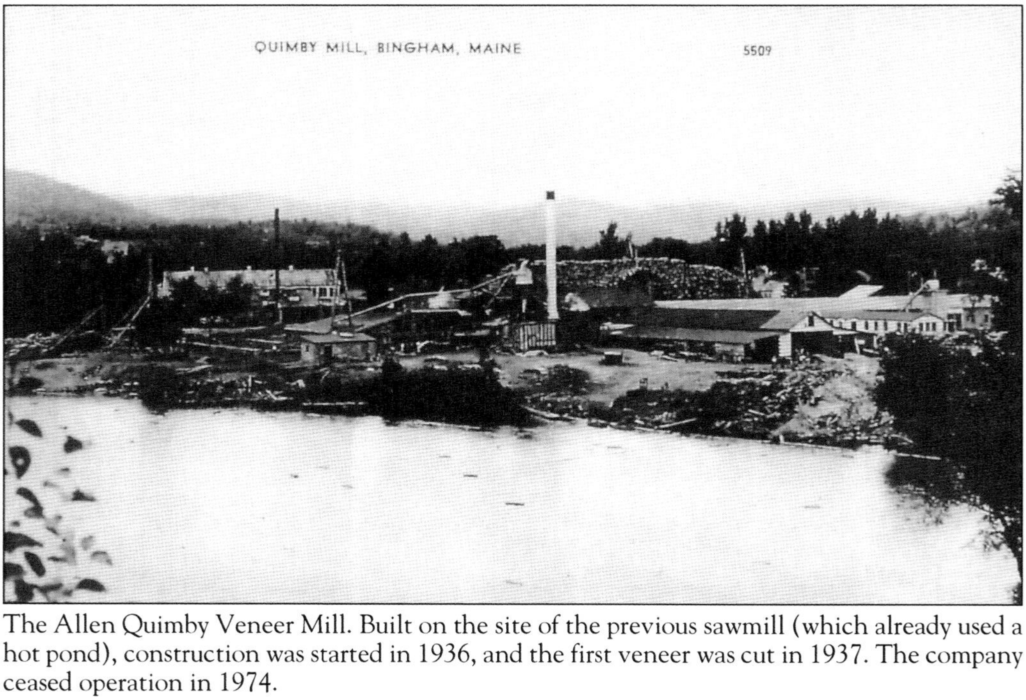

The Allen Quimby Veneer Mill. Built on the site of the previous sawmill (which already used a hot pond), construction was started in 1936, and the first veneer was cut in 1937. The company ceased operation in 1974.

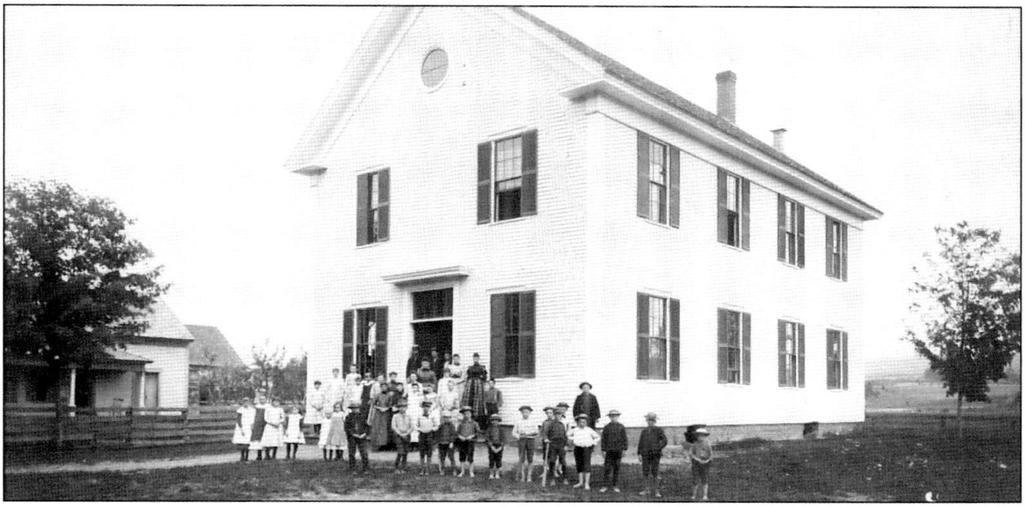

The Bingham Village School, located in front of the current Quimby Elementary School, *c.* 1885–90. This building was built *c.* 1878, and a second building, the McKinley School, was built behind it *c.* 1894. This ungraded school (at first) had the "little school" downstairs for younger children, and the "big school" upstairs. In the upper room, Sunday evening and mid-week prayer meetings were held until the Congregational church was built in 1895. A bell was added in 1902. Shown here are Miss Nellie Baker and her pupils.

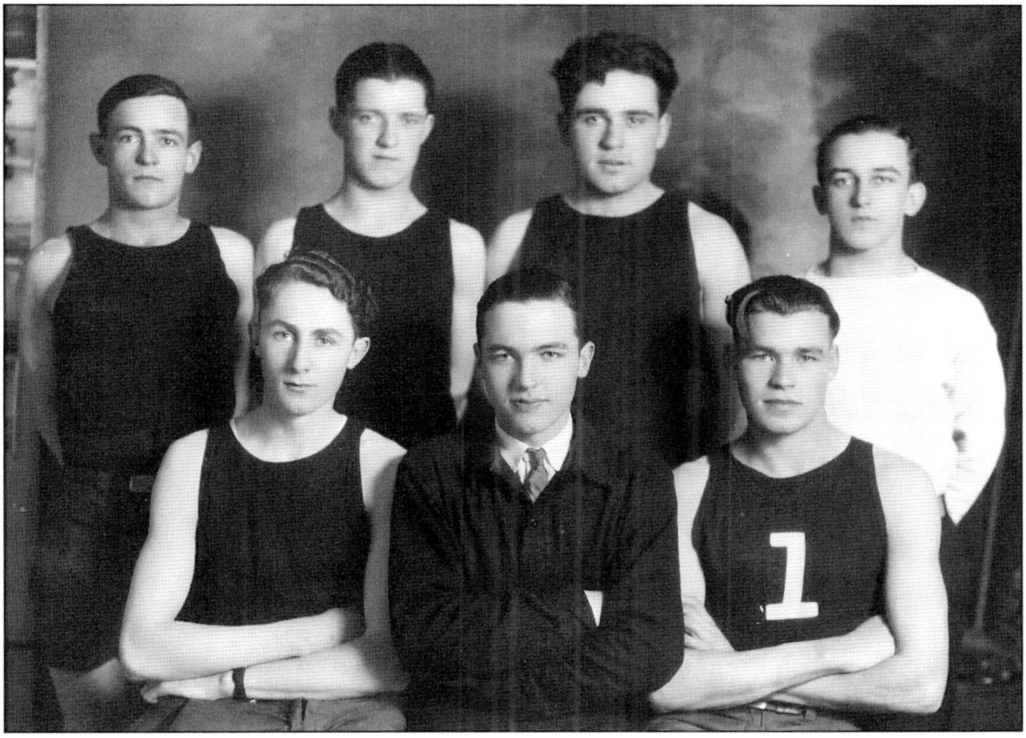

The Bingham High School track team of *c.* 1925. From left to right are: (front row) Donald Folsom, Kenneth Woodard, and Stanley Rollins; (back row) Albert Goodrich, Kendall Hunnewell, Earl Lester, and Rodney O'Brien.

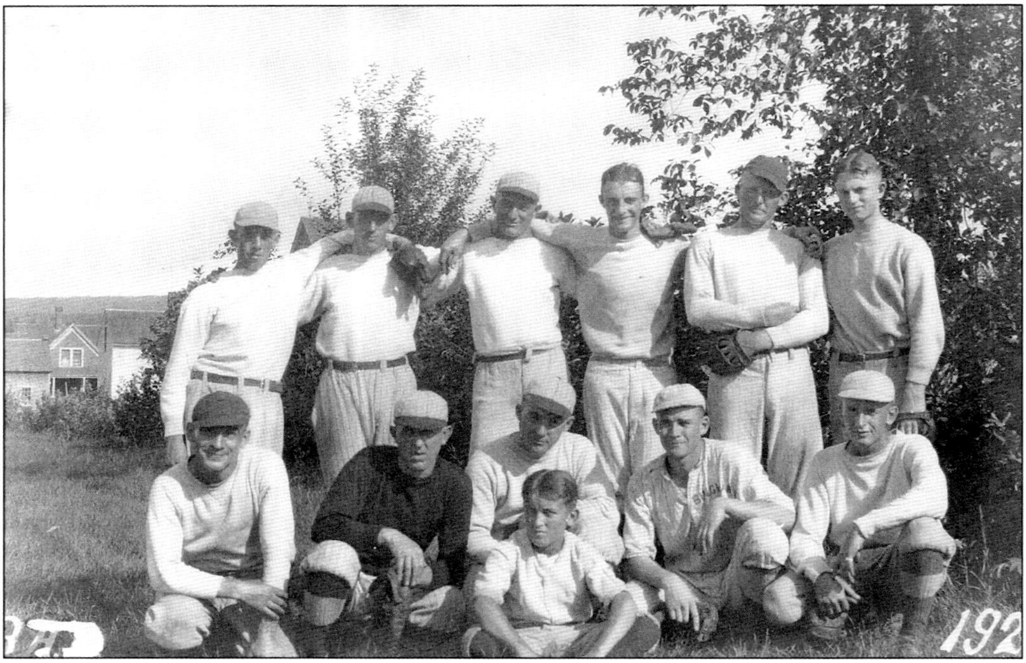

The Bingham Athletic Association baseball team of 1922. From left to right are: (front row) unidentified, Ned Moore, Bert Hunnewell, Rodney O'Brien (in front), Allen Hunnewell, and unidentified; (back row) Lester Morris, Leon Roberts, Fremont Stewart, Justin Russell, Harold Clark, and Allan Robinson. The two unidentified men may be from Skowhegan, since it was common to hire extras if the team was short of players.

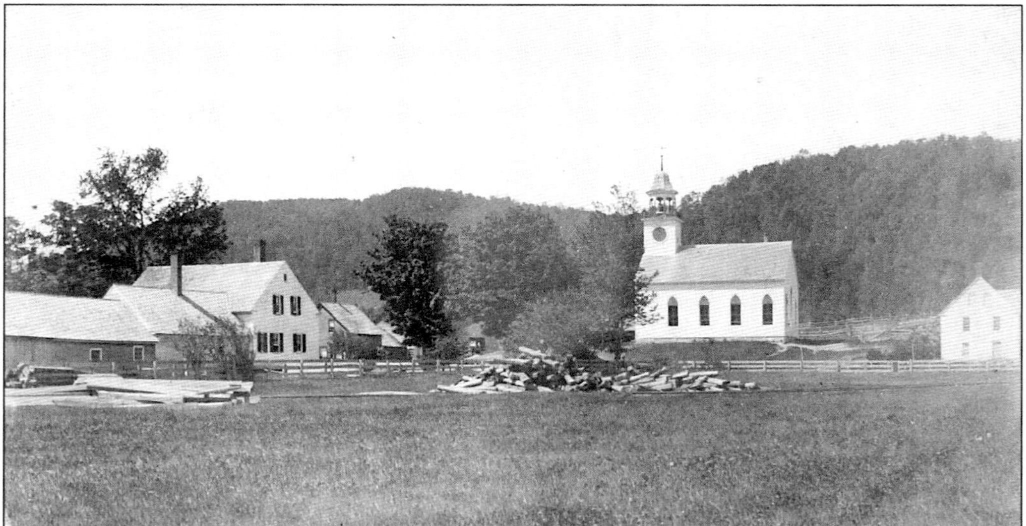

The Bingham depot grounds, June 15, 1890. The Somerset Railroad arrives in Bingham. In the foreground are the ties to be used, and the buildings have yet to be constructed. In the background is the Union Meeting House, built in 1836. The church was shared by the various Protestant denominations in town. There were fifty-two pews, one for each Sunday of the year. The Revere bell was purchased and delivered in 1863. The Cooley farm is on the left.

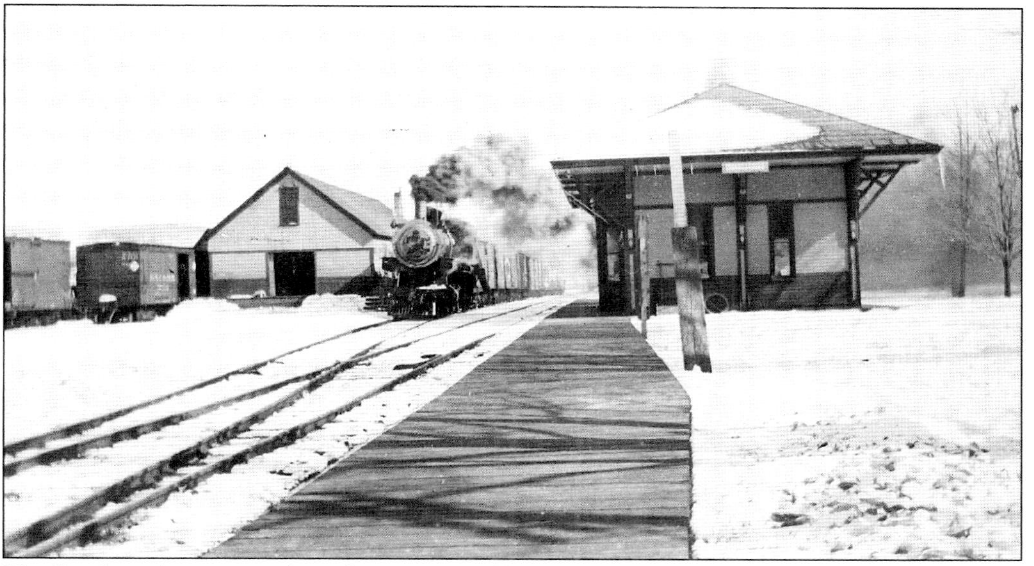

The Bingham depot grounds, early 1900s. In addition to this station, there was a passenger station on Bingham Heights, put in when the railroad was extended to Greenville in 1906–1907.

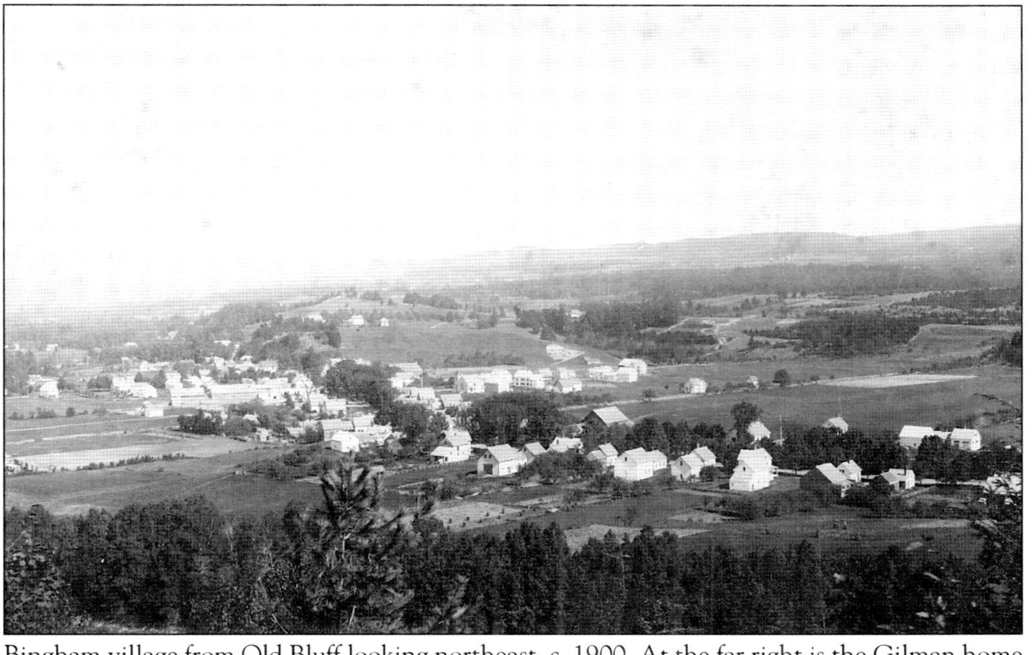

Bingham village from Old Bluff looking northeast, *c.* 1900. At the far right is the Gilman home on Owens Street. The 1902 Grange hall on Meadow Street has not yet been built.

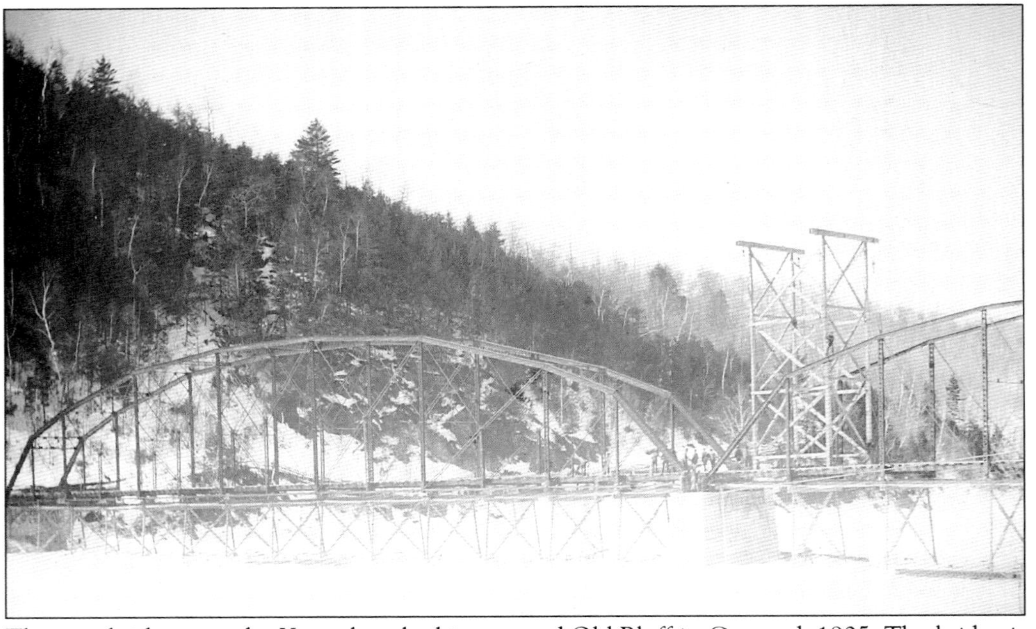

The iron bridge over the Kennebec, looking toward Old Bluff in Concord, 1905. The bridge is under construction; notice how the floor is braced against the ice in the river.

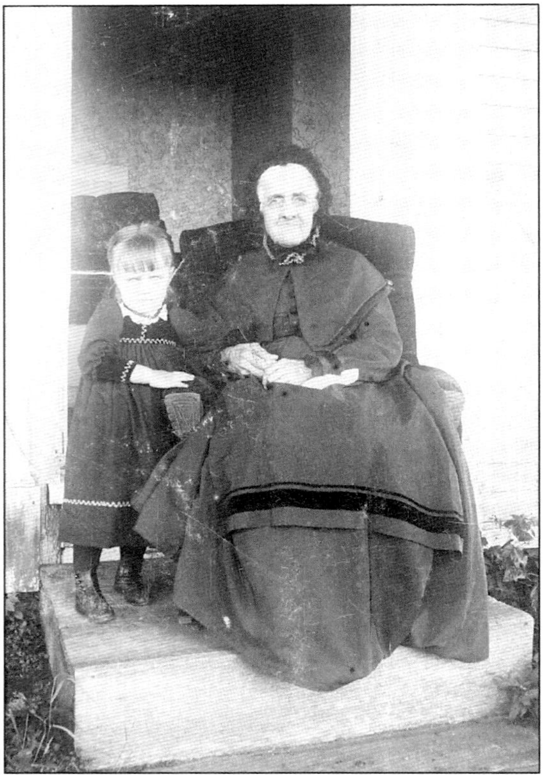

"Aunt Polly" (Mary) Wilson, the daughter of Levi and Polly (Mary) Jewett Goodrich. Aunt Polly was born prematurely in 1804, and was so small that her body was set in a quart measure and a teacup was put over her head . "She'll never live . . .," they said. Here she is shown at ninety years of age with her three-year-old great-grandchild, Minnie Jean Powers. Aunt Polly lived south of the town, in a very early home built by her father-in-law, Reverend Obed Wilson (later the home of Wilmont and Etta Doyle). Polly and Daniel Wilson had thirteen children, including two sets of twins born one year and two days apart. She died in 1898 at the age of ninety-four.

Five

Concord and Embden

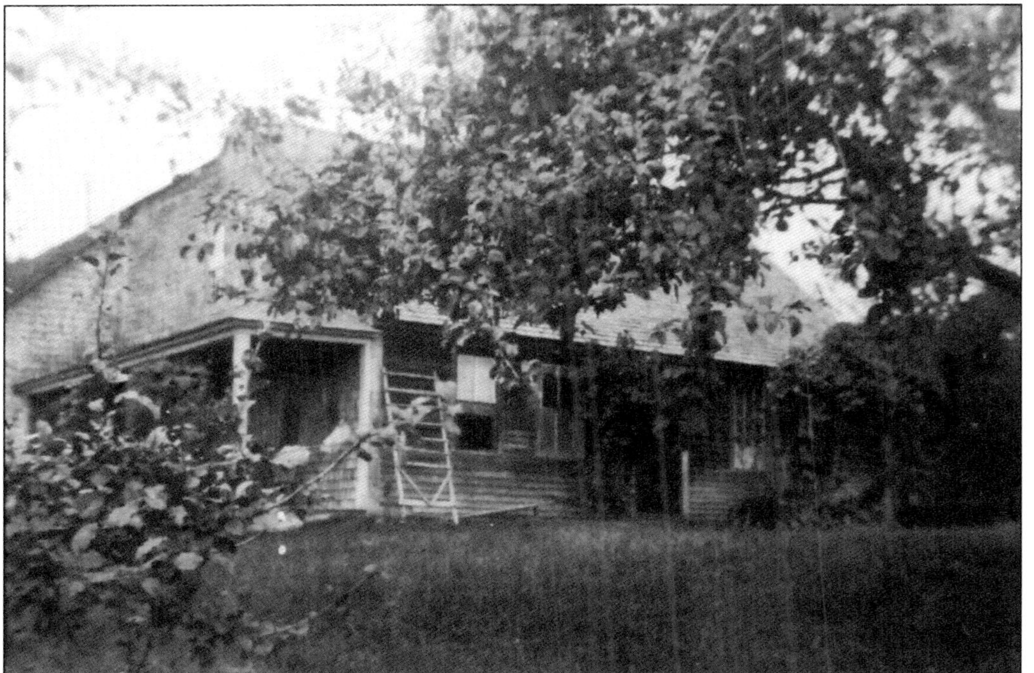

The Joseph Foss farm, located on a high bluff overlooking the river, *c.* early 1900s. For years, Foss' spring was a well-known source of drinking water, and was piped down the bluff to the road below. This building still stands, but in poor condition.

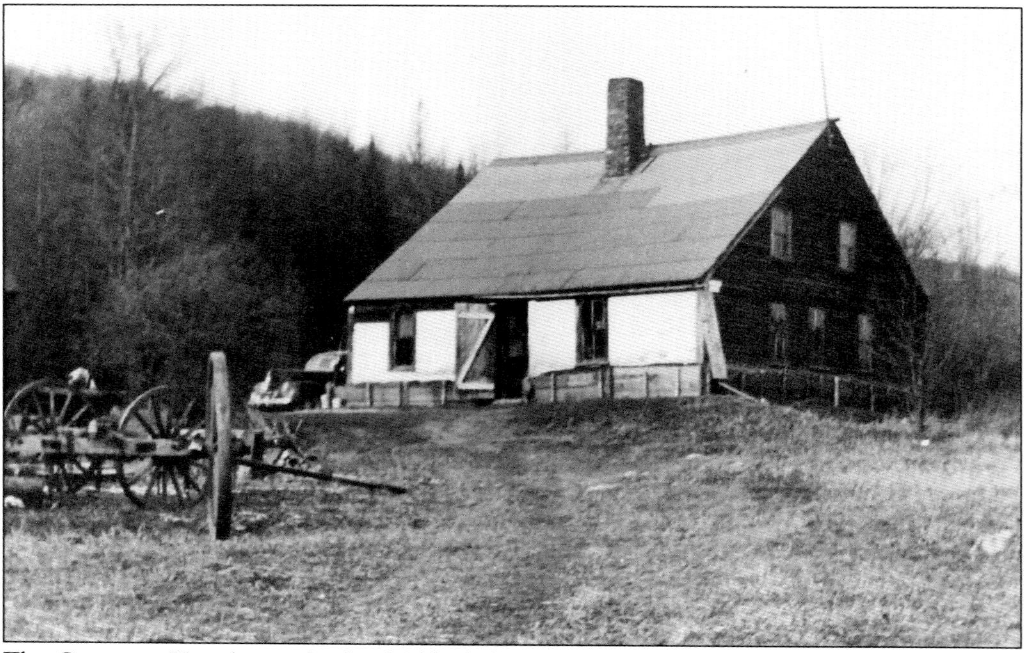

The Governor King house, back of Old Bluff, *c.* 1940s. This very early building was built by Maine's first governor, and used at first as a hunting lodge and for grain storage. For many years it was home to the Howes family. It finally collapsed in the late 1950s, after standing unoccupied for many years.

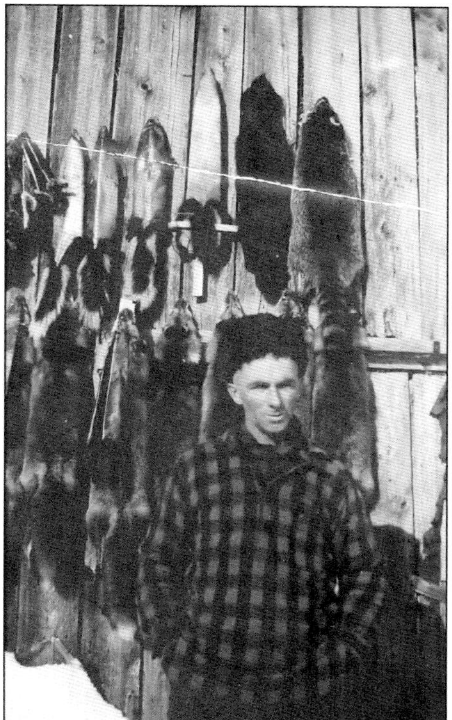

Carleton "Spider" Ellis, with pelts from his trapping, back of Old Bluff, *c.* 1930s. Mr. Ellis earned his nickname from his agility as a river driver. The Ellis farm has been renovated in recent years by his son-in-law, Donald Folsom.

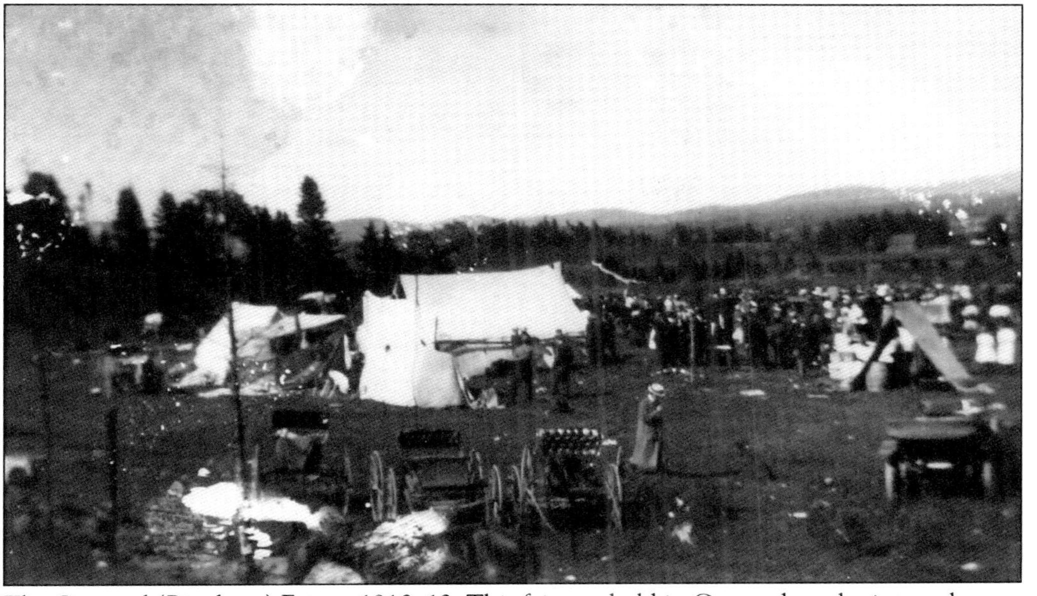

The Concord (Bingham) Fair, *c.* 1910–12. This fair was held in Concord on the intervale near the present Bingham Water District facility. It was usually called Bingham Fair, and featured horse racing at a track in this area which was owned by racing fan Clarence Dutton.

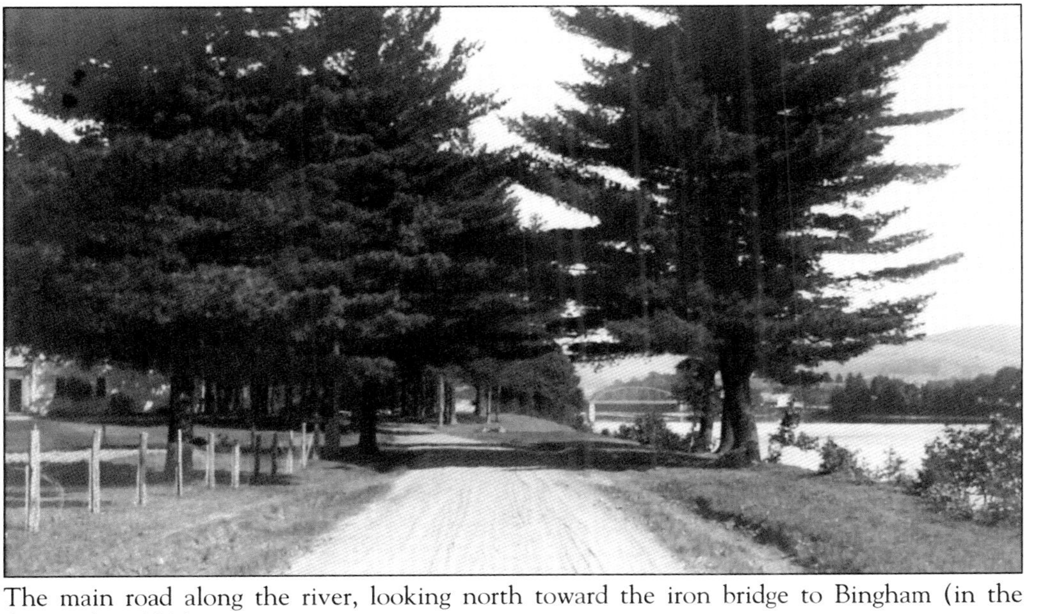

The main road along the river, looking north toward the iron bridge to Bingham (in the distance), *c.* 1910.

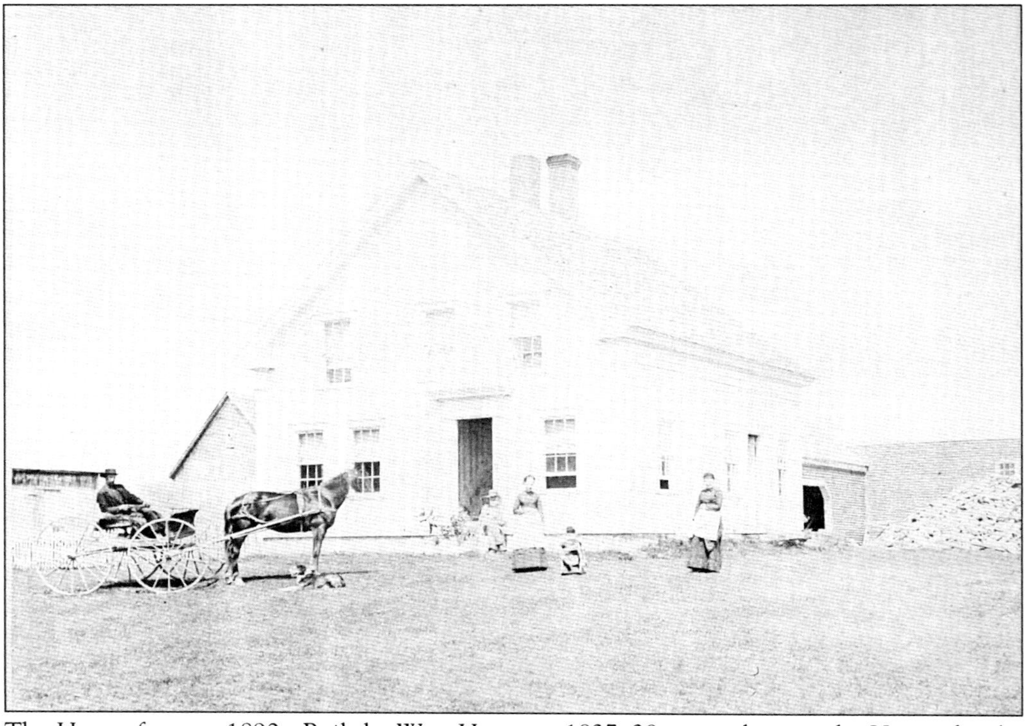

The Howes farm, *c.* 1890s. Built by Wm. Howes *c.* 1837–38, it was long in the Howes family, and was for many years the home of Davis and Dr. Anna Howes. More recently it has been the home of Harriet Hilton and Bruce and Shirley Cornue.

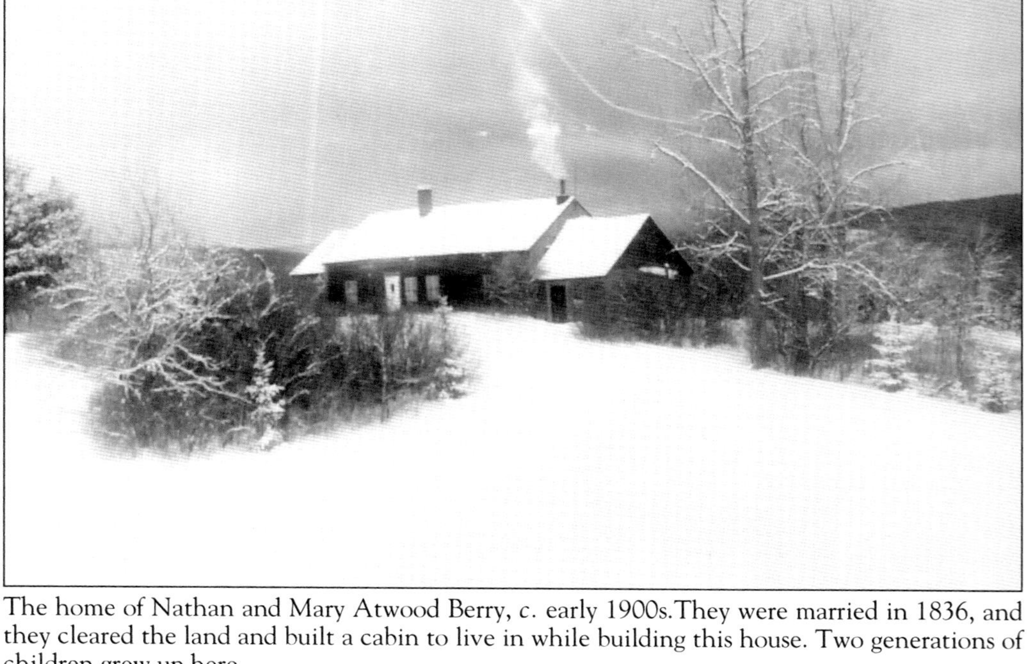

The home of Nathan and Mary Atwood Berry, *c.* early 1900s.They were married in 1836, and they cleared the land and built a cabin to live in while building this house. Two generations of children grew up here.

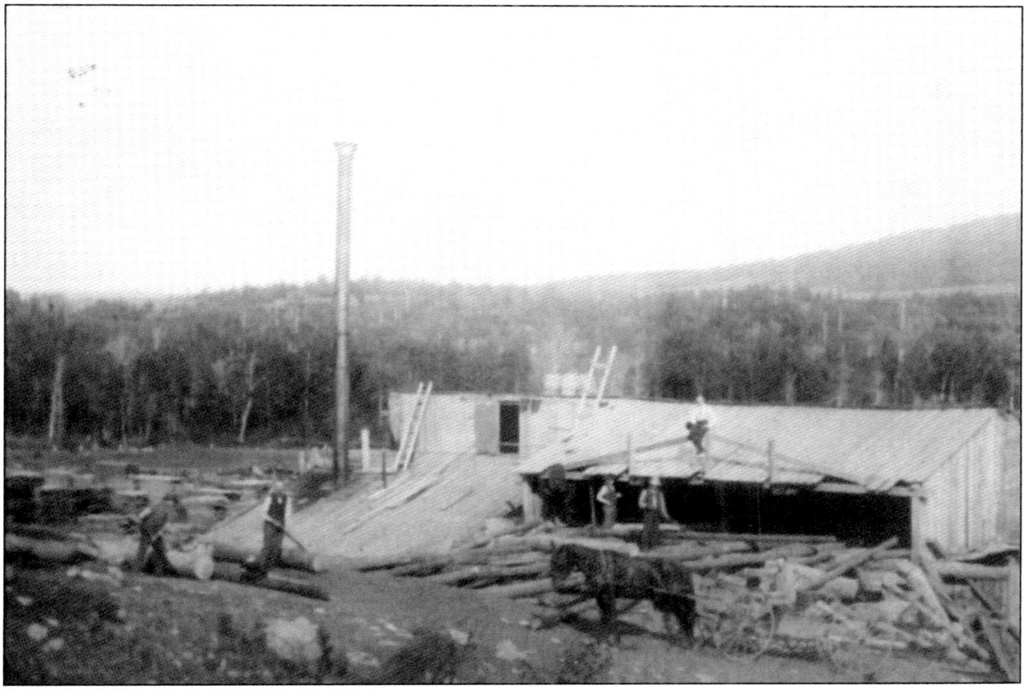

Frank A. Cleveland's sawmill, Concord, c. 1890s. Judging from the smokestack, this was probably powered by a steam boiler and engine, as were most mills of that time.

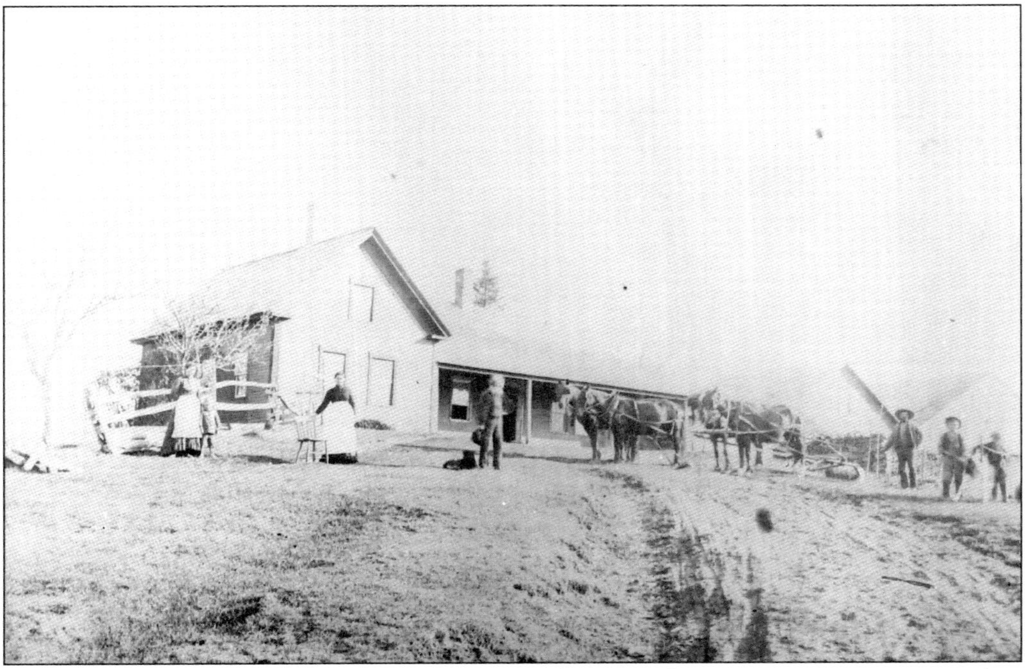

The home of Benjamin and Harriet Berry Atwood, Concord, c. 1885. It was not unusual to want both the family members and the important farm animals in a photograph. Here we see several generations, with farm buildings in the background.

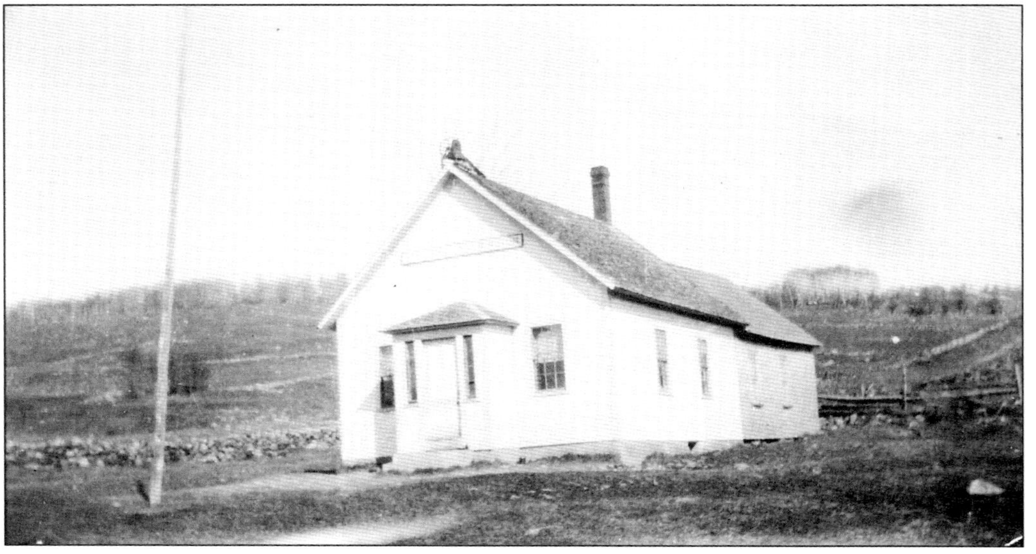

The Martha Washington School, Concord Corner, July 2, 1923, later the Larkin Dunton School. The building was first used as a church.

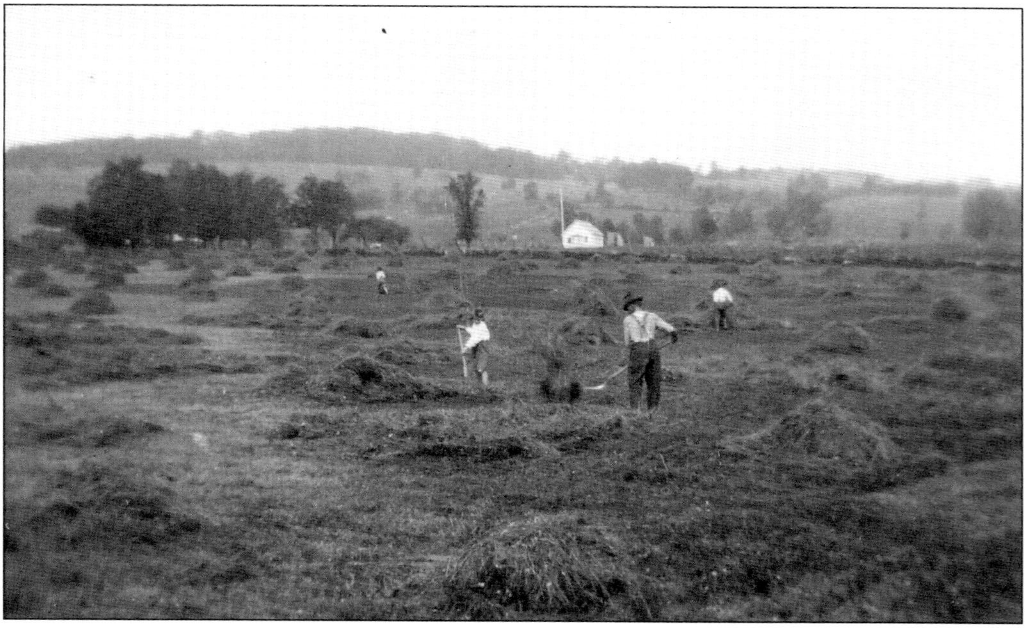

Haying, Concord, *c.* 1913–20. The crew is piling cut hay by hand. The Martha Washington School appears in the distance. The crew generally got themselves around by bicycle.

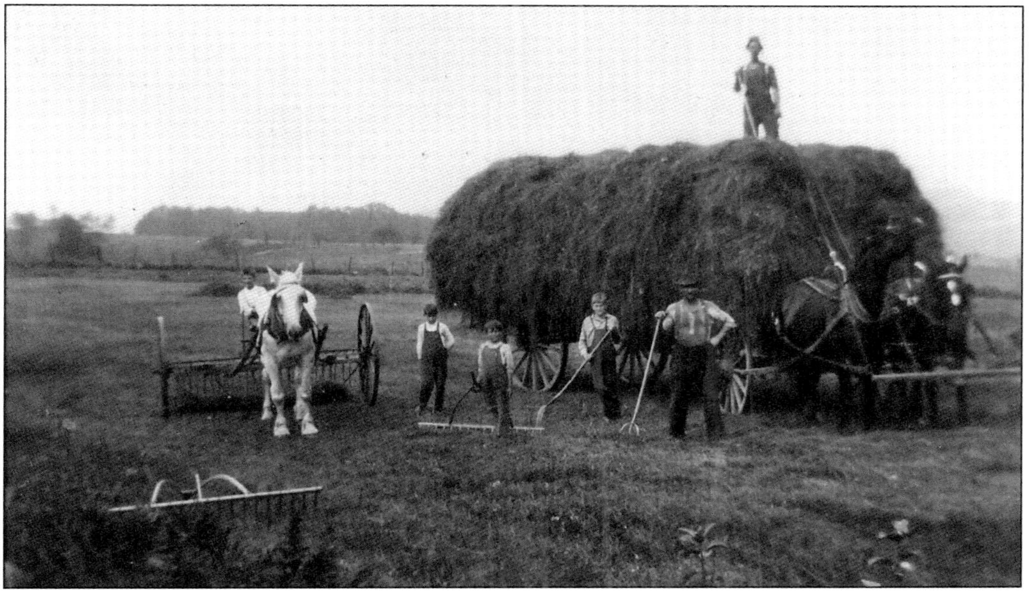

Haying, Concord, *c.* 1913–20. All the common haying implements are shown here, both hand rakes and horse rakes, as well as the hayrack.

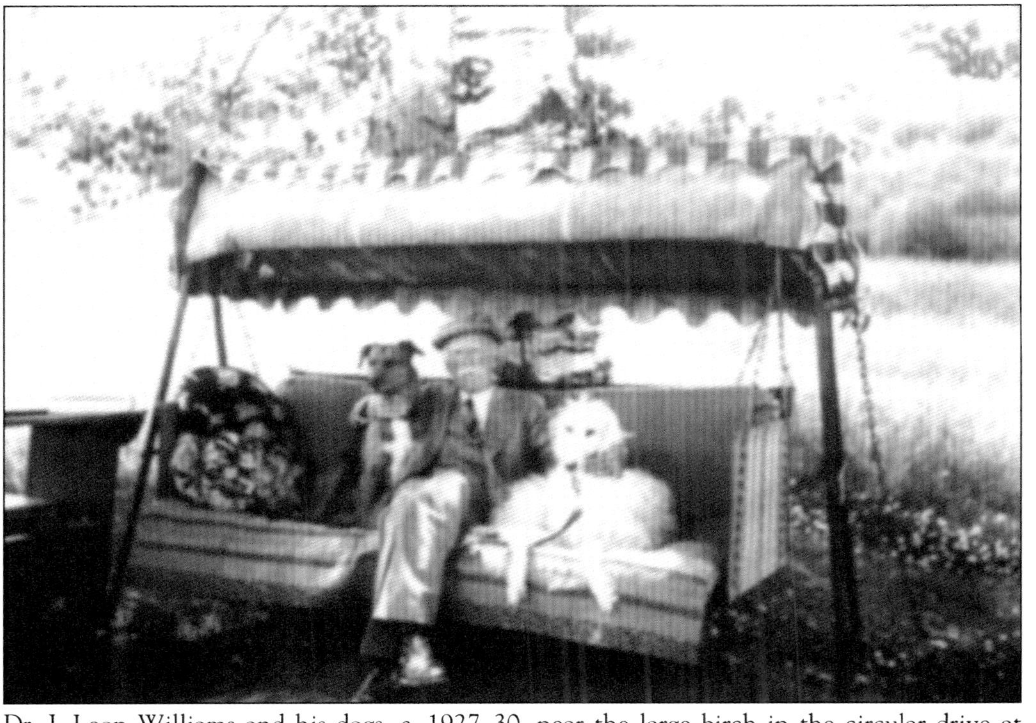

Dr. J. Leon Williams and his dogs, *c.* 1927–30, near the large birch in the circular drive at Concord Haven. Peter, the white dog, was buried nearby. Dr. Williams' inventions led to modern dentures as we know them. From his office in London, he supplied dentures to the Royal Family. Dr. Williams authored not only scientific studies, but moral and artistic works as well. The home is now owned by Amy Thorndike.

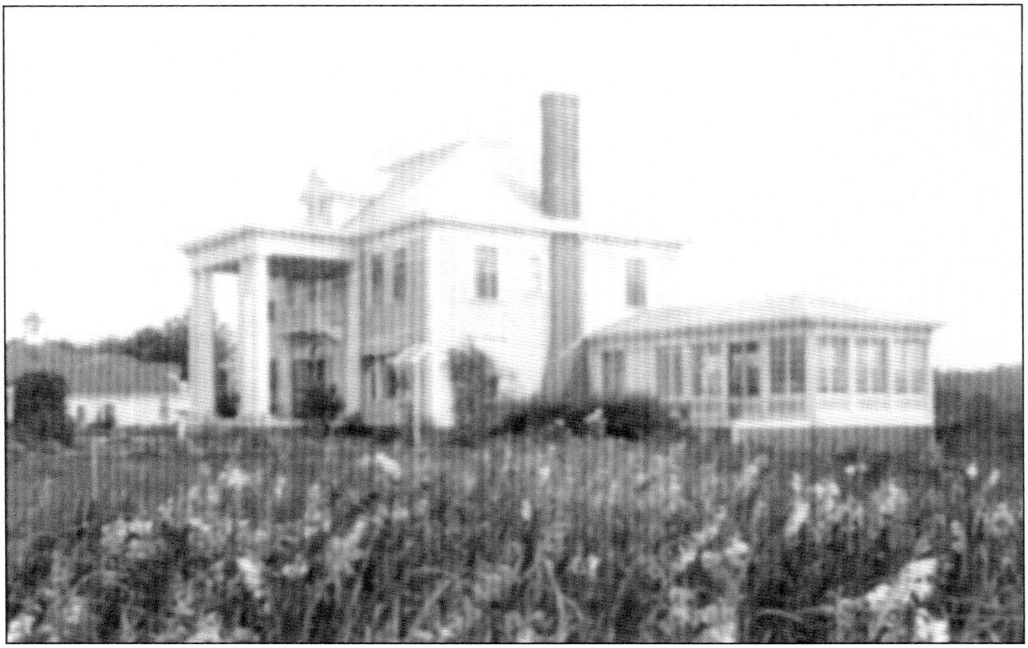

Concord Haven, the elegant summer home of Dr. J. Leon Williams (1852–1932), the world-renowned dental pioneer , researcher, and inventor. Dr. Williams had this home built *c*. 1915–18 near the site of his boyhood home, on a spot overlooking the Kennebec, where he had tended cows as a lad. The house is actually in Embden, though the stables (on the left) are in Concord.

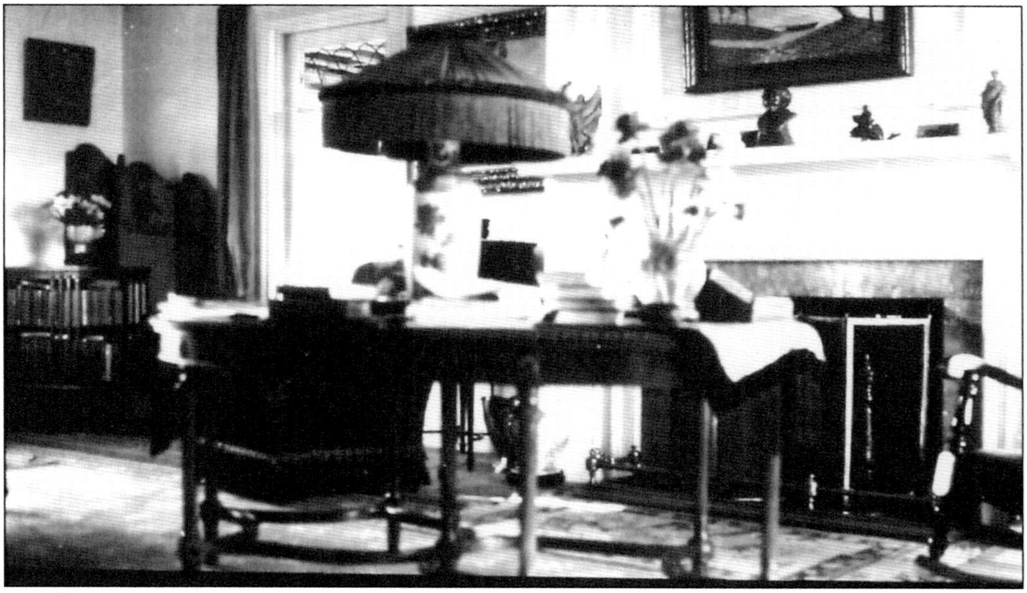

The living room at Concord Haven, 1920s. This stylish fifteen-room summer home in the Colonial Revival style had a large solarium (door to the left) and spacious high-posted rooms. A bust of Shakespeare is on the mantel (Dr. Williams wrote a work on Stratford-on-Avon, the poet's birthplace).

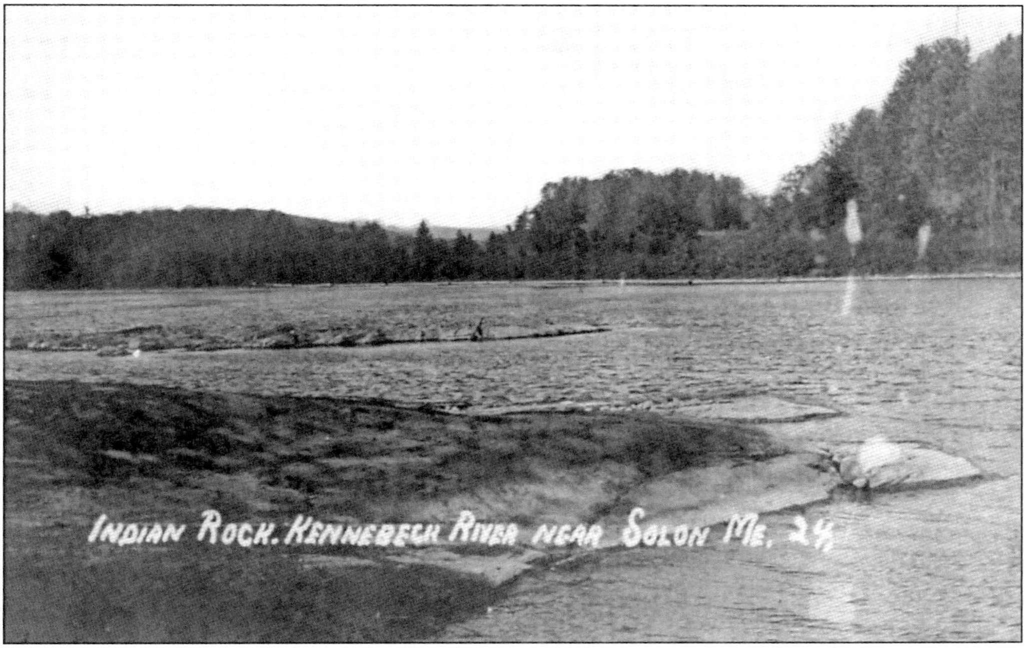

Indian rock, in the Kennebec, on the Embden side below the Solon bridge. This rock shows petroglyphs of great antiquity, carved into the rock by the earliest inhabitants of the upper valley.

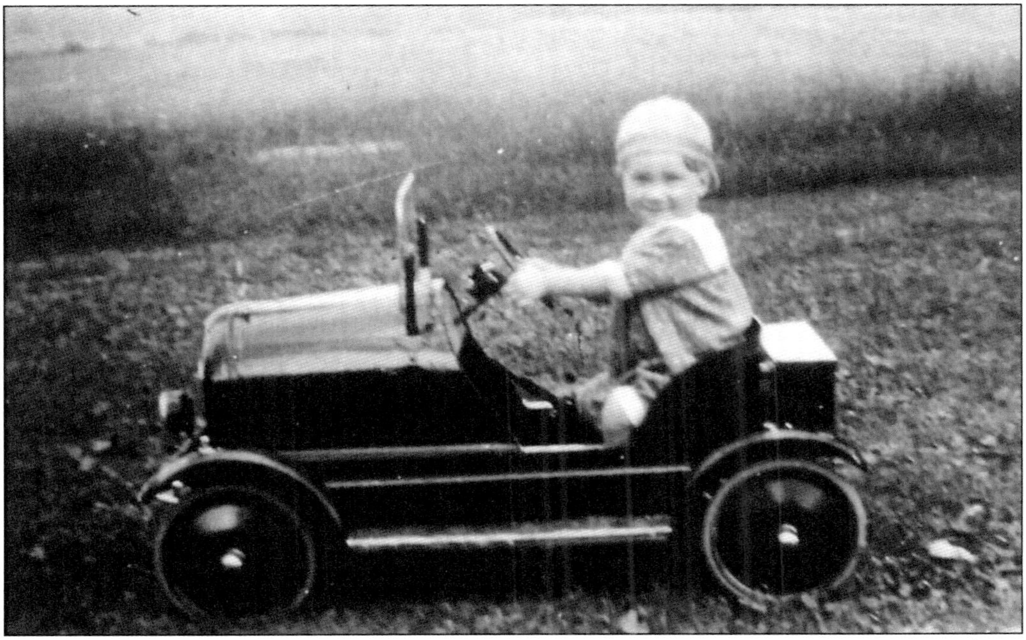

Owen Croteau in his shiny pedal car, c.early 1930s. Many of the pedal cars were made to resemble a particular make of automobile. Owen was the grandson of Inzie and Harry Hilton.

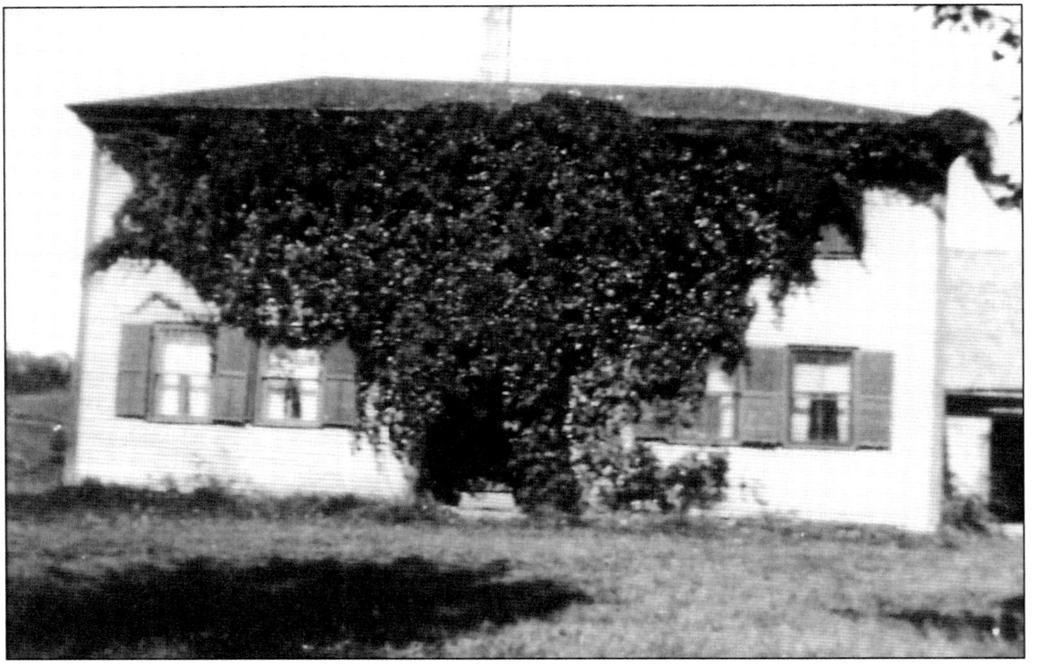

The home of Inzie and Harry Hilton, *c.* 1920s. The house has been taken over by a voracious vine. This early Federal-style house burned in 1931.

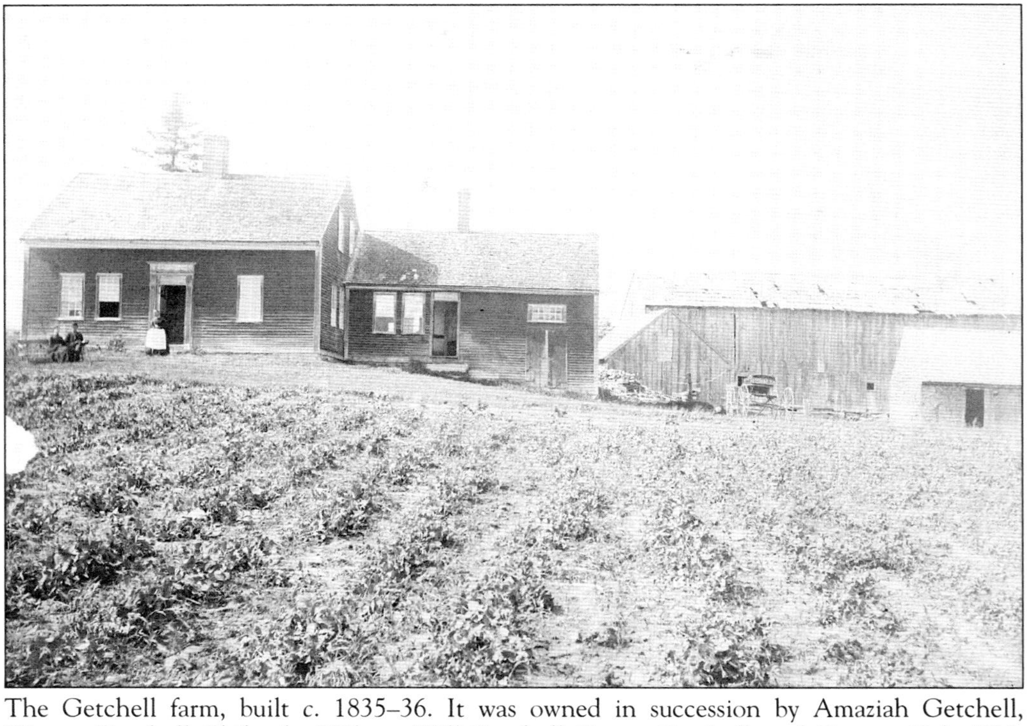

The Getchell farm, built *c.* 1835–36. It was owned in succession by Amaziah Getchell, Warren Getchell, Philander Wilson, Will Getchell, Ernest Getchell, and Gustave Kelm.This photograph showing both home and barns dates from *c.* 1880s.

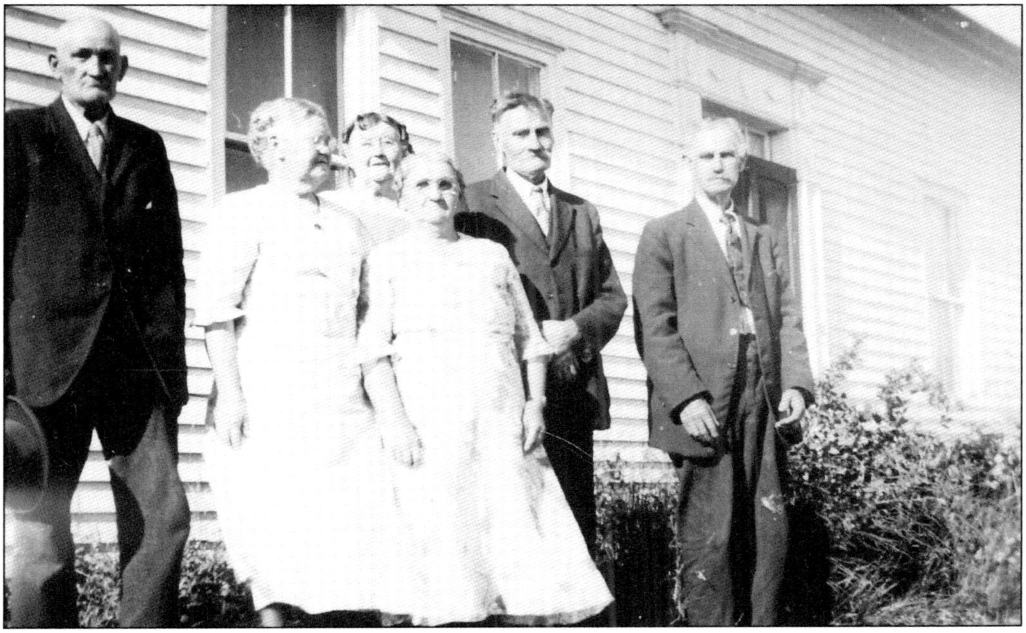

A gathering of cousins at the Getchell farm, c. 1950. They are, from left to right, Danny Walker, Della Sampson, Zadee Barrott, Lizzie Wentworth, Will Getchell, and Fred Getchell.

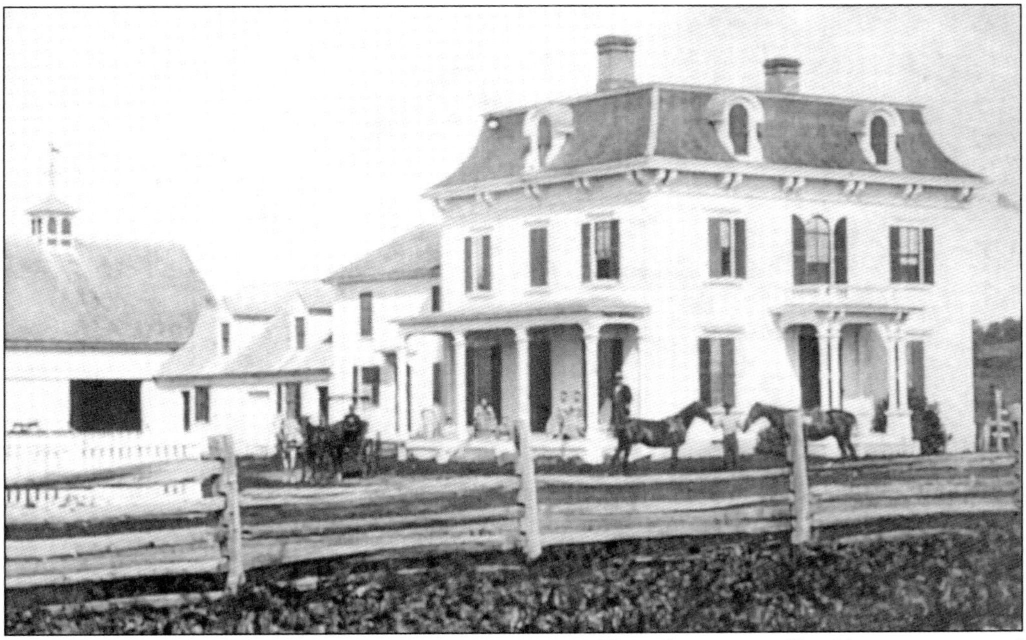

The Joel Gray farm, from a stereo photograph, c. 1880s. This elegant set of buildings was erected on the farm of his father, Joseph Gray, by Joel, who built and owned the first Carrabassett Hall at North Anson in 1870. He was also an urgent advocate of the building of the Somerset Railroad. When he died at age forty-four, his remains were conveyed with ceremony from Boston to Carrabassett Hall for a large funeral. In 1888, the farm buildings were purchased by Randall Ellis of Belfast, who conducted a large and profitable dairy farm.

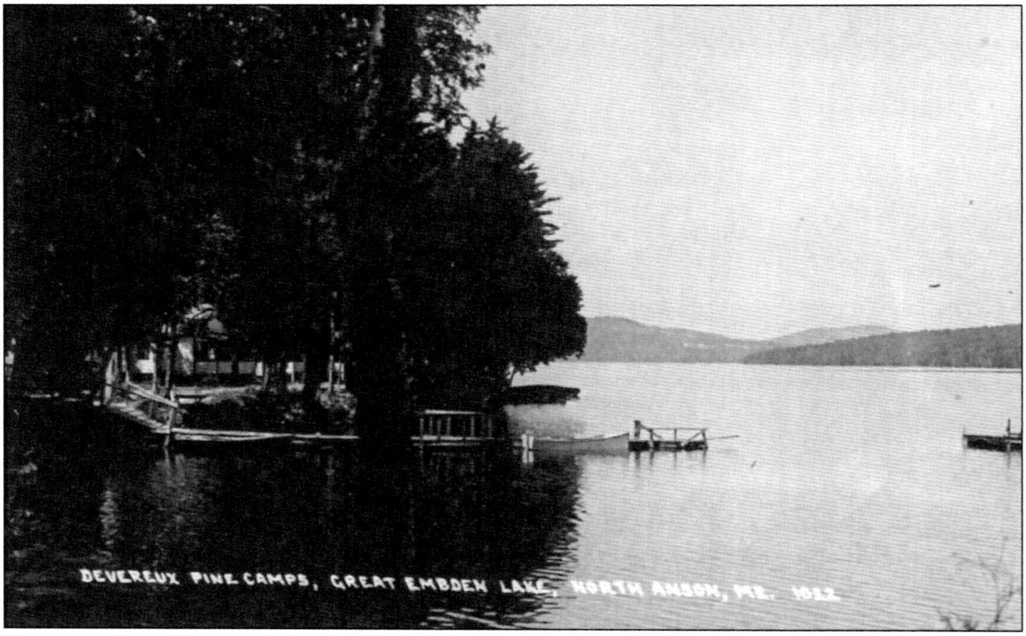

Devereux Pine Camps, Lake Embden, *c.* 1940–50. The lake has long been a popular summer attraction with many cottages. Summer campers returned to camps like these all over Maine.

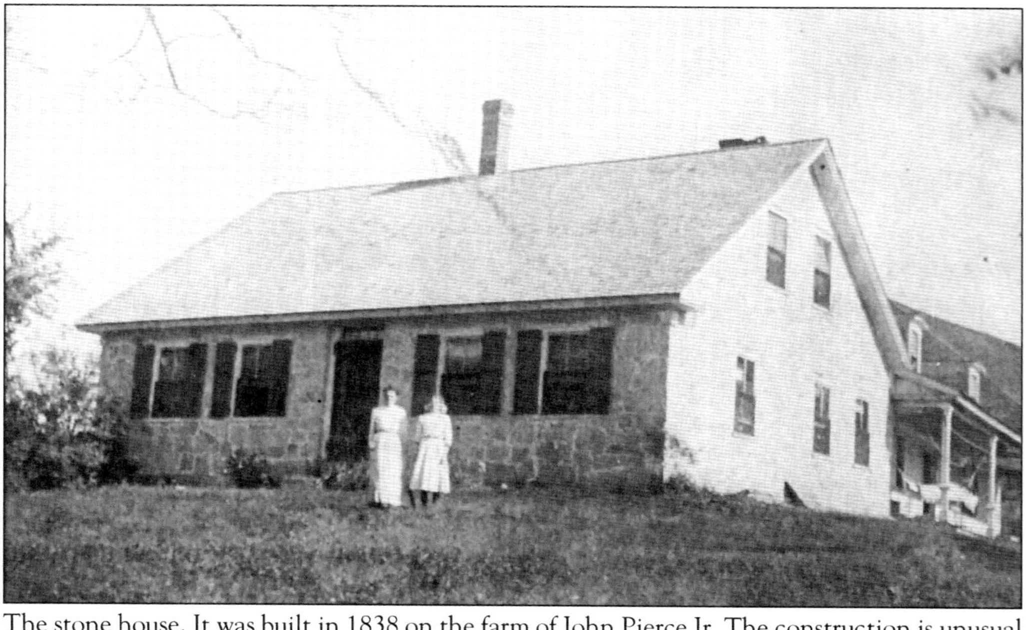

The stone house. It was built in 1838 on the farm of John Pierce Jr. The construction is unusual for this part of the state. This building still stands and is presently the home of Mr. and Mrs. Richard Allen.

Six

Solon

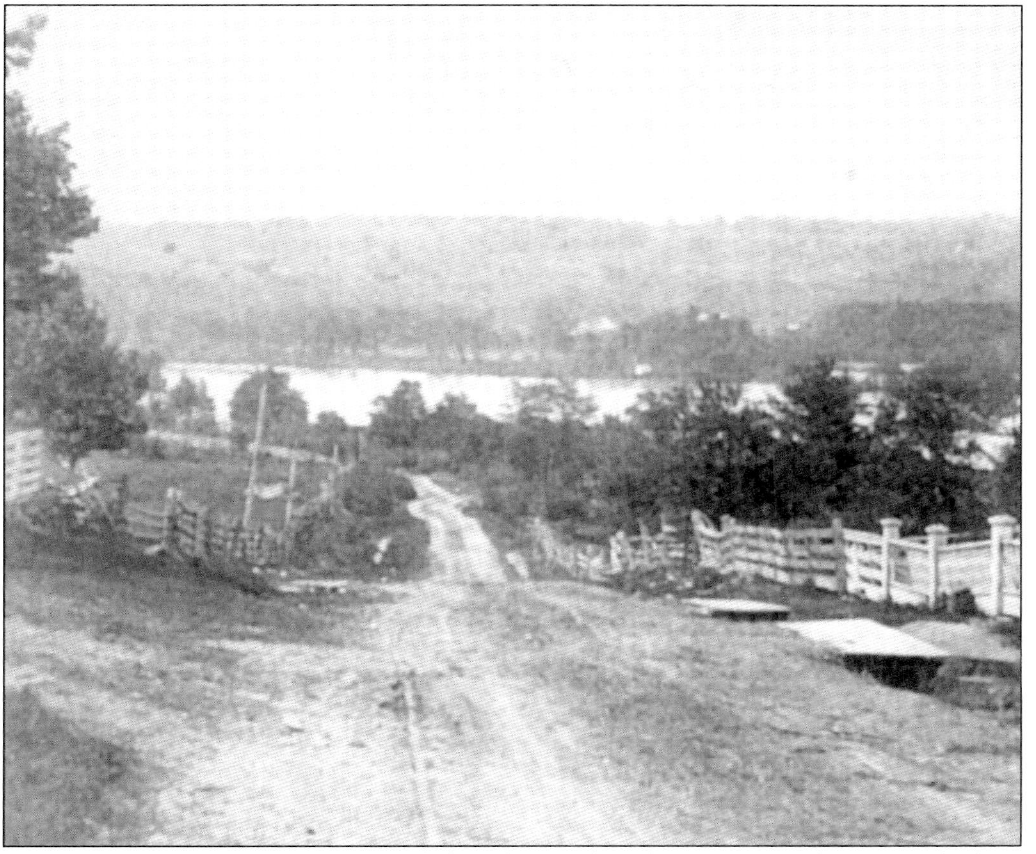

An early stereo view of the road just below the Bingham line, *c.* 1875. The view is looking south, with the river (above Caratunk Falls) visible in the distance.

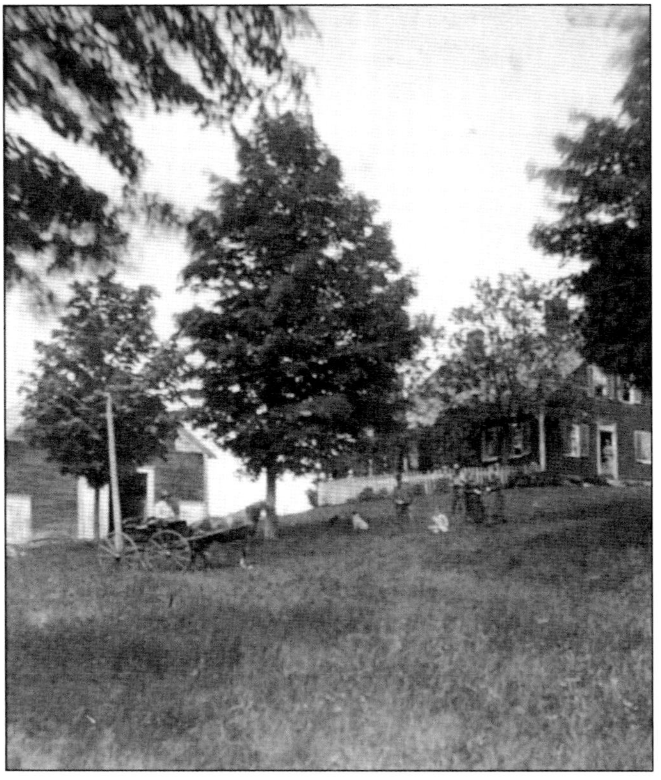

The Withington farm, just south of the Tilden Davis farm, on the hill above Route 201, north of Solon village. This stereo photograph from the 1880s shows the early Cape Cod house and barn, with residents posed in the dooryard with their animals. The present Linwood Tuscan home is in this location.

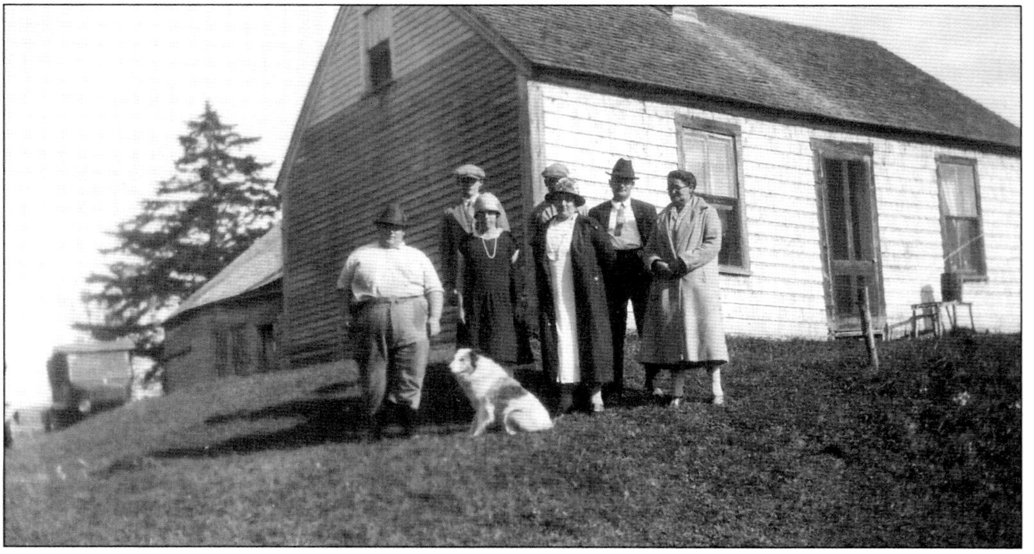

The Arlie McClintick farm, McClintick Road, off Hardscrabble Road and the Lake Road, September 15, 1927. From left to right are Lawrence McClintick, unidentified, unidentified, Leroy McClintick (at rear), Emma McClintick, Arlie McClintick, and unidentified. All the farms in this part of town are now overgrown and fallen in.

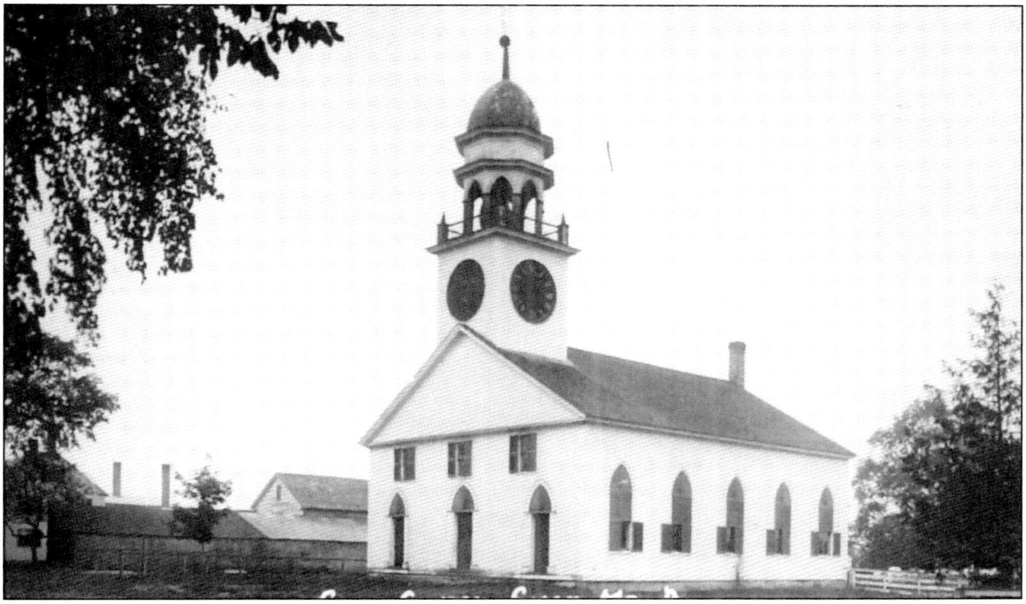

The Solon Congregational Church, *c.* early 1890s, with a clock face but apparently never a clock. Built in 1837 as the Solon Free Meeting House and originally owned jointly by the Baptists, Methodists, Congregationalists, and Universalists, it is thought to have the oldest pipe organ in the state, which was purchased used for $250, and was first installed in 1859 in the rear gallery. The organ came from the Chestnut Street Methodist Church in Portland, and dates from the 1830s. The old horse sheds (torn down *c.* 1899) can be seen to the south of the church.

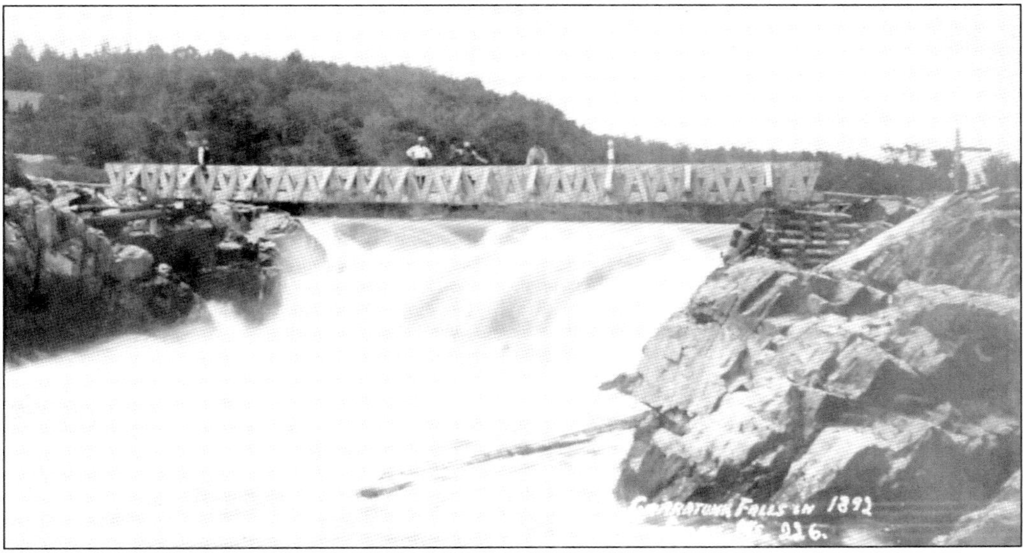

Caratunk Falls with footbridge, probably before 1892. The pulp mill and railroad bridge were built in 1889, and this photograph may precede that. The Abenaki name for the Kennebec valley, from the falls to Moosehead, was Caratunk (variously spelled as Carrituncк and Carratunk). This has often been translated as "a rough and broken place." The character of the valley changes at this point to be more narrow and rocky. Tales of death over Caratunk Falls can be traced to the earliest settlers, who had to use the river for transportation.

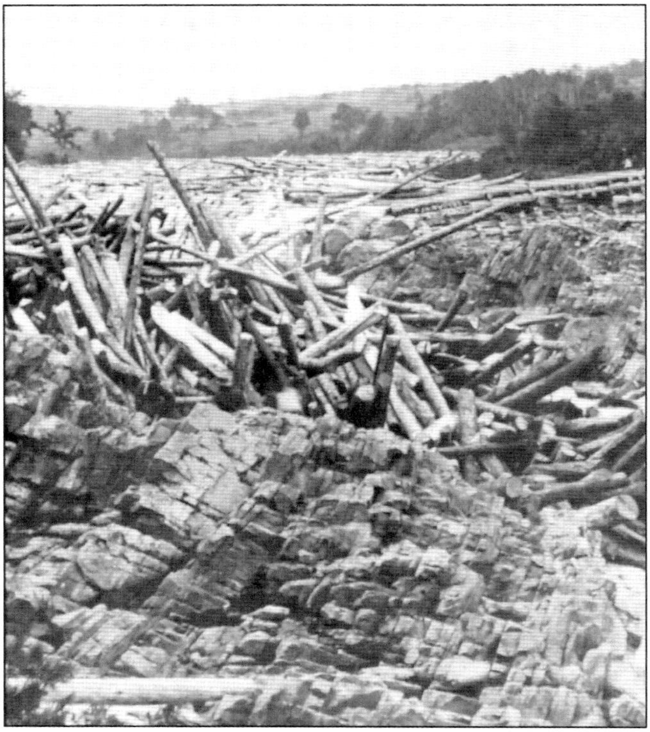

A log jam at Caratunk Falls, c. 1875–85. It's easy to see why this narrow point in the river was a real headache for river drivers, particularly when large logs were being moved.

The pulp mill at Caratunk Falls, c. 1890s. Built in 1889 by the Moosehead Paper and Pulp Company, this mill was later part of the International Paper Company. The 120-by-70-foot mill was built of native stone. The old driving dams were removed and a new dam was built in the shape of a horseshoe. Behind the railroad bridge at right is the mill superintendent's house.

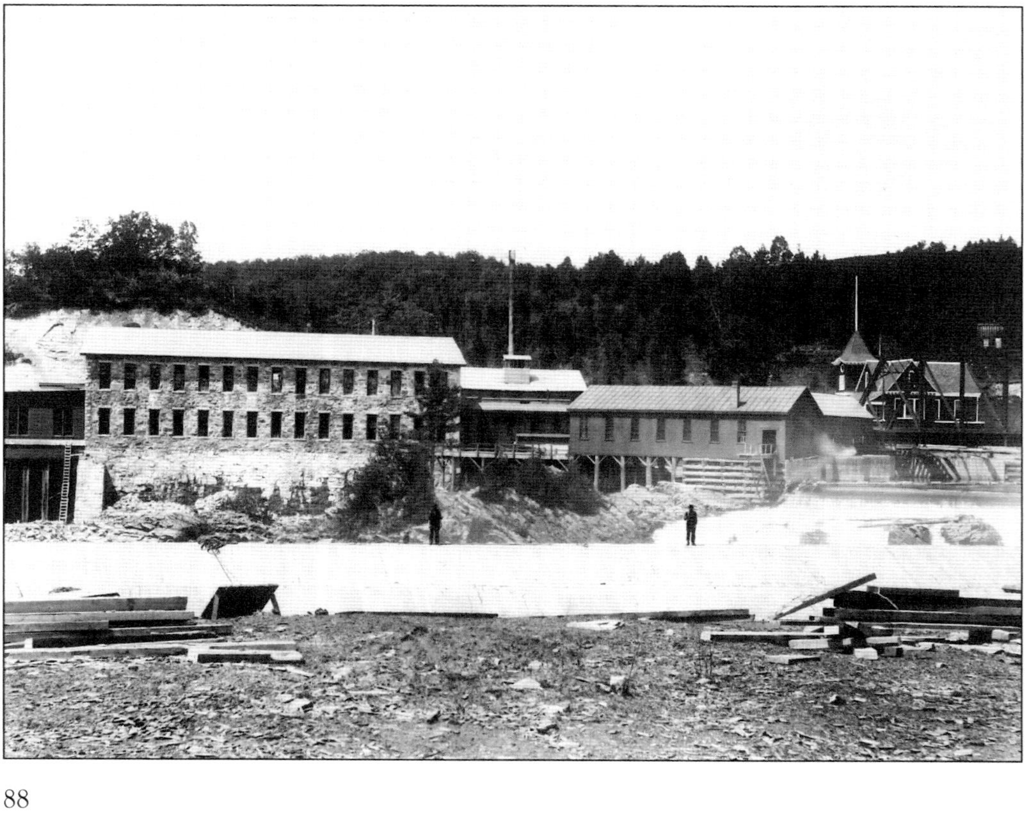

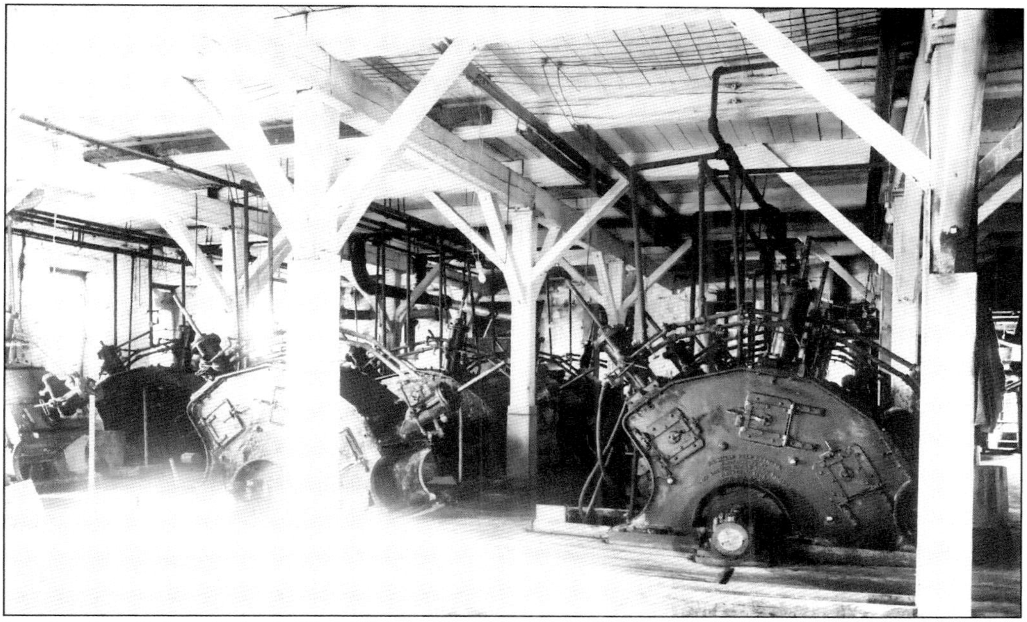

Inside the Solon Pulp Mill, 1890s. The large machines say "D.T. Mills Pulp Grinder/ Manufactured by the Dayton Globe Iron Works Co./Dayton O. 1888 (or 98)." David T. Mills was one of the original owners of the mill.

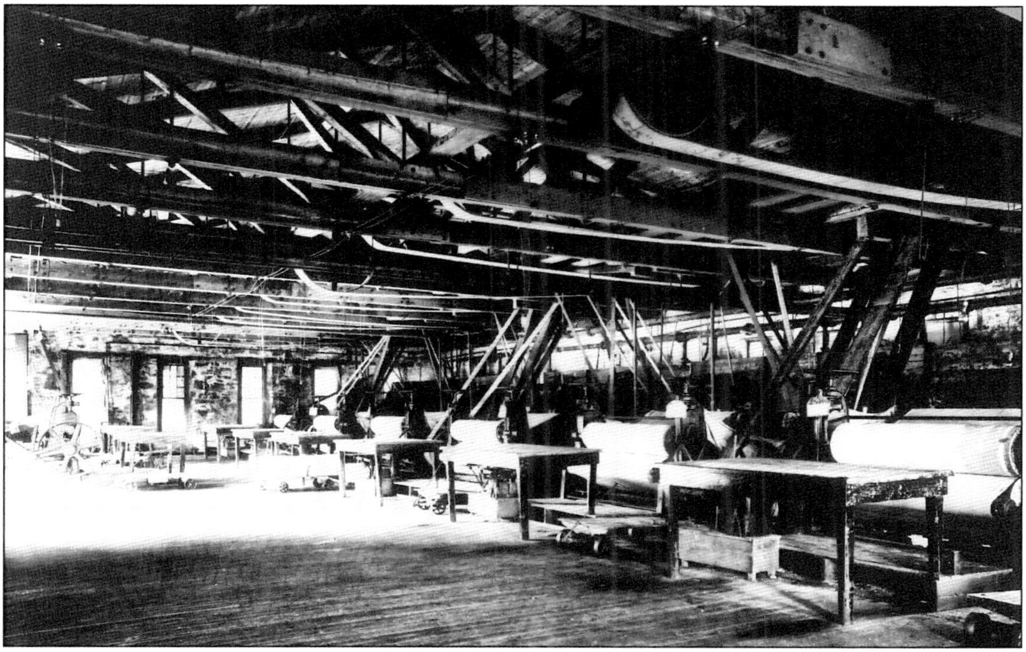

The second floor of the Solon Pulp Mill. Here sheets of compressed pulp were rolled out, quickly cut, and folded on low carts to be taken elsewhere and have more water pressed from them. The mill burned on January 31, 1920. John Walker, fireman in the boiler room, when the heat was too intense to stay, tied down the mill whistle and it blew until there was no more steam.

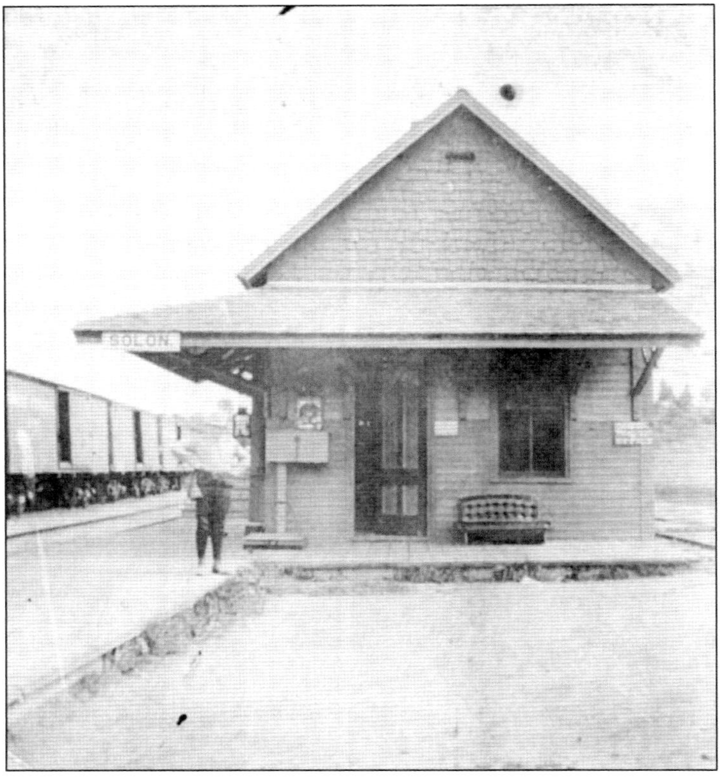

Solon Station, located near Caratunk Falls where the railroad crossed the river. The depot was not located near the village , since Solon had not supported the building of the railroad at that time. Long in disuse, it was burned in the 1940s.

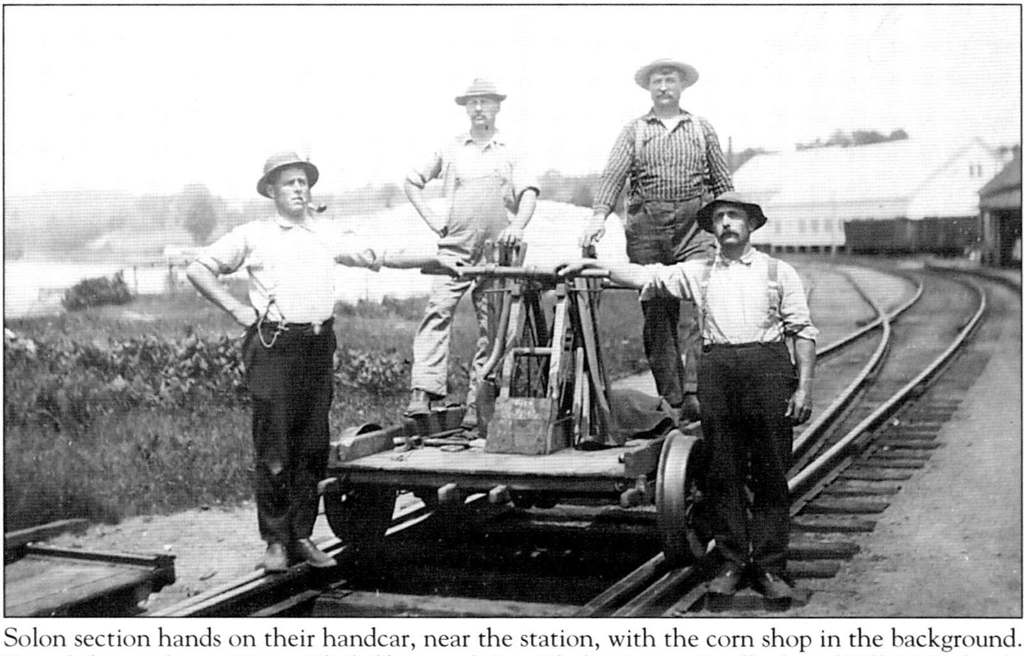

Solon section hands on their handcar, near the station, with the corn shop in the background. From left to right are Harry Clark (foreman), Les Clark, George Spofford, and Bill McFarland.

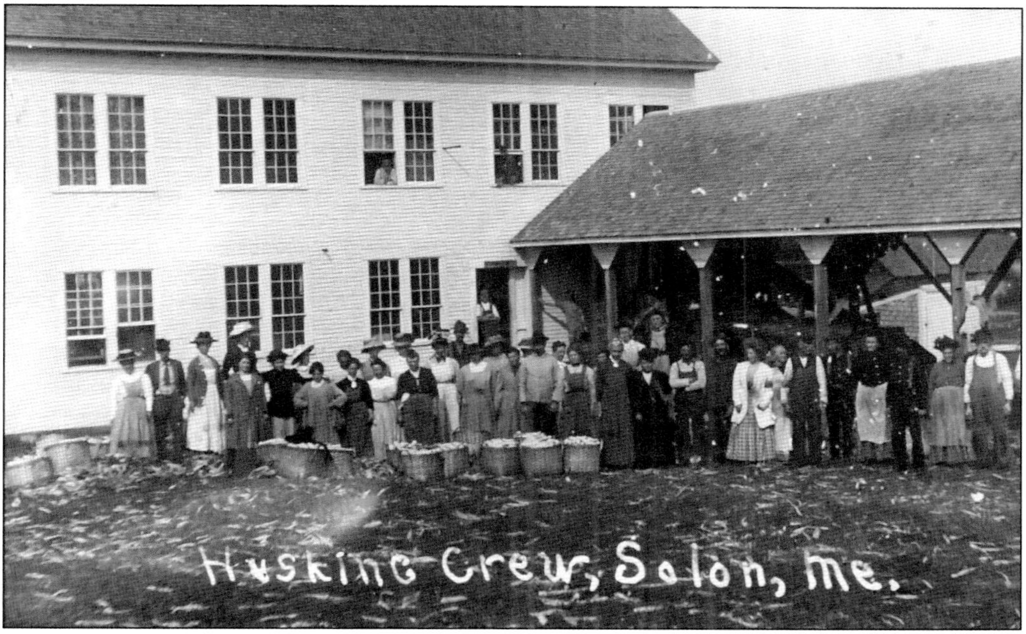

The husking crew, Solon Corn Shop, postmarked 1910. Many towns had corn shops, particularly after the railroad came, making it easier to get crops to mass markets. The Northern Maine Packing Co. plant was built in 1908 for the purpose of canning corn, beans, and other farm products. There was also a nearby building used for storing and shipping potatoes.

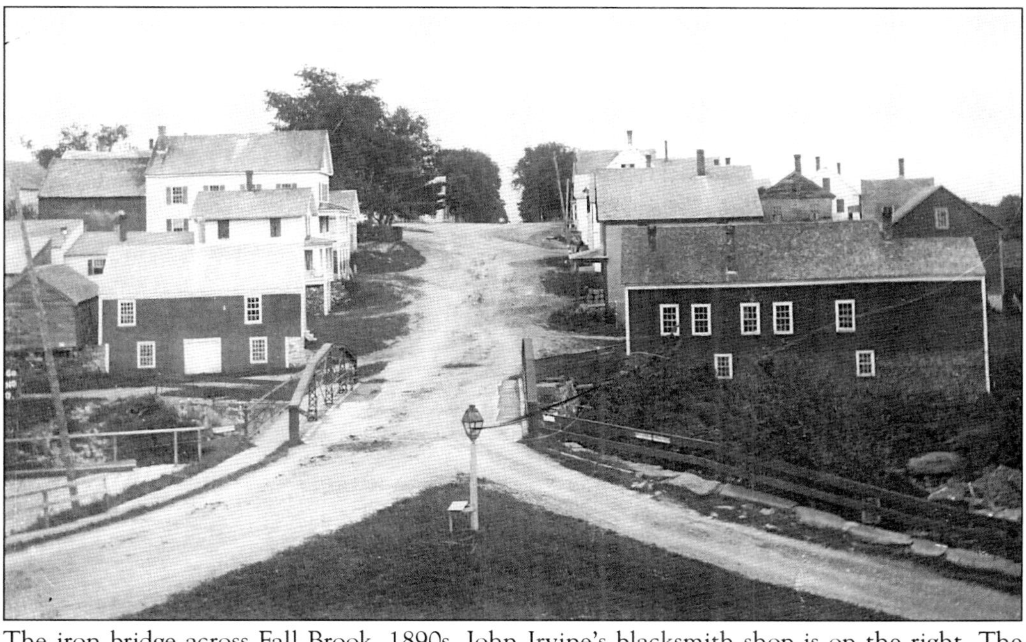

The iron bridge across Fall Brook, 1890s. John Irvine's blacksmith shop is on the right. The store across from it was later owned by Fred Coolidge. On the left at the upper end of the hill is old Union Hall, where the first Masonic meeting in town was held on January 3, 1855.

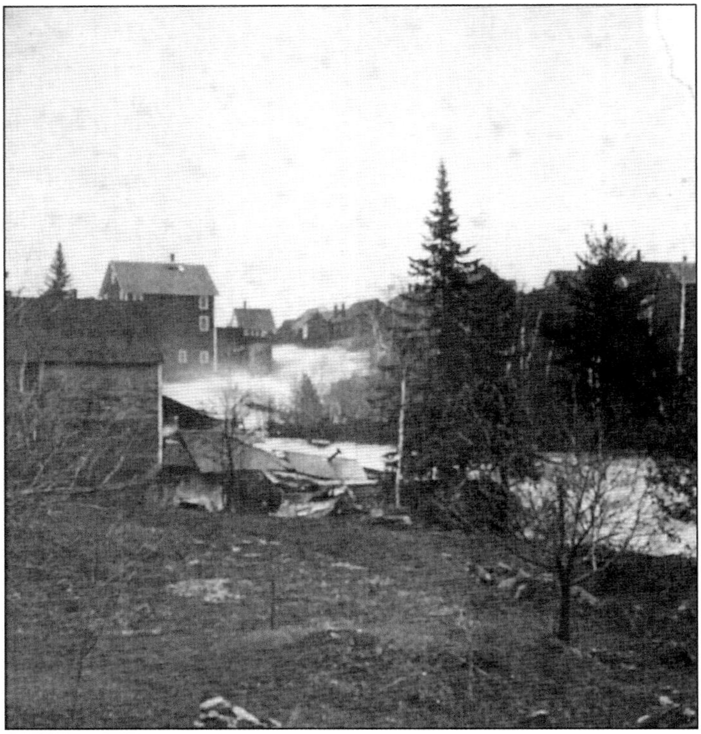

A freshet on Fall Brook, c. 1875, looking upstream toward the bridge. Visible are the surging high waters and wreckage (left bank). There were a gristmill and a carding mill on this section of the stream.

The Solon Brass Band crossing the bridge, heading south, *c.* 1890s. At left center across the bridge is the carriage shop of Henry Redmond.

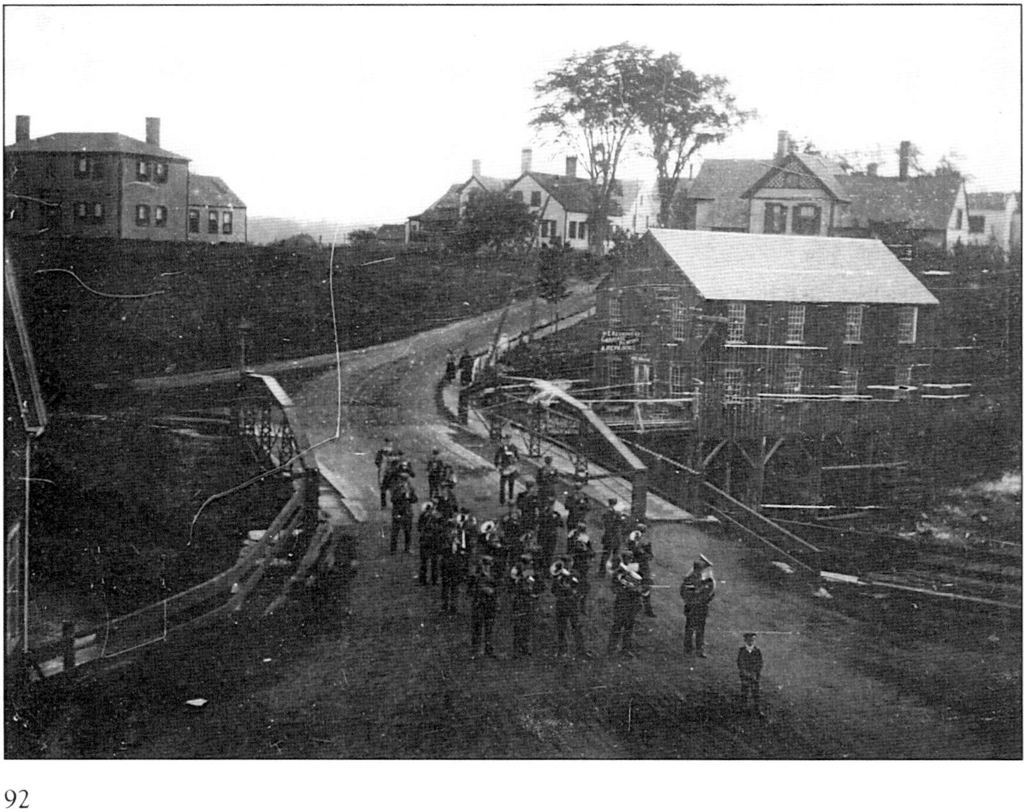

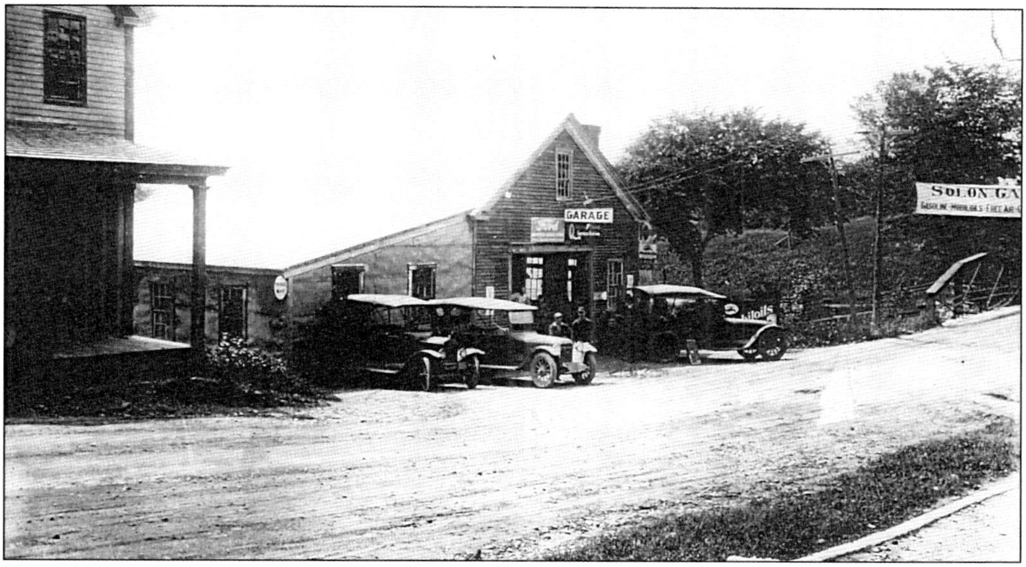

Kendall Cross' garage, 1922–23, southwest of the bridge. The two men are Roland Tozier on the left and Kendall Cross on the right. The car on the left is a *c.* 1918 Model T Ford belonging to Walter Cram; the car in the middle is a 1920s Oakland belonging to Mahlon Robbins; the car on the right is a 1918–20 Chevrolet belonging to John Irvine. This building was the Irvine blacksmith shop before technology caught up with it.

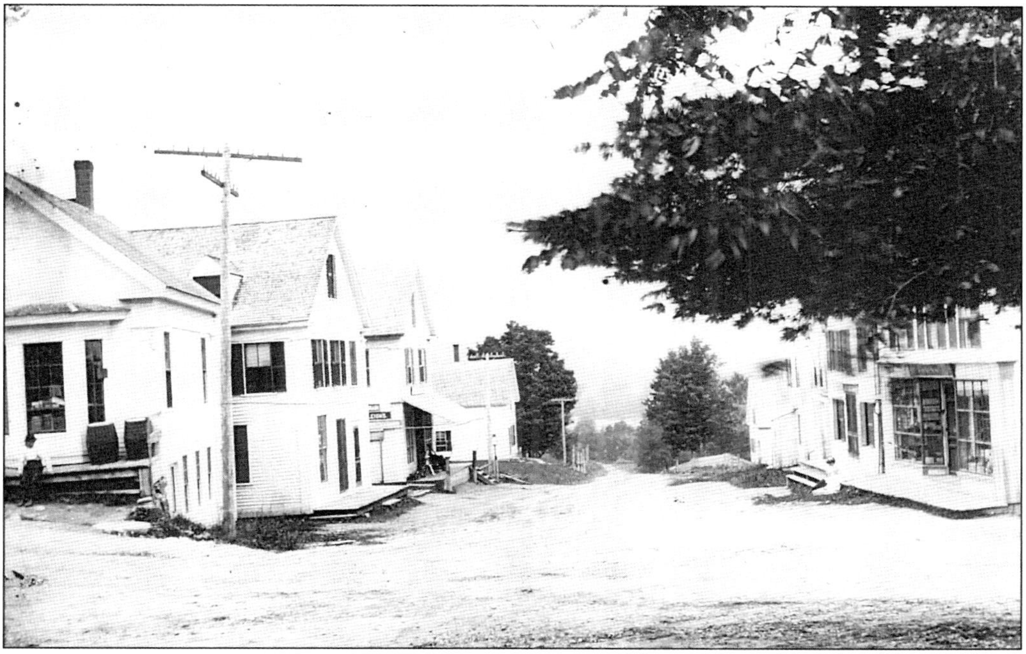

Looking down Ferry Street, *c.* 1890s. On the right corner is the Moses Townsend store, later run by his son-in-law, Azel Jones. On the right is the dry goods store of F.C. Clark, with the telephone office in the lower level. Next comes Timothy Smith's casket shop, later Azel Jones' storehouse. Beyond is O.O. Vittum and Sons grocery, later John Lawrence's American Express Agency.

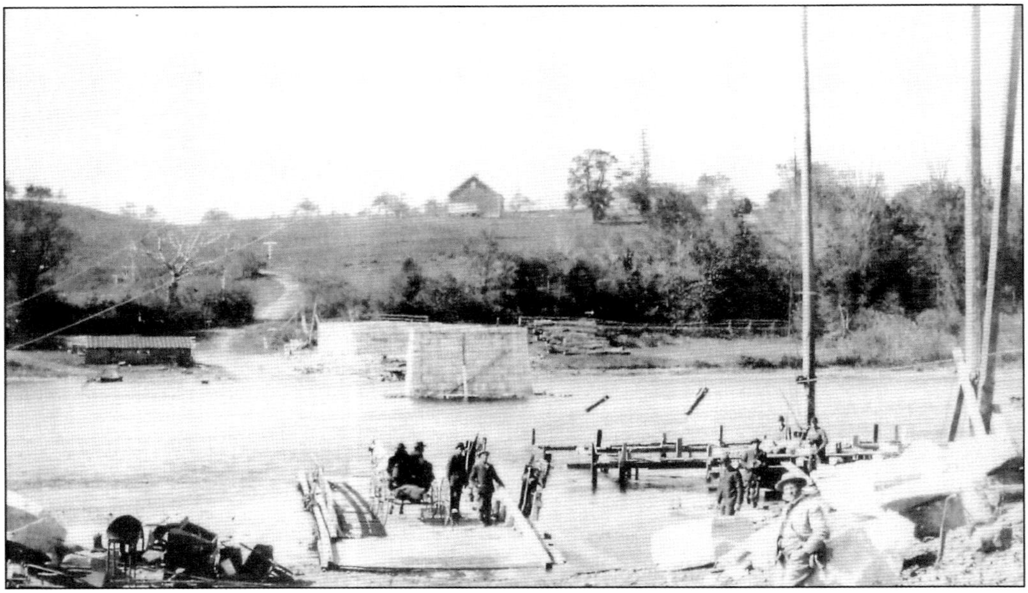

Solon Ferry over the Kennebec looking toward Embden, c. 1910. The ferry was still operating while the stone piers for the new iron bridge were being built (constructed 1910–11). In the upper center, partly hidden by trees, is the old Moses Thompson tavern (the "yellow house"). The railroad tracks go by partway up the hill but are hard to see here.

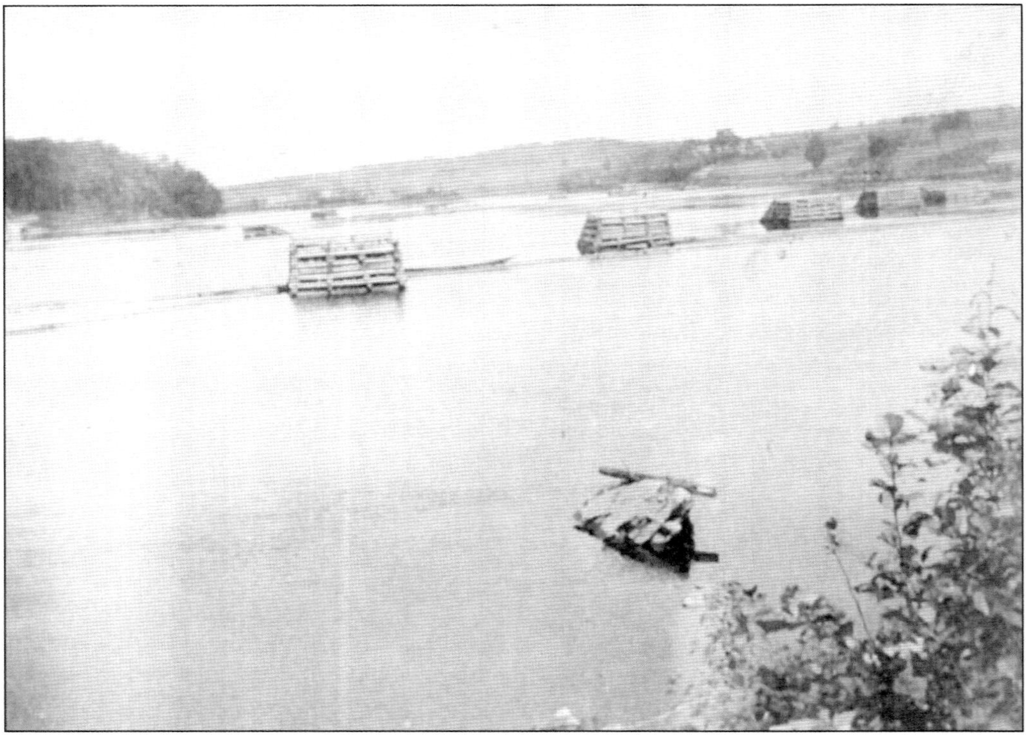

Piers in the Kennebec, below the railroad bridge at Caratunk Falls. Long a familiar sight on the river during the logging days, these have largely vanished.

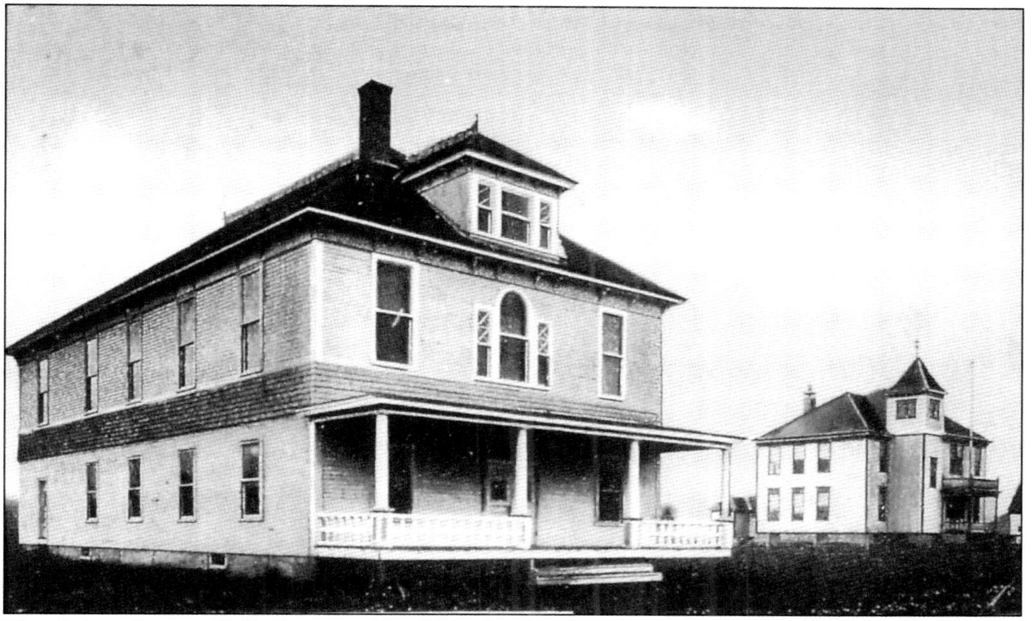

The Solon Grange Hall, showing the old high school, early 1900s. The school was constructed c. 1900 at a cost of $5,122 and burned the night of October 29, 1911.

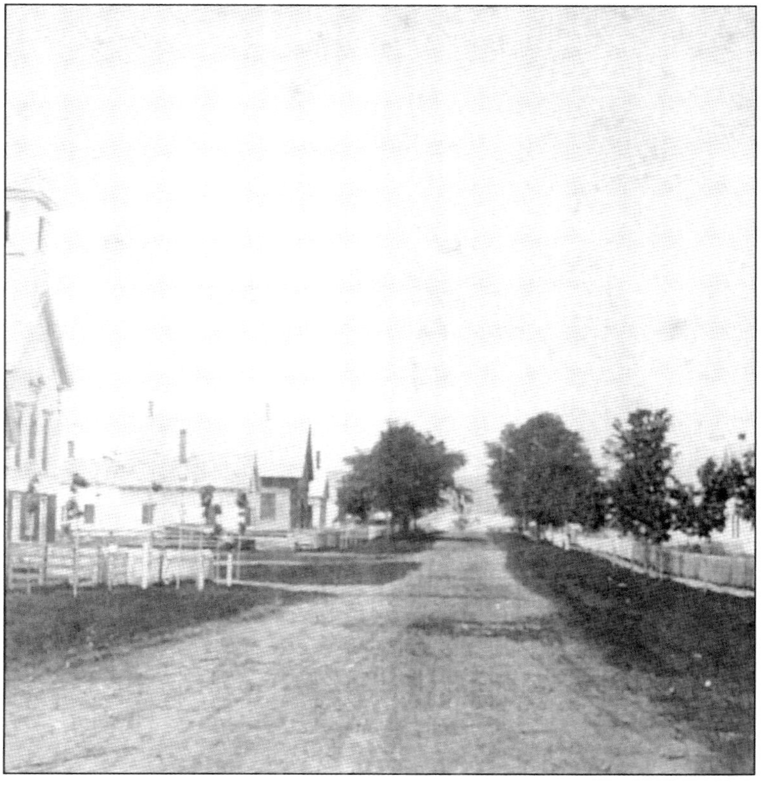

A stereo photograph of Pleasant Street, *c.* 1875–85, showing the Methodist church on the left (built 1859).

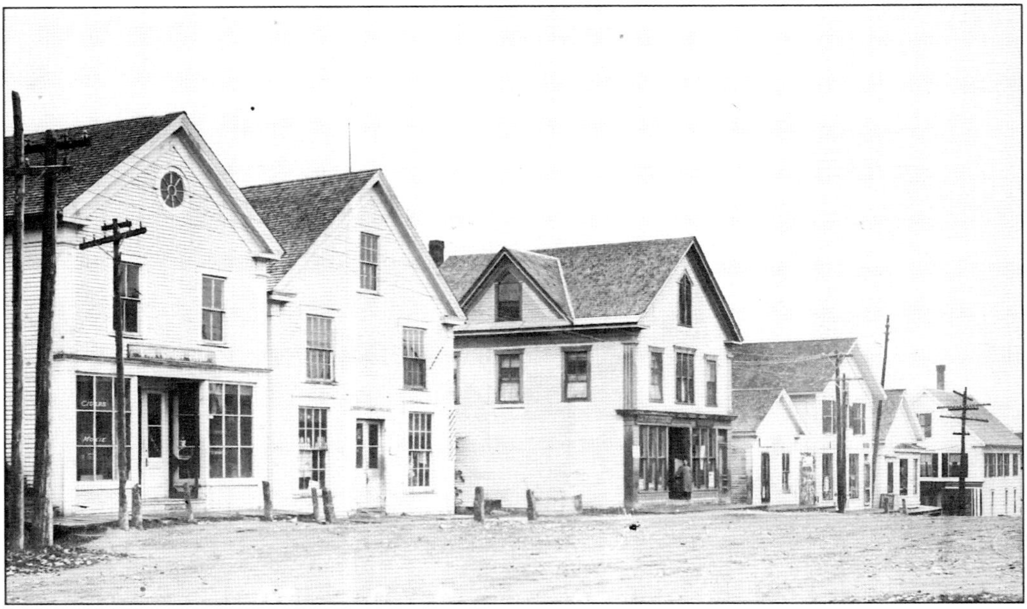

The west side of Main Street looking north toward Ferry Street, *c.* 1905–10. The two stores to the left survived the fire of 1925. From left to right are as follows: Wilder Pettengill's grocery store; Roland French and Thomas Tuskin, later Ernest Powell; the Leslie McIntire Drugstore featuring yard goods, hardware, and a post office; Turner Buswell's law office (small building); and M.H. Andrews Clothing, with T.J. Young's law office above.

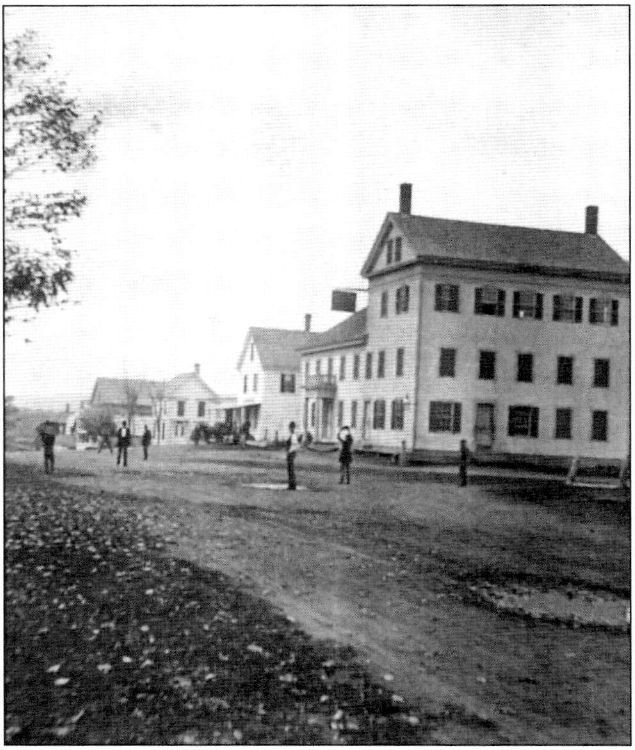

The original Carratunk House, *c.* 1880s, Main Street, looking north. It burned on October 31, 1893. Beyond the hotel are L.L. Patterson's grocery store, then the John Rowell (later Beryl Cram) house on the north corner of Pleasant Street.

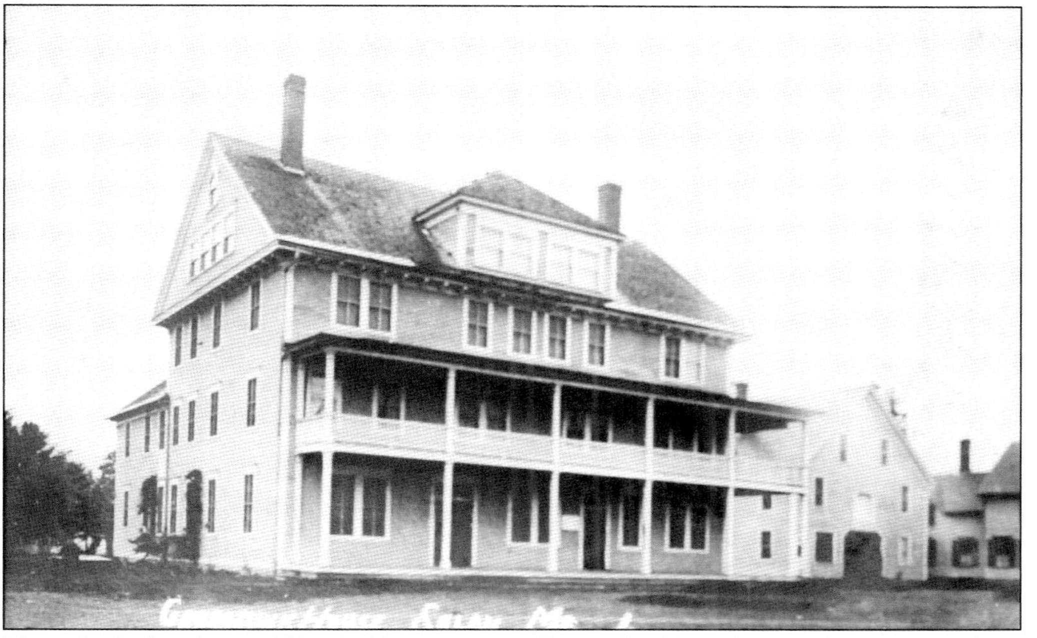

The rebuilt hotel, c. 1900–10. Known originally as the New Carratunk House, it later became Gray's Tavern (for the Grays who built and operated it), and is now known as the Solon Hotel.

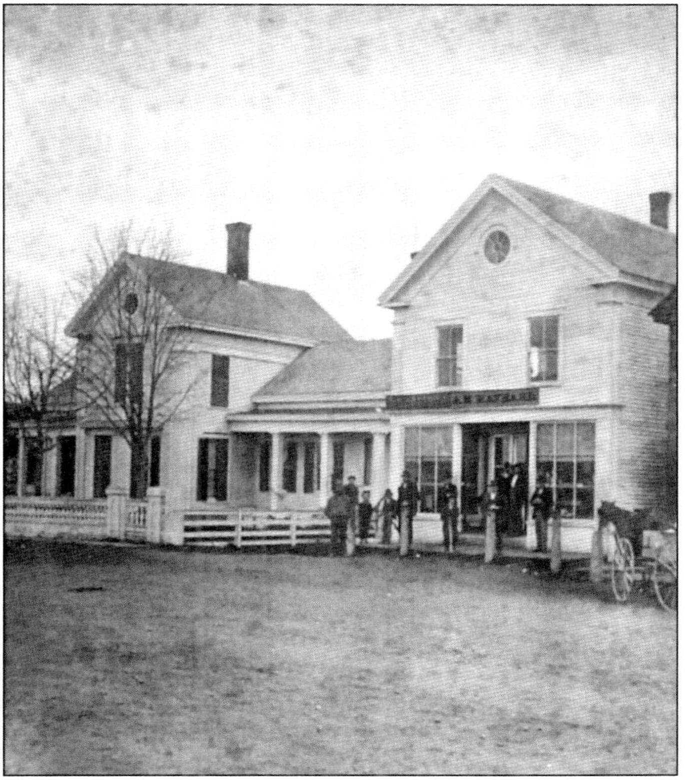

Main Street across from the hotel, c. 1890. The house on the left was used as a hotel and connected via a second-story walkway to Maynard's store on the right (later known as Pettengill's). Both buildings survived the fire of September 29, 1925, which destroyed nineteen buildings on the west side of Main Street and both sides of Ferry Street.

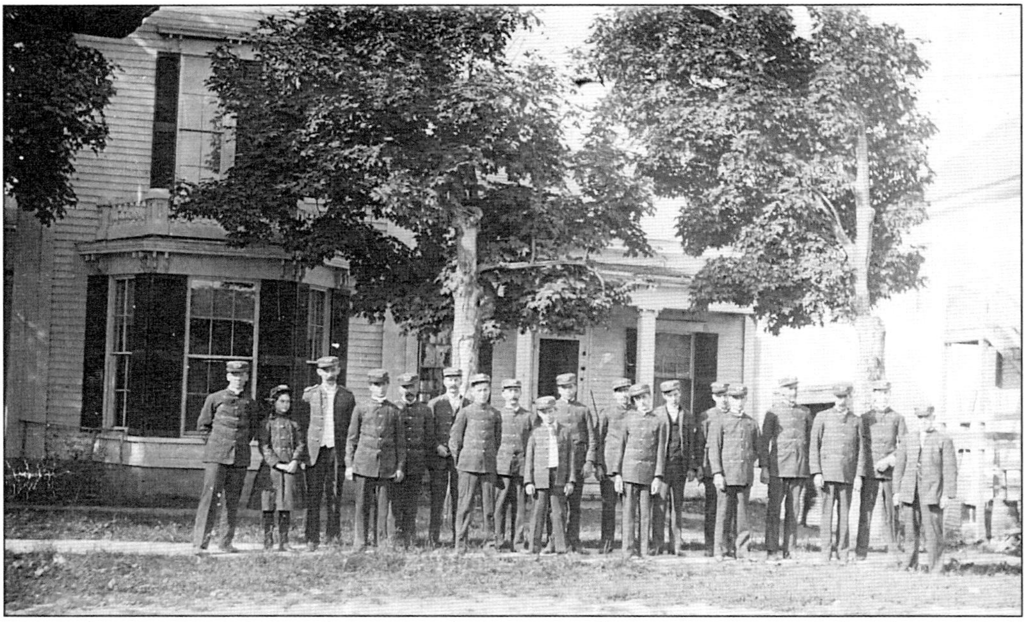

The Solon Brass Band, *c.* early 1900s. Shown are Will Soper, Geneva Clark, Charles Clark (leader), Herbert Young, Everett Clark, Bert Gray, Angus Davis, Will McFarland, Harold Randlett, Perley Priest, Luther Albee, Mahlon Whipple, George Longley, George Moulton, Marcellus Irvine, Sumner Wilson, Alston Rowell, Charles Cates, and Joseph Lander.

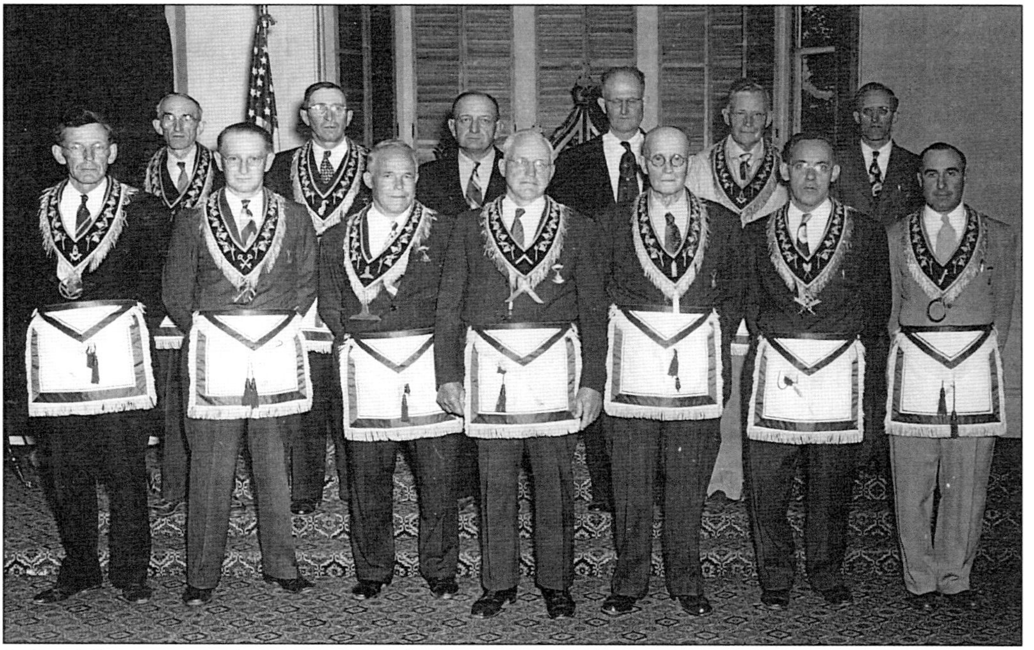

Solon Masons, *c.* early 1930s. From left to right are: (front row) Ira R. Adams, Malcolm M. Hall, Harold M. Starbird, Elwyn W. Starbird, Ernest L. Paul, George E. Lincoln, and Roland E. Tozier; (back row) Leon M. Wyman, Leon E. French, Eldred C. Heald, Kendall E. Cross, Bert W. Paul, and Neil O. Hunnewell.

Seven

North Anson

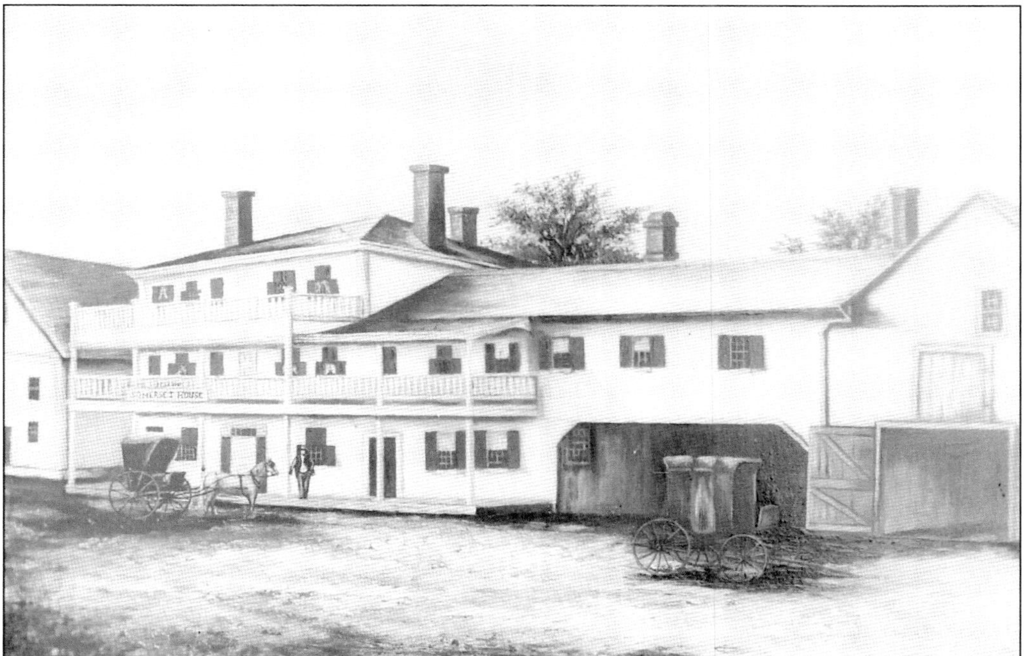

The Somerset House, drawn *c.* mid-1800s. This hip-roofed, Federal-style hotel with large verandas appears to date from near 1800.

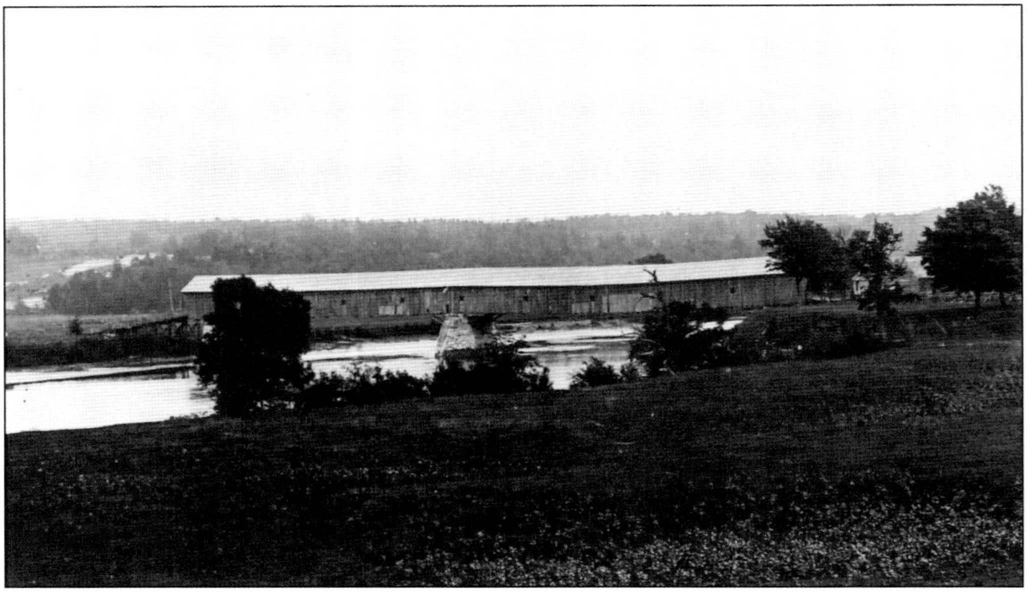

The Patterson toll bridge, built *c.* 1840. Early toll rates were as follows: each foot passenger 2¢; one person and one horse 6¢; one horse and cart or one horse and sleigh 12 1/2¢; each horse and chaise or sulky 17¢; each additional horse 6¢; each team including cart, wagon, sled, or sleigh drawn by two oxen 22¢; each additional beast 2¢; four-wheel carriages with two horses 25¢; each additional horse 6¢; meat cattle and beasts of burden exclusive of those rode upon or in carriages or teams 2¢ each; sheep and swine 6 1/4¢ per dozen.

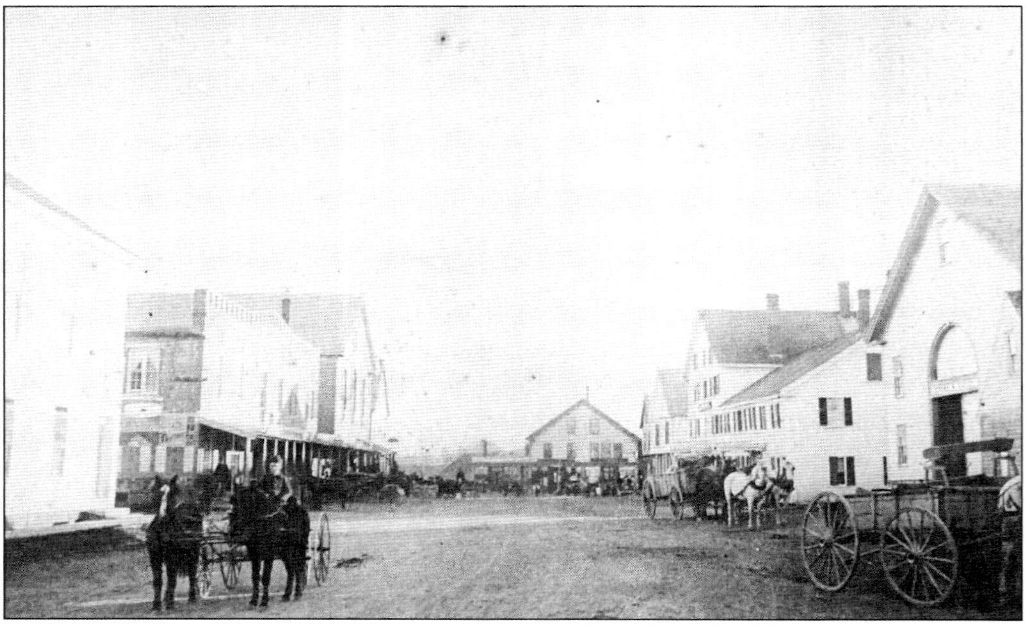

Main Street, North Anson, *c.* 1875–80. The Somerset Hotel is on the right, much changed from the earlier drawing. The white building on the left is Central Hall; Music Hall was upstairs in the brick building next door. The tall building beyond is Joel Gray's Carrabassett block with a hall over the stores.

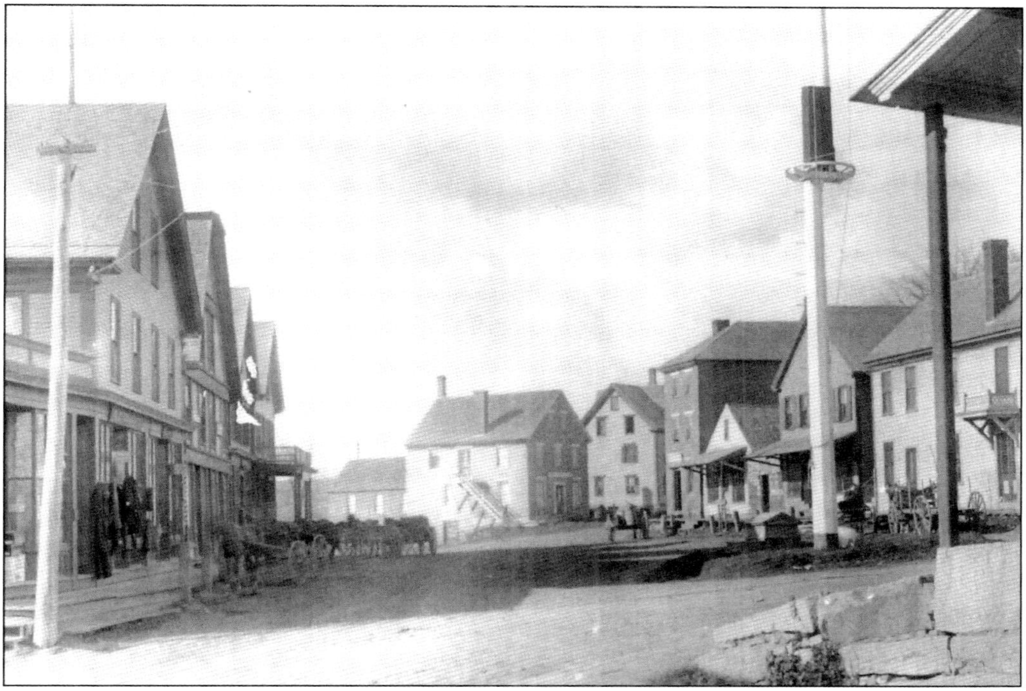

Elm Street, looking west before 1900. The stores on the right are the Bodfish Drugstore (with the *Union Advocate* paper printed upstairs), Stickney Gray's store, Spooner's Boots & Shoes (small building), Luke Emery's workshop, Wells' apartments, and Grange Hall.

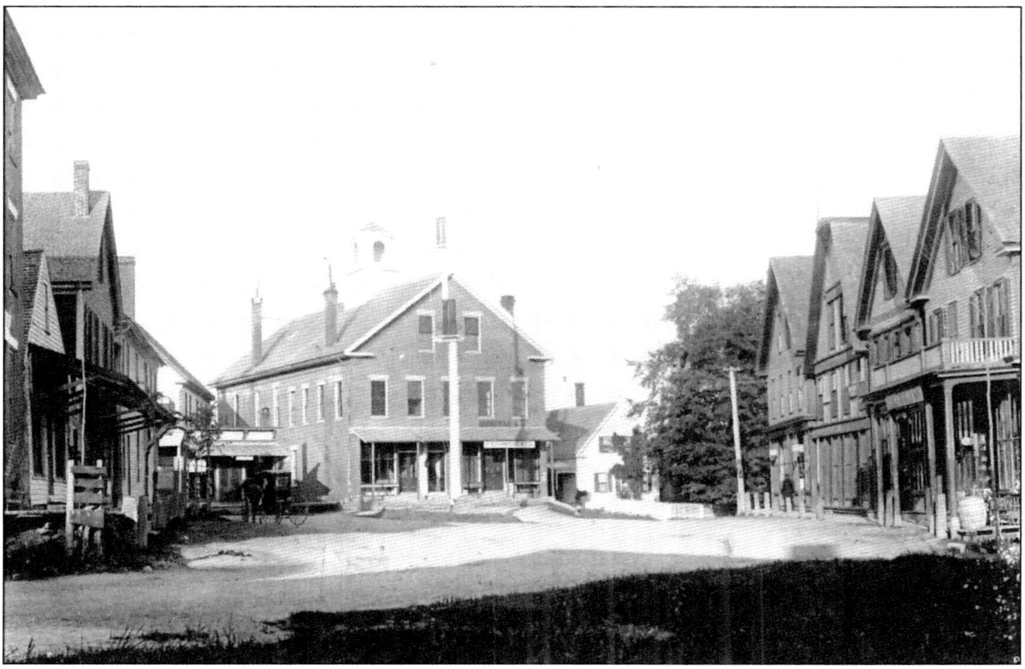

Elm Street, looking east, before 1900. Note the very large flagpole, which has a perch partway up. Behind it is the F.S. Parsons & Co. Store.

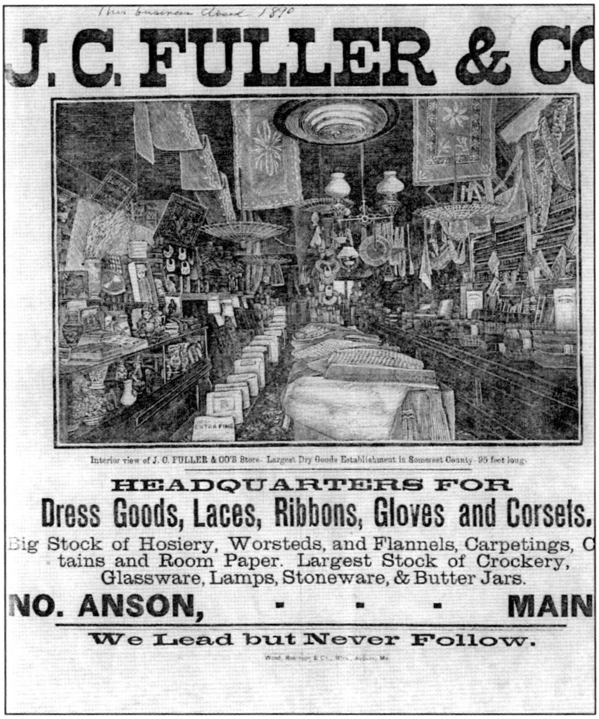

A broadside of the 1880s. Fuller's store was in the Carrabassett block, and the business closed in 1910.

The smoldering ruins of North Anson, after the fire of August 19, 1913. The town has had several disastrous fires, but this was the worst. The entire center of town was destroyed.

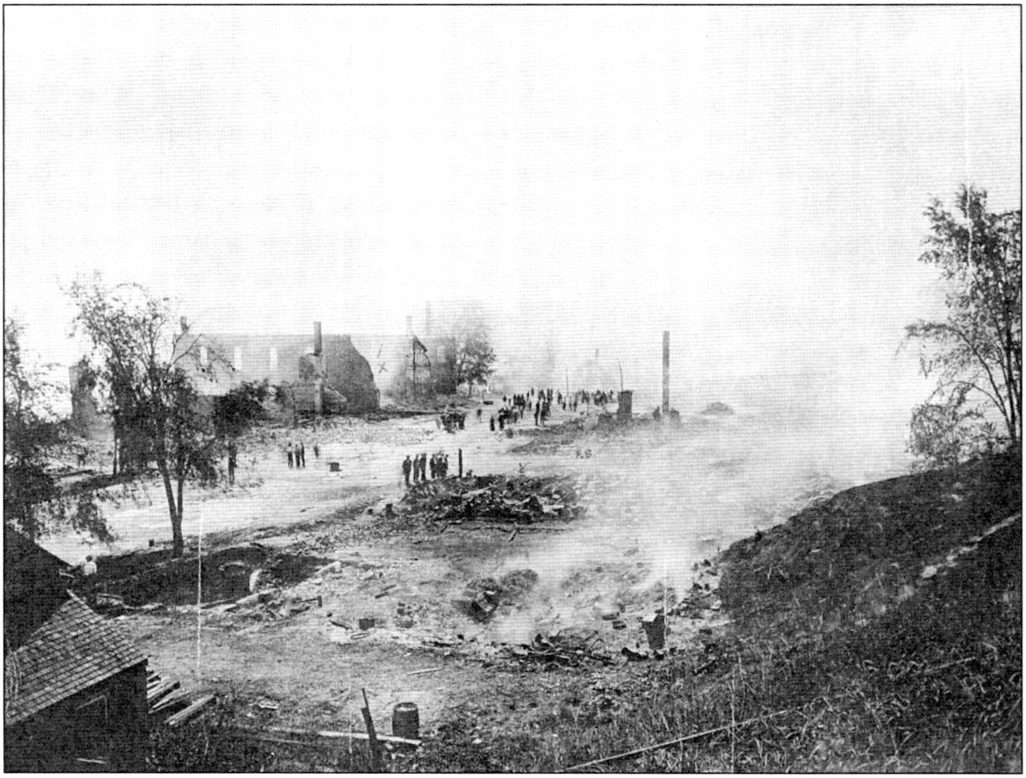

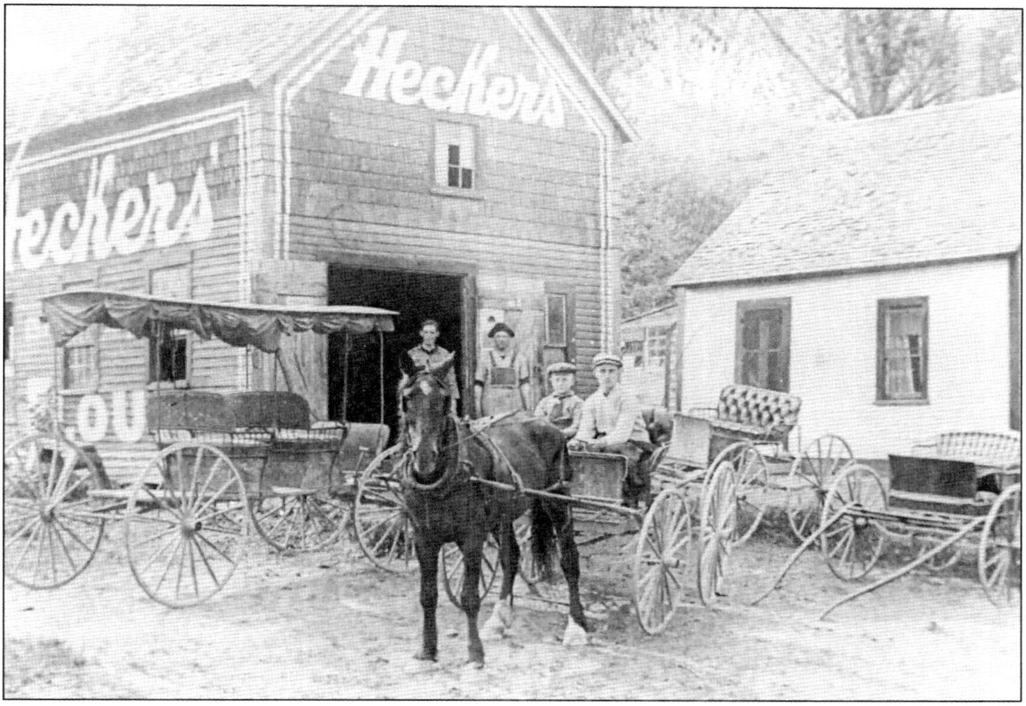

Charles Pullen's blacksmith shop, c. 1900–1910. Companies often paid building owners to allow advertising to be painted on their walls. Here the ad for Hecker's Flour has little to do with blacksmithing.

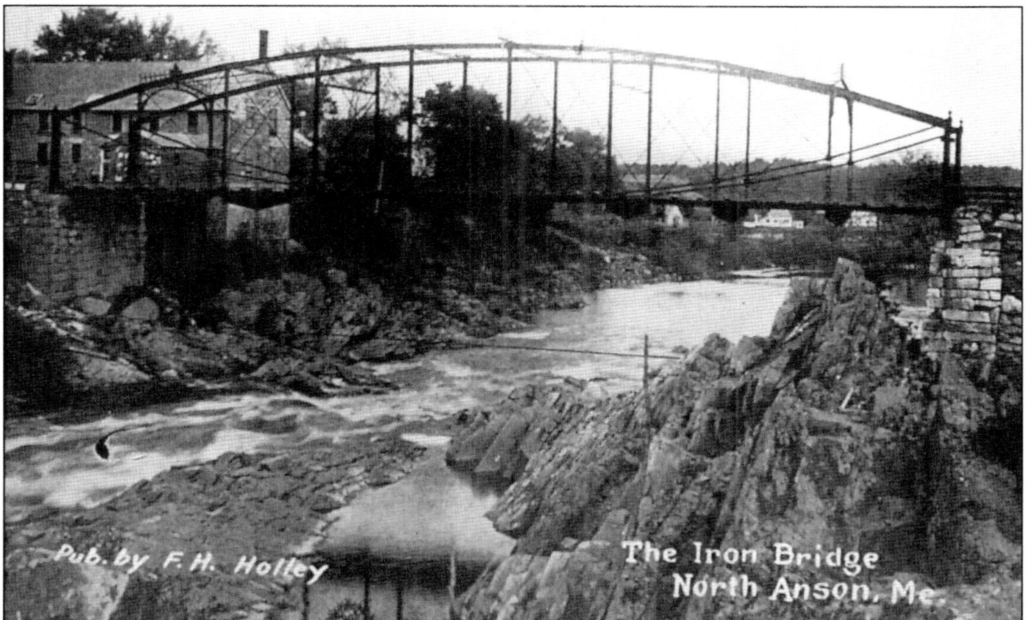

The iron bridge across the Carrabassett, postmarked 1909.

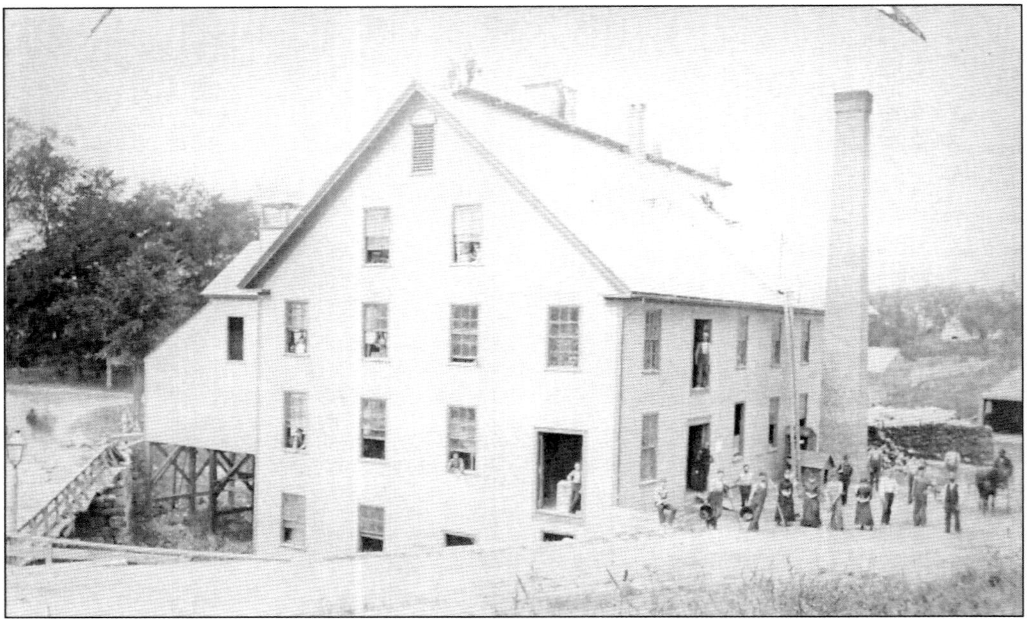

The shank factory and workers, *c.* 1890s. This factory, built in 1881–82 and expanded in 1892, was where wooden shoe shanks were made. The mill employed twenty to twenty-five men and women. The equipment was moved to Bingham 1906–1908. The factory was torn down after 1914, and the tall chimney was taken down by Keith Partridge in 1960.

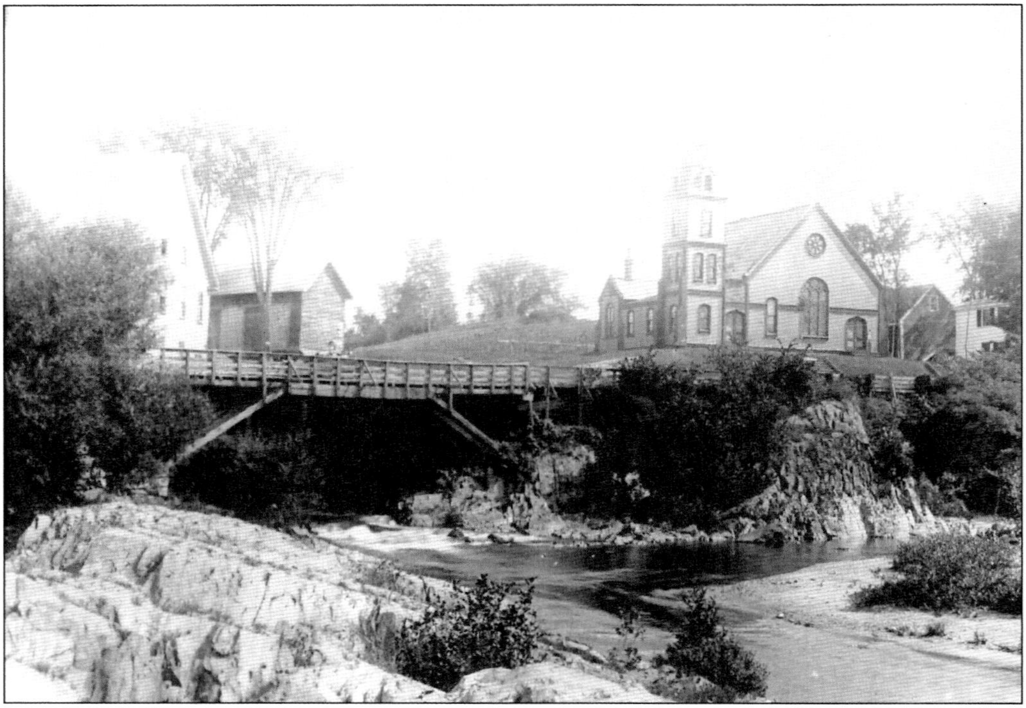

A wooden bridge across Mill Stream, *c.* 1900. The bridge (it was not the first) was built in 1886. The Congregational church dates from 1884.

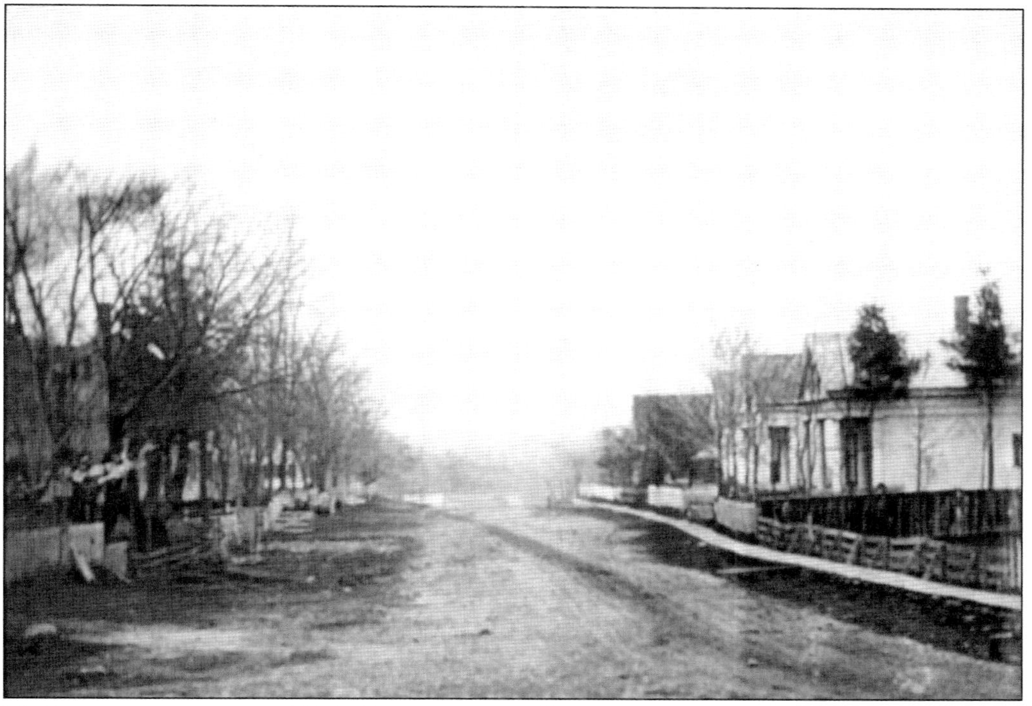

Madison Avenue in a c. 1870–80 stereo view. The unusual three-columned Greek Revival houses still stand along this street, which was the route to the Patterson bridge. Note the wooden sidewalks, a necessary protection from frequent mud in the days before paving was common.

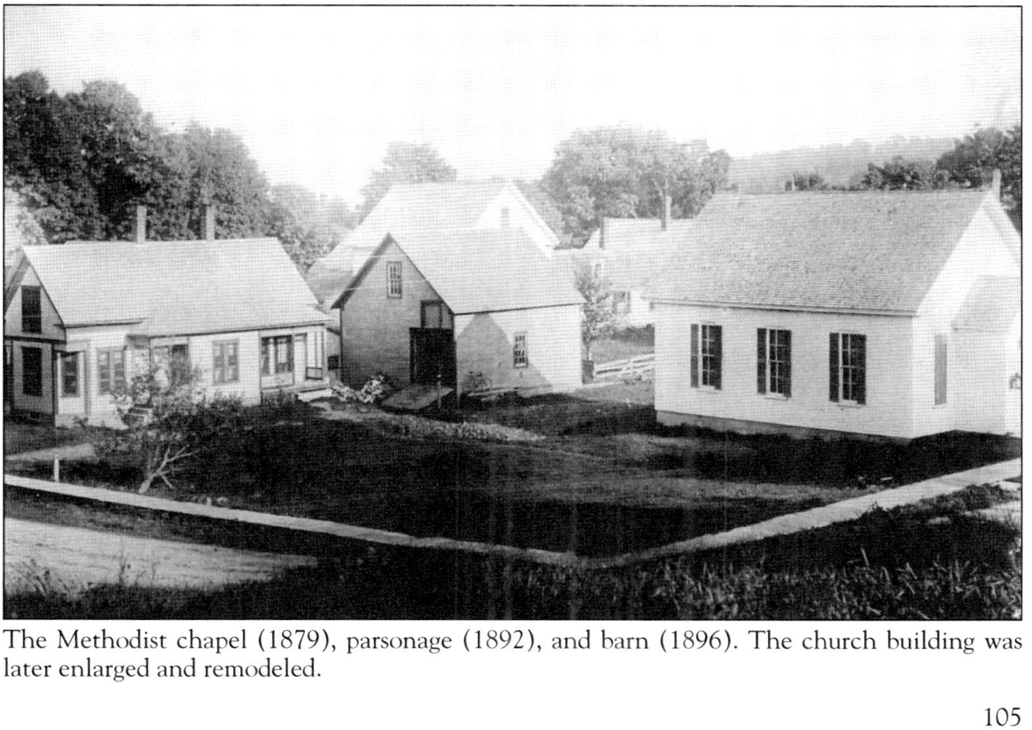

The Methodist chapel (1879), parsonage (1892), and barn (1896). The church building was later enlarged and remodeled.

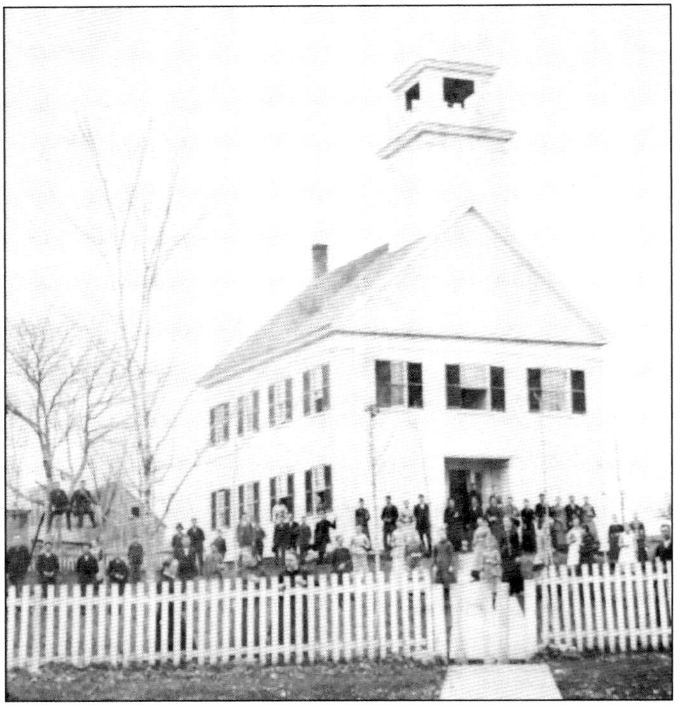

A stereo view of old Anson Academy, *c.* 1880. The students are clearly older and more well-dressed than those in the village grammar schools.

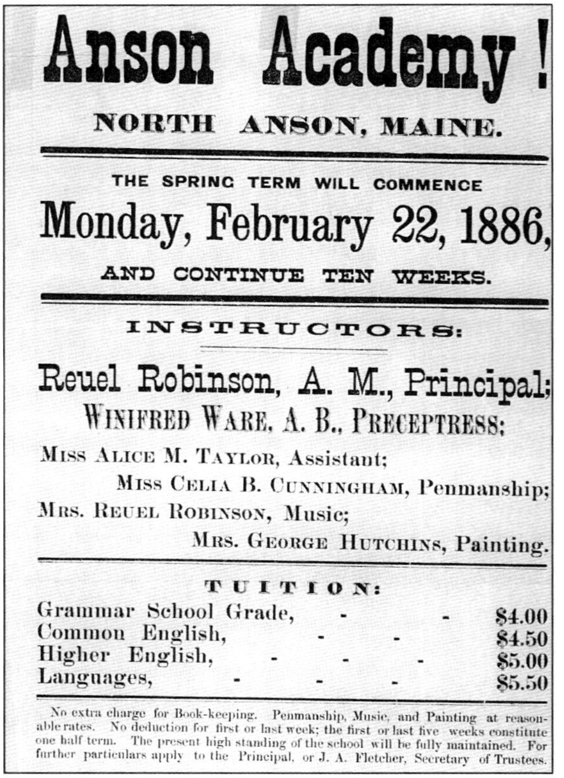

Anson Academy!

NORTH ANSON, MAINE.

THE SPRING TERM WILL COMMENCE

Monday, February 22, 1886,

AND CONTINUE TEN WEEKS.

INSTRUCTORS:

Reuel Robinson, A. M., Principal;

WINIFRED WARE, A. B., PRECEPTRESS;

MISS ALICE M. TAYLOR, Assistant;

MISS CELIA B. CUNNINGHAM, Penmanship;

MRS. REUEL ROBINSON, Music;

MRS. GEORGE HUTCHINS, Painting.

TUITION:

Grammar School Grade,	$4.00
Common English,	$4.50
Higher English,	$5.00
Languages,	$5.50

No extra charge for Book-keeping. Penmanship, Music, and Painting at reasonable rates. No deduction for first or last week; the first or last five weeks constitute one half term. The present high standing of the school will be fully maintained. For further particulars apply to the Principal, or J. A. Fletcher, Secretary of Trustees.

A Broadside advertising the academy. Tuition costs have escalated considerably since 1886.

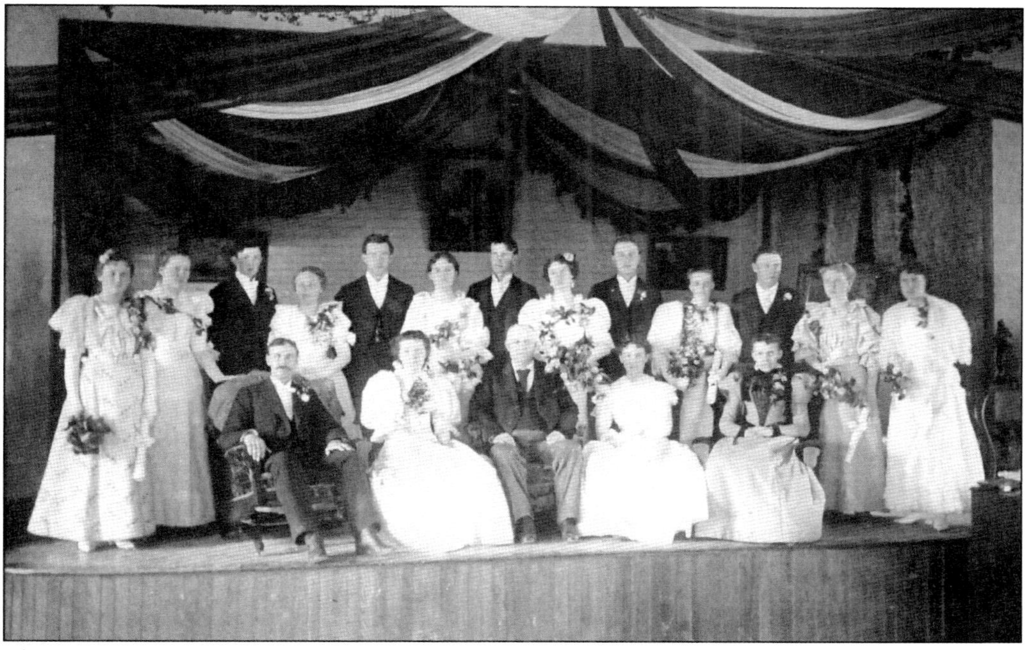

The Anson Academy Class of 1897, in Carrabassett Hall. From left to right are: (front row) Lena Smith, Winnie Hall, principal Walter Poore, assistant principal Ellen Poore, President of the Trustees Judge A. Simmons, assistant teacher Mabel Marston, a visiting former teacher (name unknown), Jennie Paine, and Edee Davis; (back row) Dan Steward, Vesta Moulton, Raymond Mayo, Eda Baker, Morrell Walker, Frances Simmons, Charles Luce, Bertha Caswell, and Mahlon Moore.

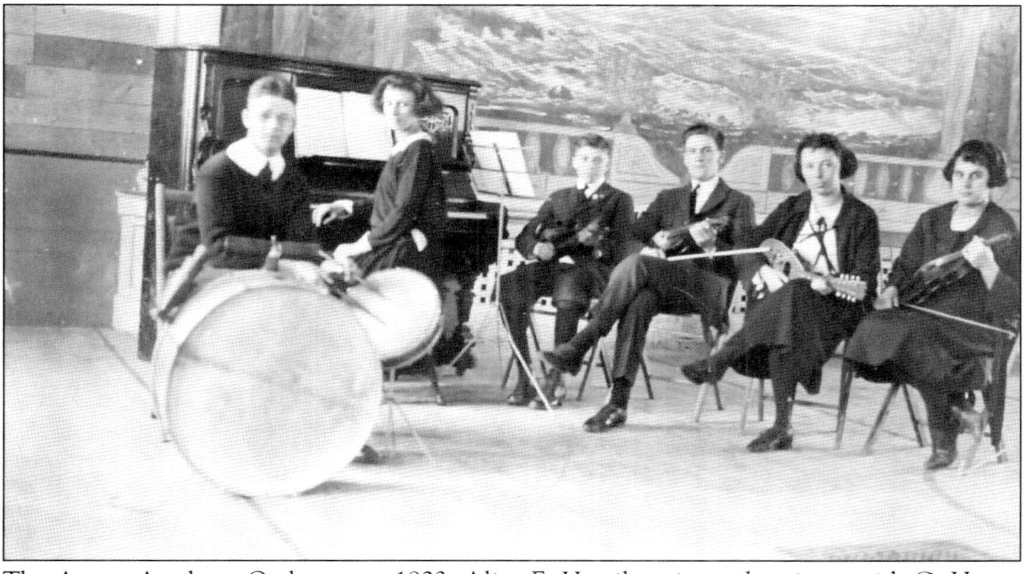

The Anson Academy Orchestra, c. 1923. Alice E. Hamilton is on the piano, with G. Hovey Barnaby on the drums. The violinists, from left to right, are Prescott Baker, C. Wadsworth Mraz, and Alice M. Brown. Evelyn M. Bridges is holding the mandolin.

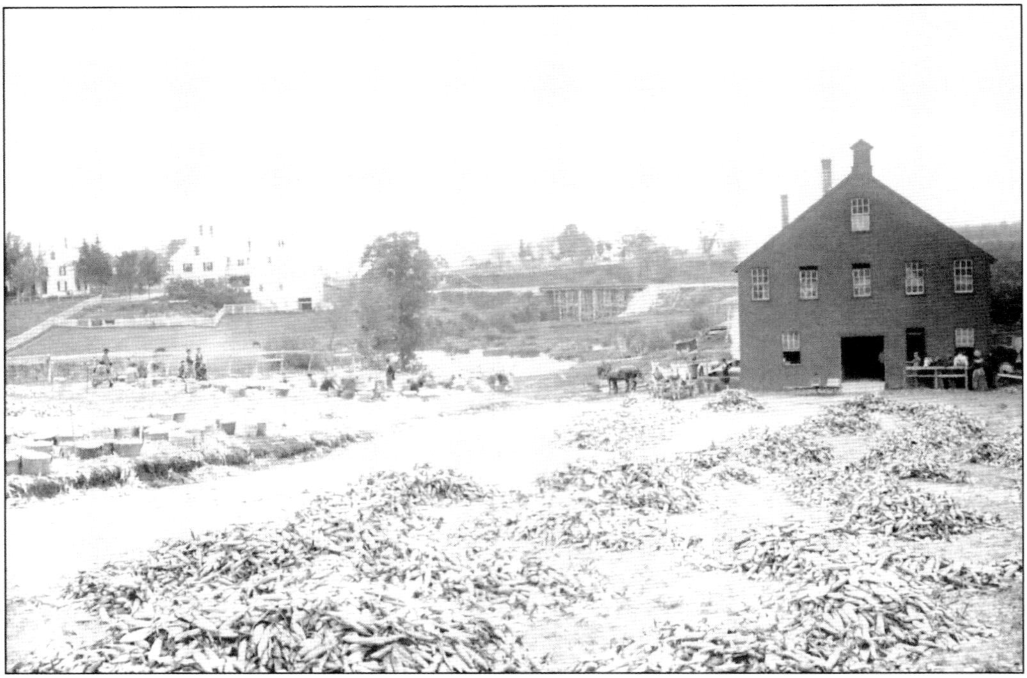

The corn shop, behind Anson Academy, c. 1885–95. In the center is the railroad trestle across Mill Stream; to the left is the Donlay house (owned later by Granville and Lucinda Berry, and by Sidney Sharp), which has since burned. The house on the far left was the J.A. Fletcher house, built in 1869.

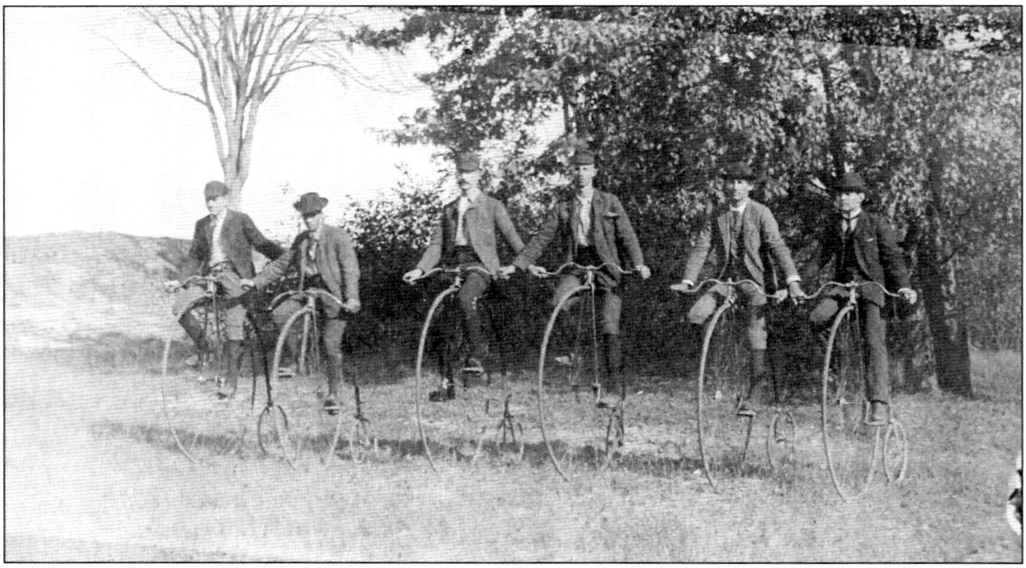

High-wheel bicycles, c. 1885–90. Wheeling was popular even in the hilly parts of Maine in the 1880s, even though a new wheel cost about $125 in 1885. The wheelmen are, from left to right, unidentified, unidentified, Chauncey Adams, Bert Witham, George or Ben Marshall, and unidentified. The wheels, except those second and third from left, appear to be Columbias (most popular at the time); the other two seem to be by Gormully & Jeffrey.

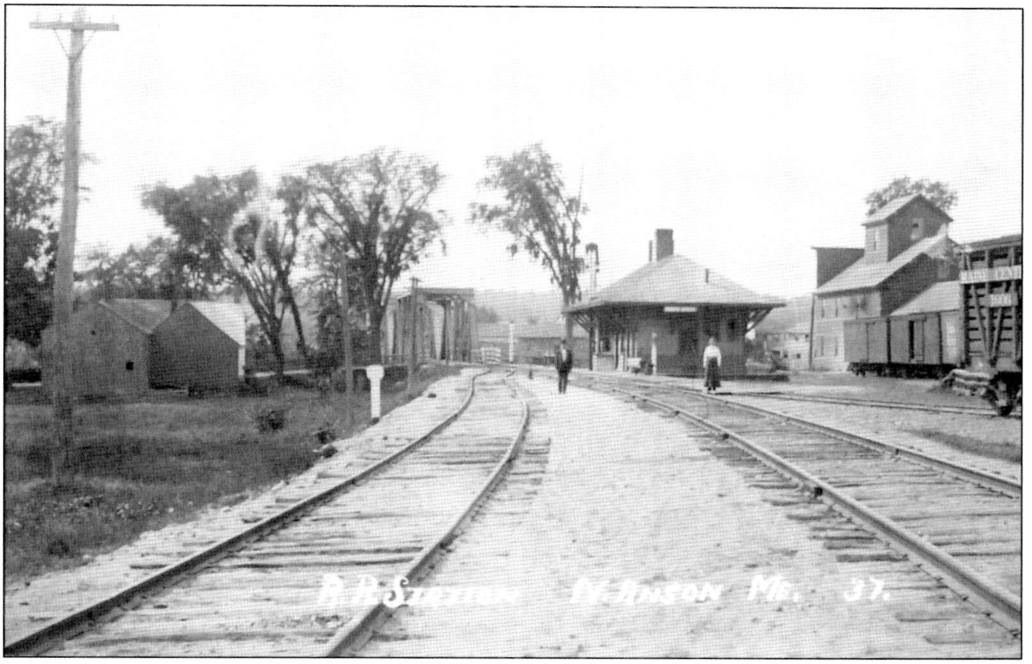

North Anson Depot (note the nearby bridge), *c.* 1915–20

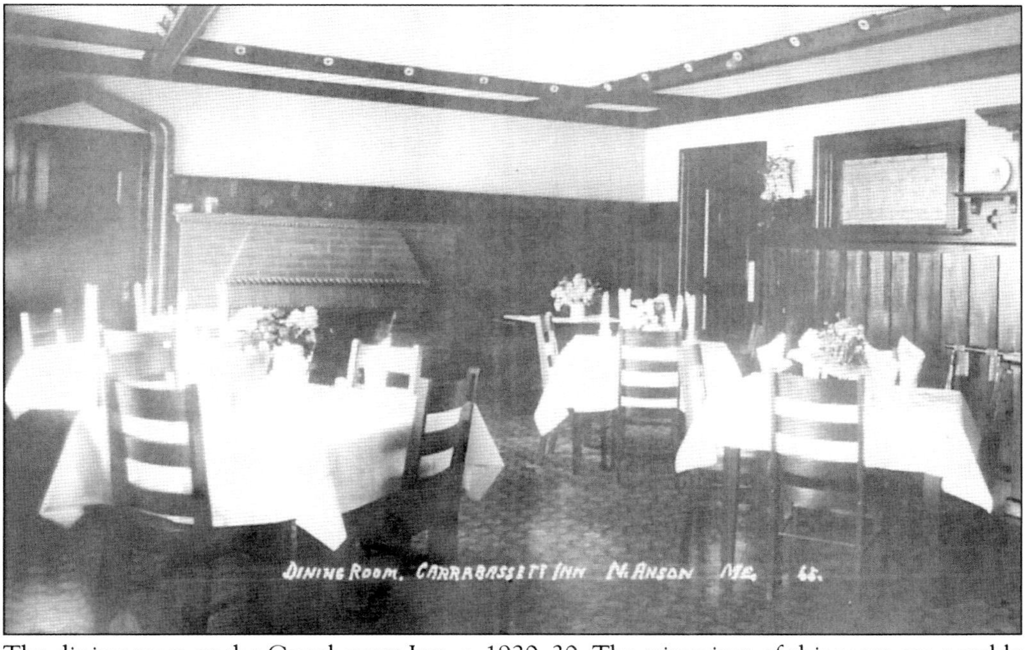

The dining room at the Carrabassett Inn, *c.* 1920–30. The trimmings of this room are notably more stylish then those of the sporting camp dining rooms farther north in the valley.

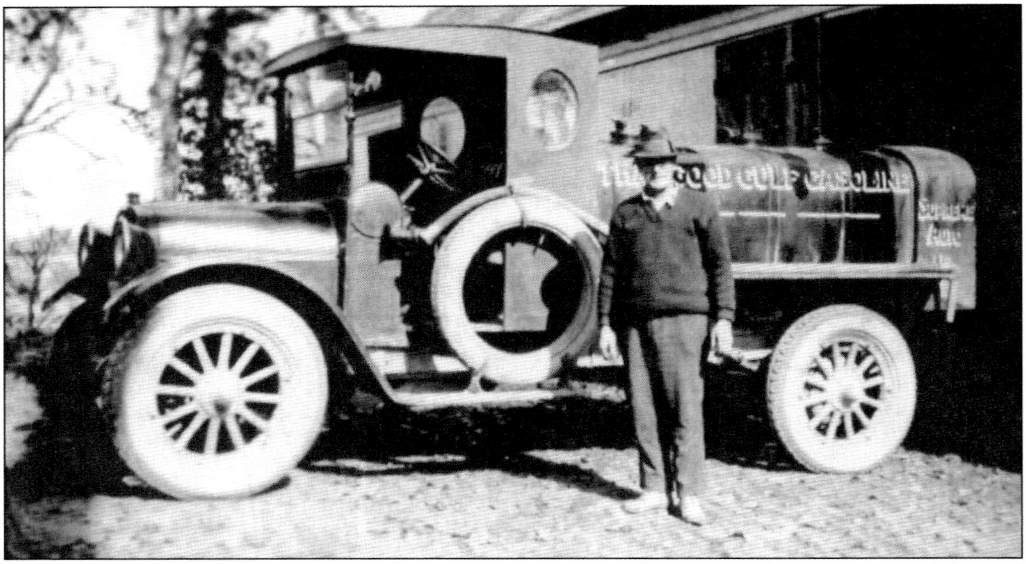

Walter M. Deane, veteran oil distributor, with his 1920 Reo Speed Wagon. Mr. Deane delivered oil, starting with a horse-drawn wagon, through the upper valley for a very long time. In the days before Wyman Dam, he negotiated the treacherous "dugways," always with a gun aboard, thinking them ideal for holdups. This truck, his first, is still in family hands.

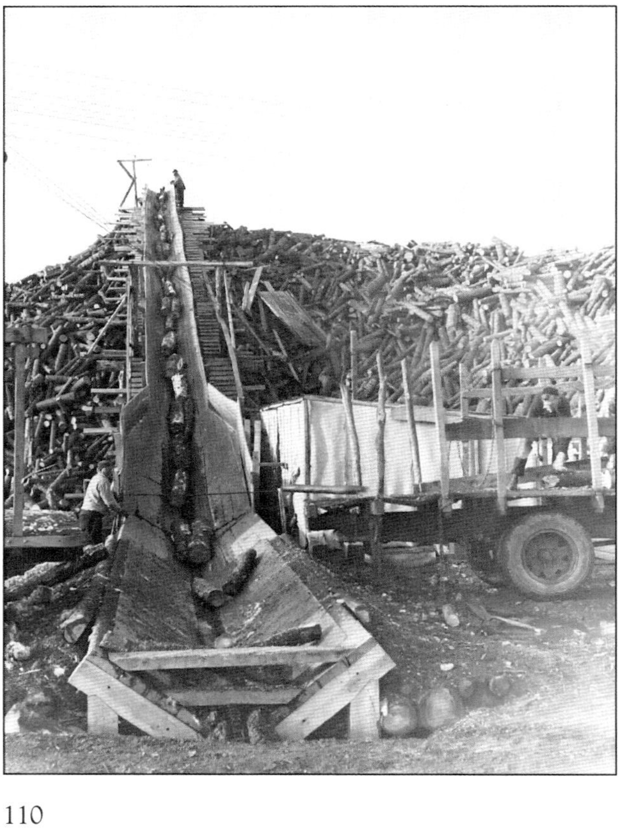

The "stacker," located on the south bank of the Carrabssett, c. 1940s. Pulpwood would be trucked in and stacked, as shown here, through the winter. In the spring, powerful pumps would reverse the process and sluice the pulp into the river.

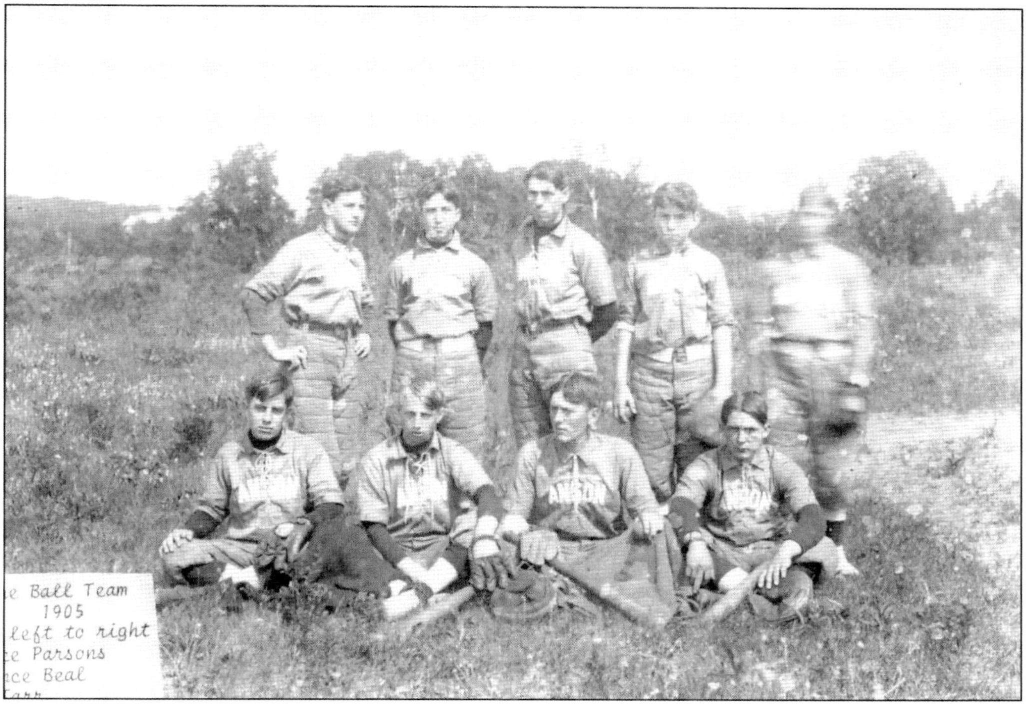

The Anson Academy ball team of 1905. From left to right are: (front row) Wallace Parsons, Lawrence Beal, John Tarr, and unidentified; (back row) Jim Thorne, unidentified, unidentified, Elmer Sawyer, and unidentified.

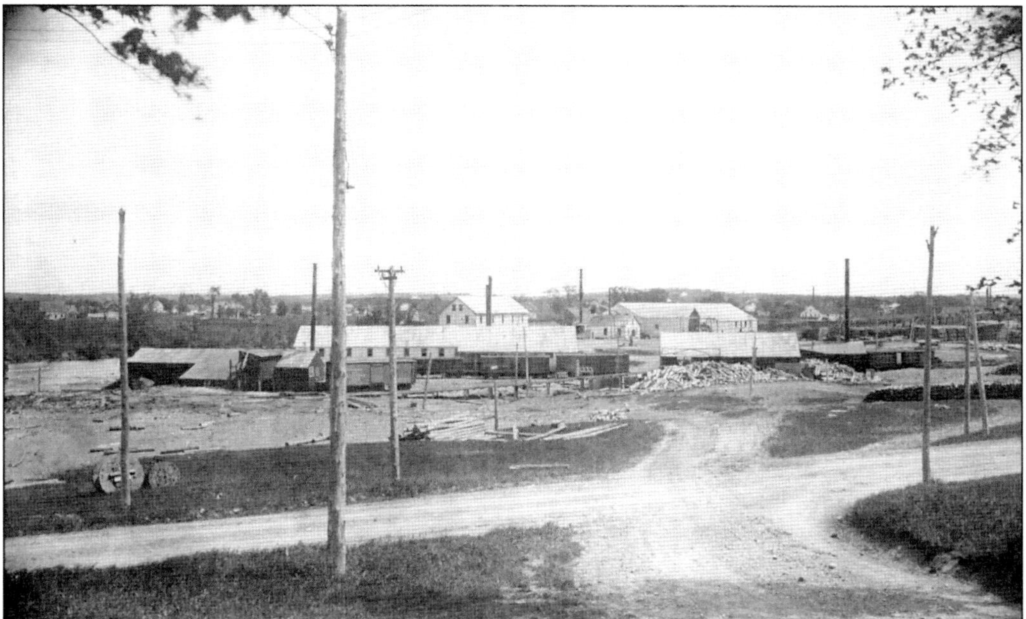

The North Anson Lumber Company, early 1900s. The whistle blew for the first time here on April 26, 1906.

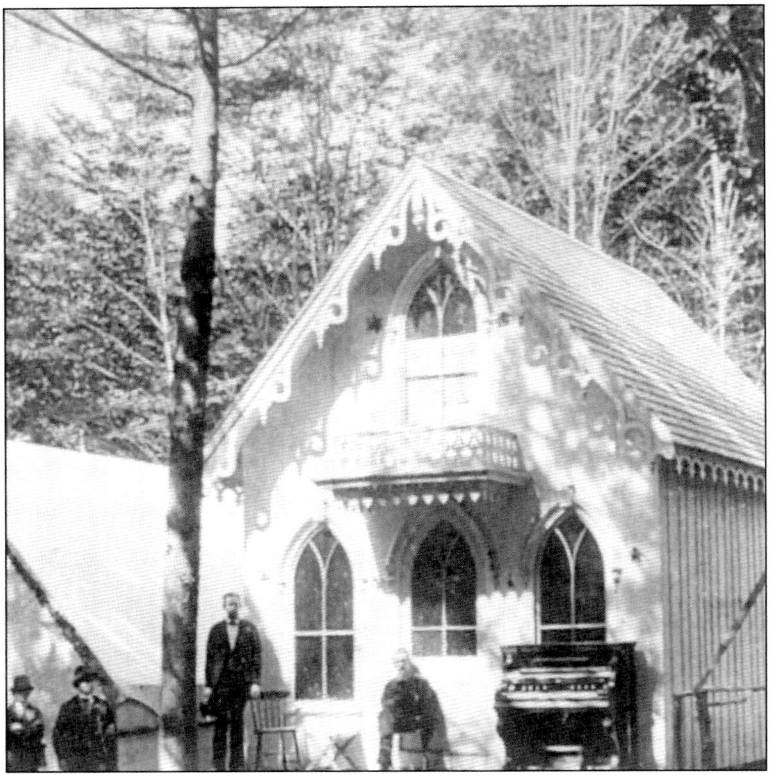

A stereo view from the Methodist campground, North Anson, c. 1880.

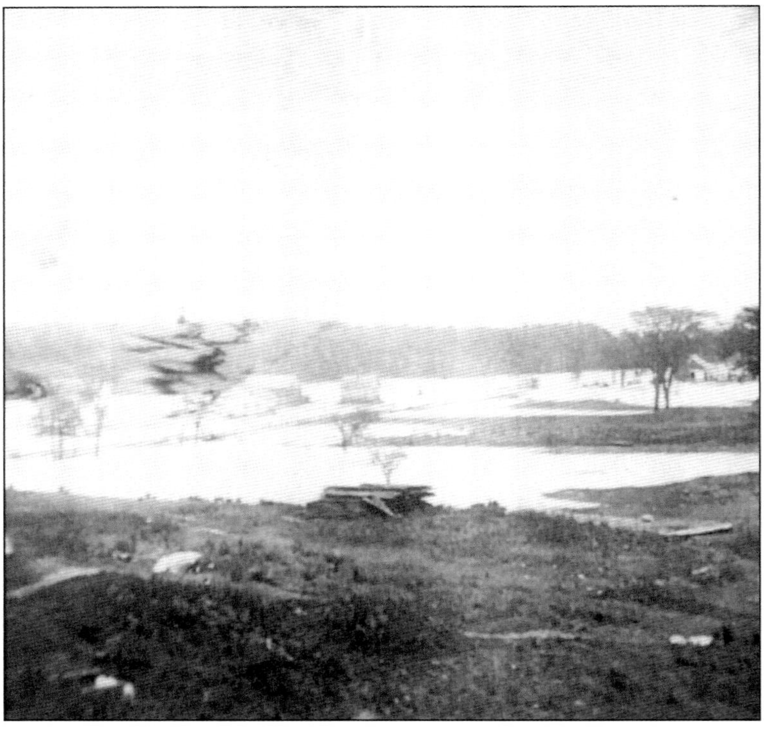

The "pumpkin freshet" in October of 1869. It was so named because of the large number of pumpkins washed downriver off the intervale farms. This stereo view is along the road from Anson to North Anson.

Eight

Madison and Anson

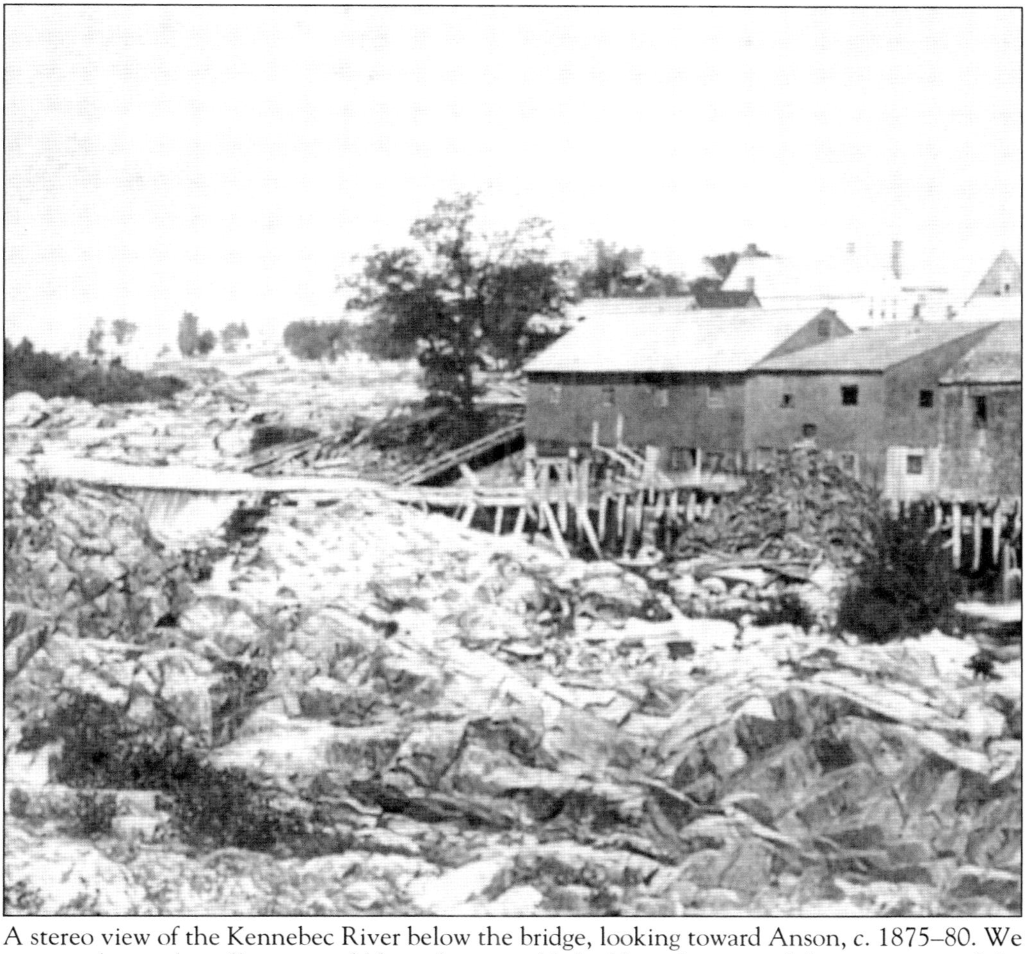

A stereo view of the Kennebec River below the bridge, looking toward Anson, *c.* 1875–80. We can see that early mill sites would have been established here because of the narrowing of the river and the ease of building dams.

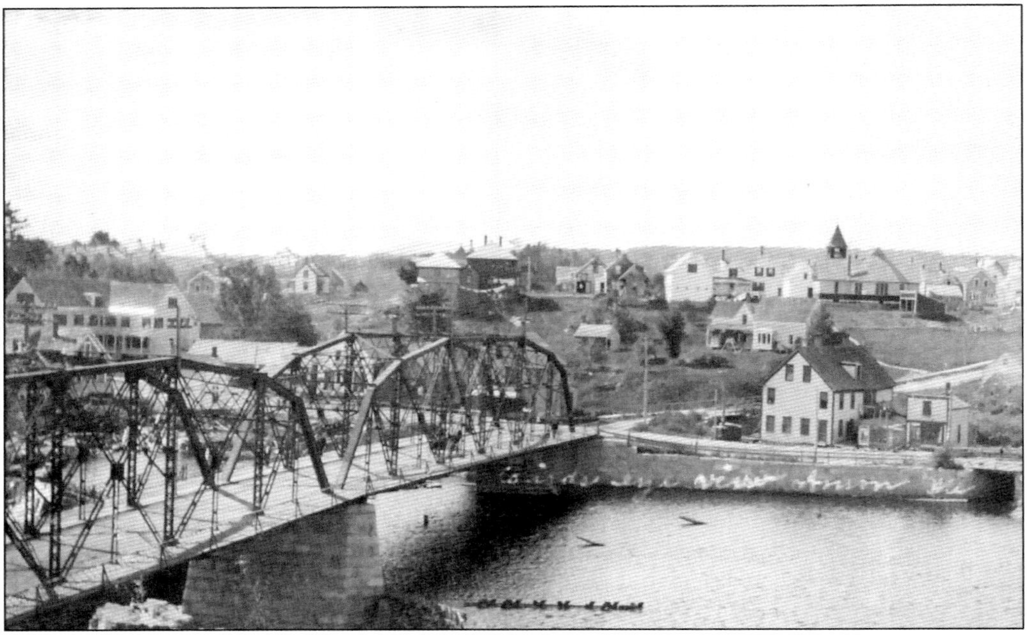

Anson, from the Madison side of the steel bridge. This bridge was erected in 1902–1903. On July 4, 1903, a mile-long parade with fifty-two floats, three bands, and ninety-nine horses, accompanied by 320 people, drew a crowd that was estimated between 8,000 and 10,000 people. The large building on the left is the Hotel Howard.

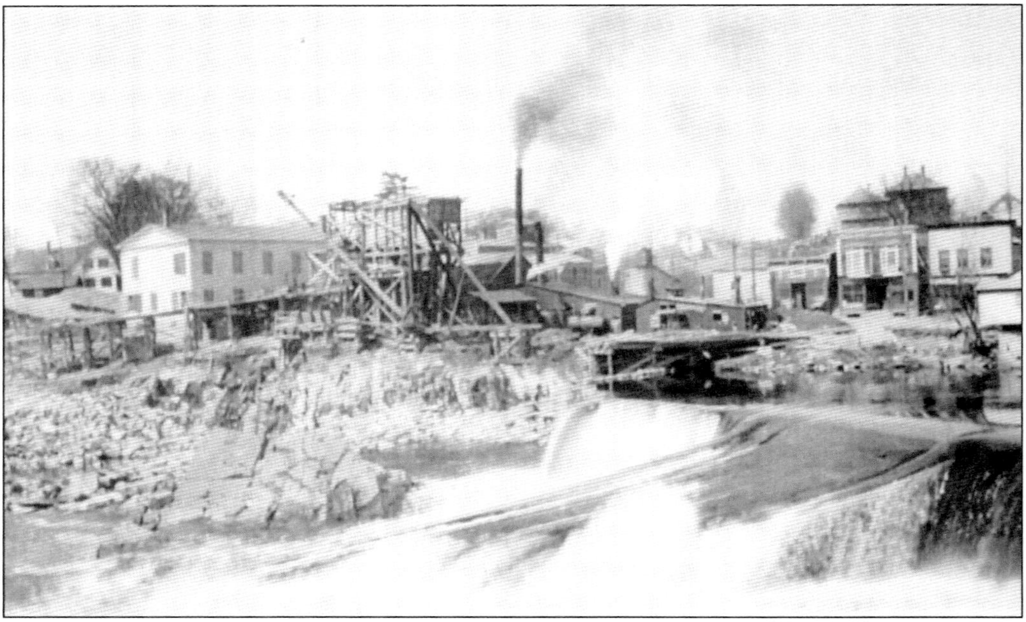

Construction of the Great Northern Paper Company power house, Anson, 1922–23. This 80-by-140-foot structure held four generators, which could provide 4,000 horsepower, with room to expand to seven generators and 7, 000 horsepower.

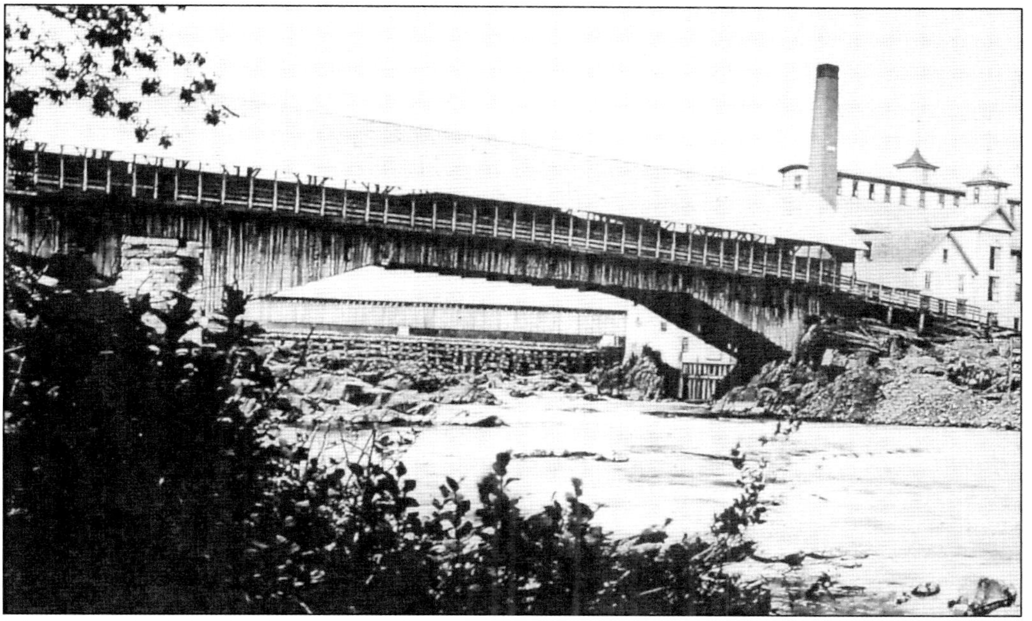

The covered toll bridge between Madison and Anson. Owned by the Norridgewock Falls Toll Bridge Company, it was removed to make way for the 1903 steel bridge, which was toll free. Part of the Indian Springs Woolen Mill is visible at the right. The first toll bridge was chartered in 1825. It was partially destroyed by a freshet in 1832. The first roof was put on the bridge about 1878.

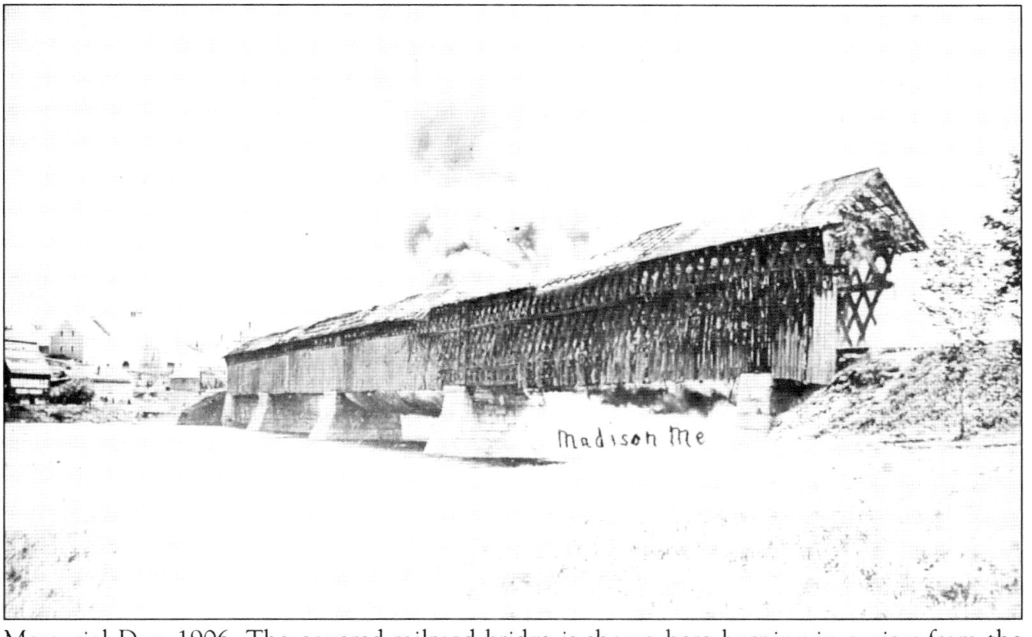

Memorial Day, 1906. The covered railroad bridge is shown here burning in a view from the Anson side. Sparks from locomotives were a great fire hazard to bridges of this type.

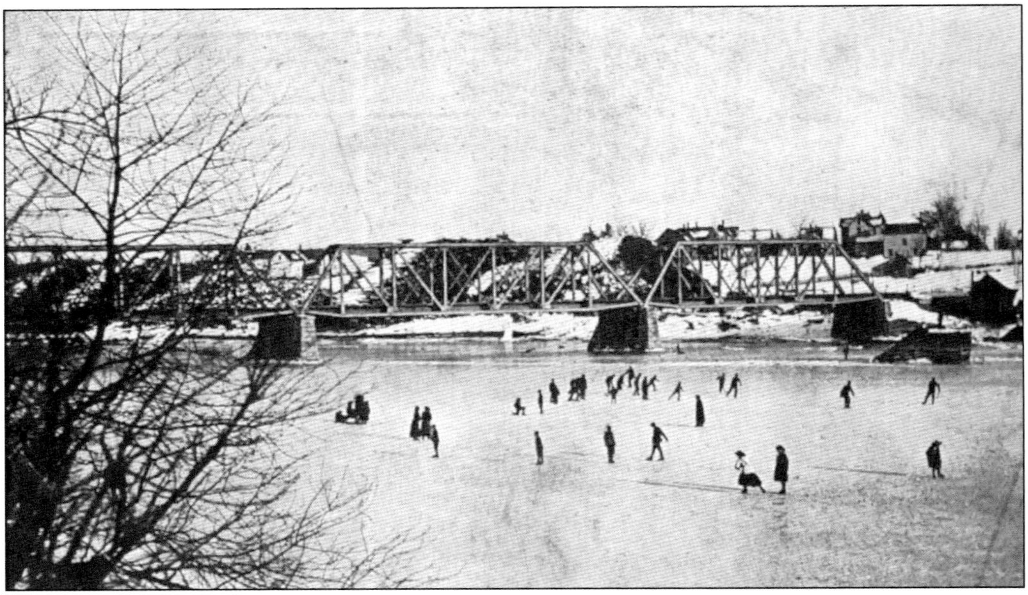

The new steel railroad bridge. This bridge was built later in 1906, using the same piers. The card, postmarked 1910, shows that winter on the Kennebec could be fun when the weather was temperate.

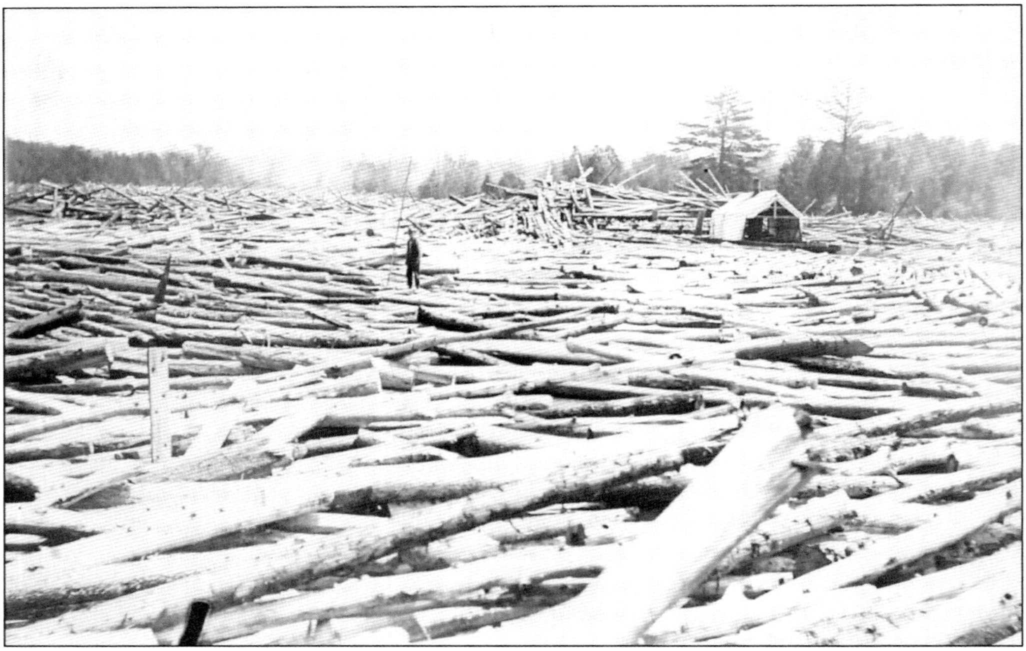

A giant log jam at the Madison sorting gap. The legend on the photograph says "Taken June 1, 1912." This started with a jam that was said to contain 5–7 million feet of lumber. It was caused by high water and a fear of letting the logs go all at once, in case they should go out to sea and be lost. This picture was taken after they had been trying to break the jam for two weeks, by which time it had built up to 12–14 million feet.

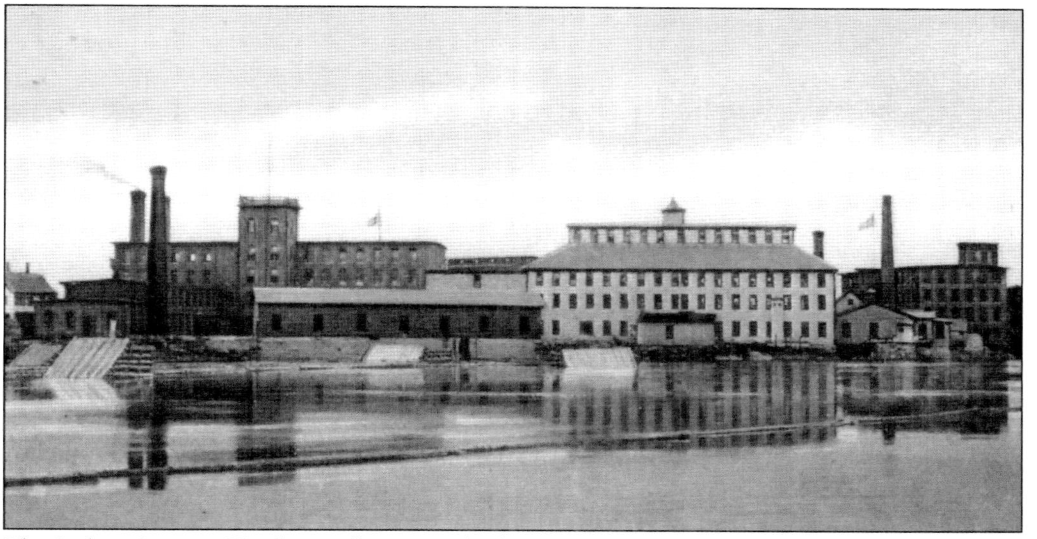

The Indian Springs Woolen Mill, postmarked 1907. The wooden part of the mill (the lighter section) was built in 1881; the brick section was built *c.* 1887–88. The mill continued to produce cloth into the 1940s. In 1949, the main building and storehouse were bought for a shoe factory by Melvin Lane of Waterville for $9,500.

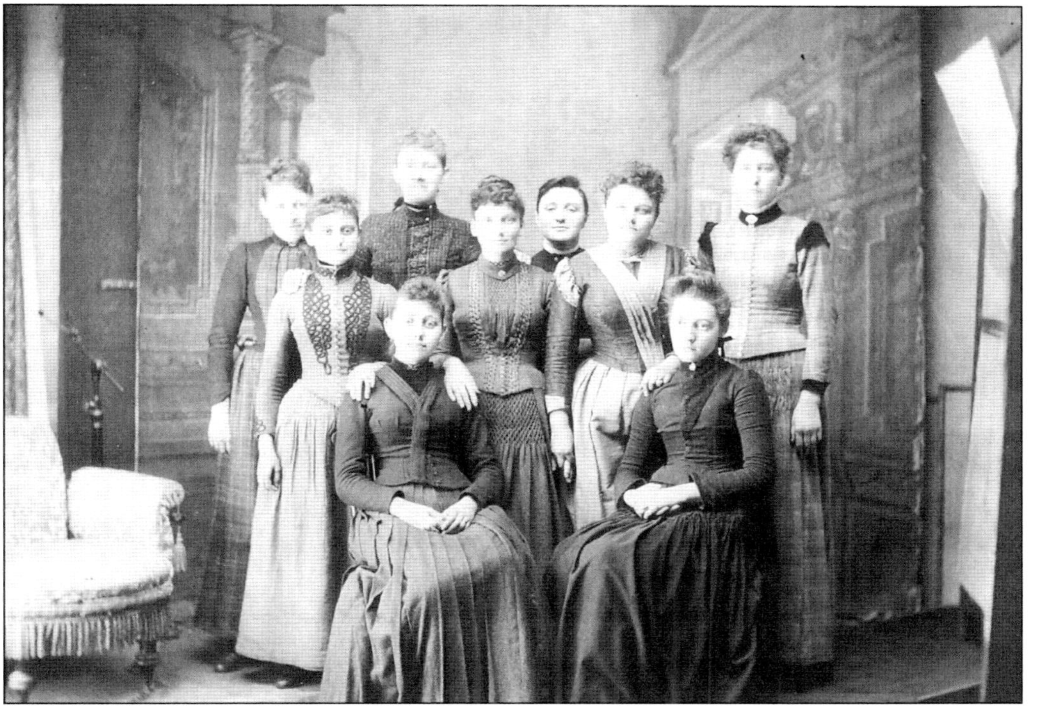

Women workers at the Indian Springs Woolen Mill, *c.* 1890. They are Nellie Wade, Nettie Wade, Edith Nye, Lizzie Booker, Emma Wood, Mrs. Hinckley, Della Greenleaf, and Bertha Randall.

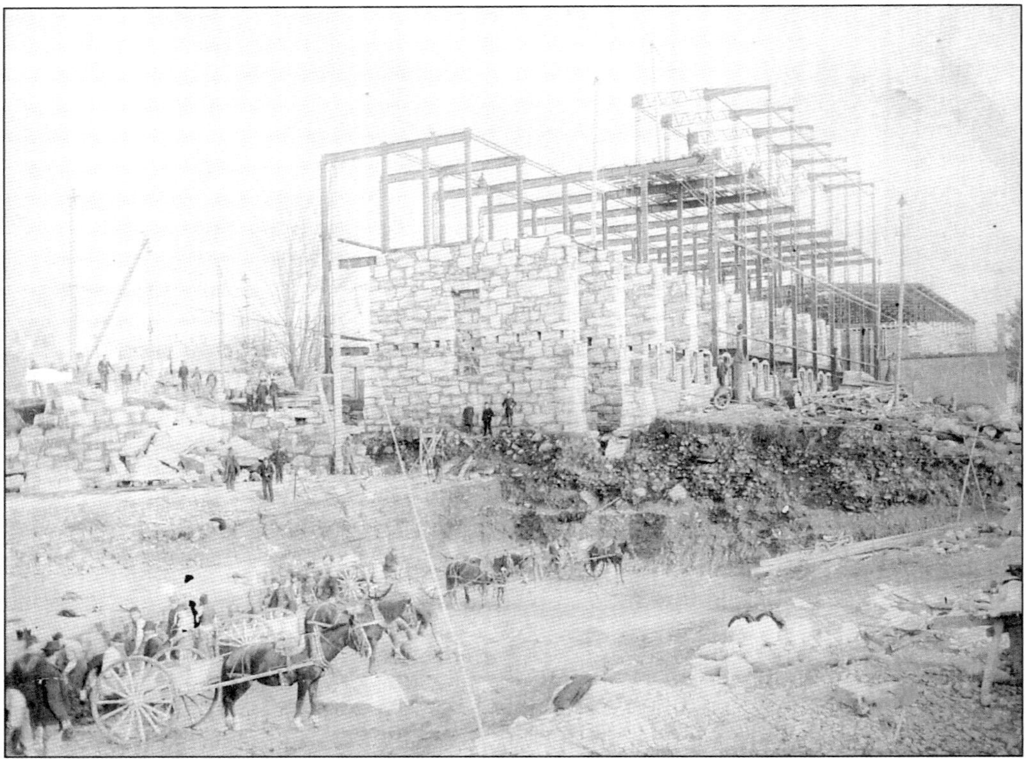

Construction of the digester pits at the Great Northern Paper Company's New Economy Mills, *c.* 1900. Horses still supplied a lot of the labor, even with steelwork and rail transport.

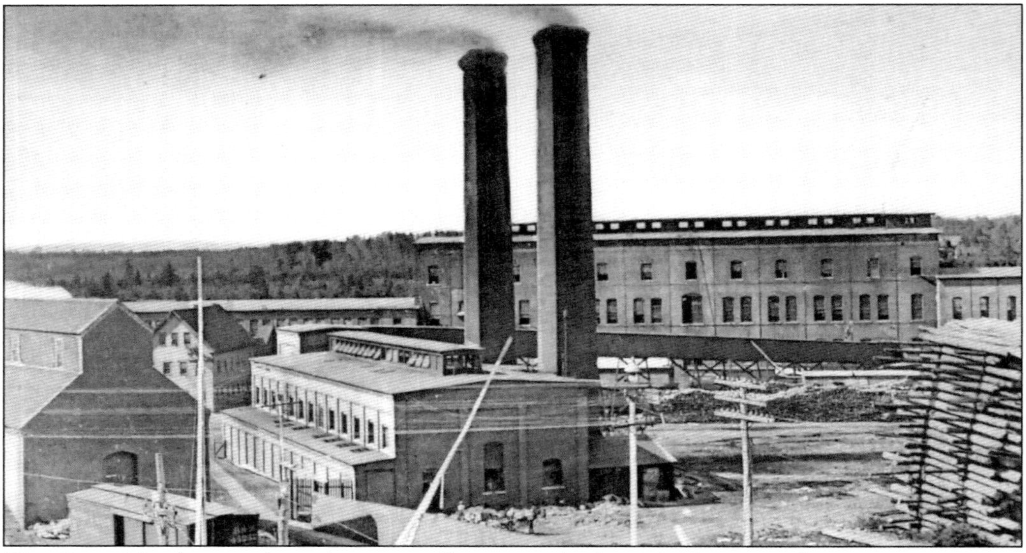

The Great Northern pulp and paper mills, postmarked 1905. The Manufacturing Investment Company built the first pulp mill in Madison in 1890. They went into receivership in 1899, and Great Northern rebuilt the mill.

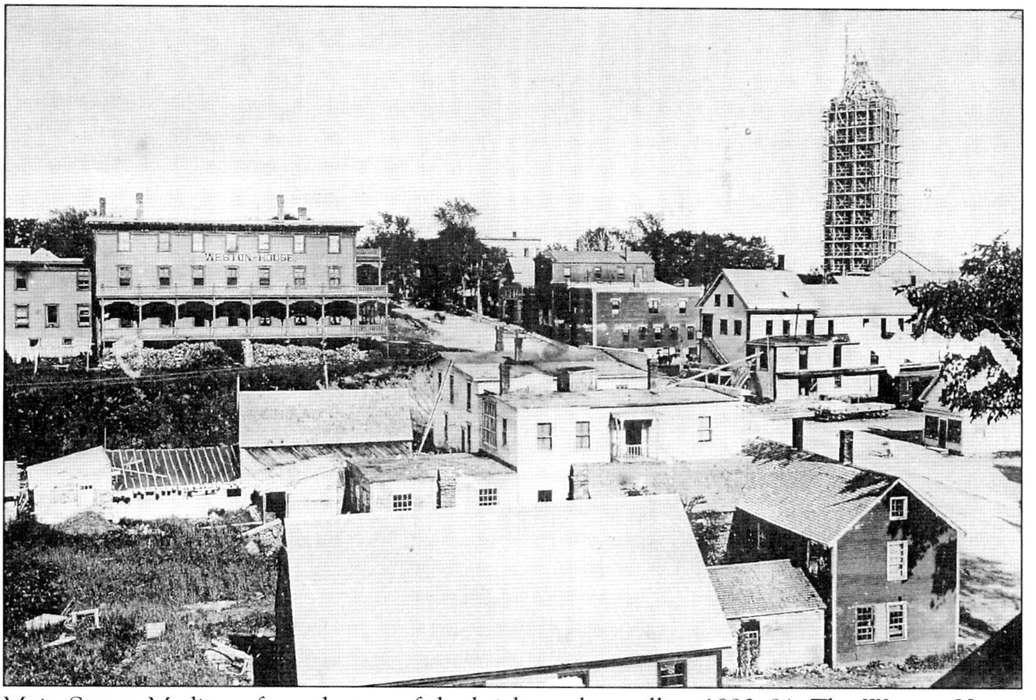

Main Street, Madison, from the top of the brick woolen mill, *c.* 1890–91. The Weston House (center left) was opened in 1887 with Abail Thompson as proprietor. It was later run by Cephas Hilton, and then Harry Hilton. It was badly damaged by fire in 1924 and subsequently torn down. On the far right is the sulphite tower for the pulp mill. It was torn down in 1899.

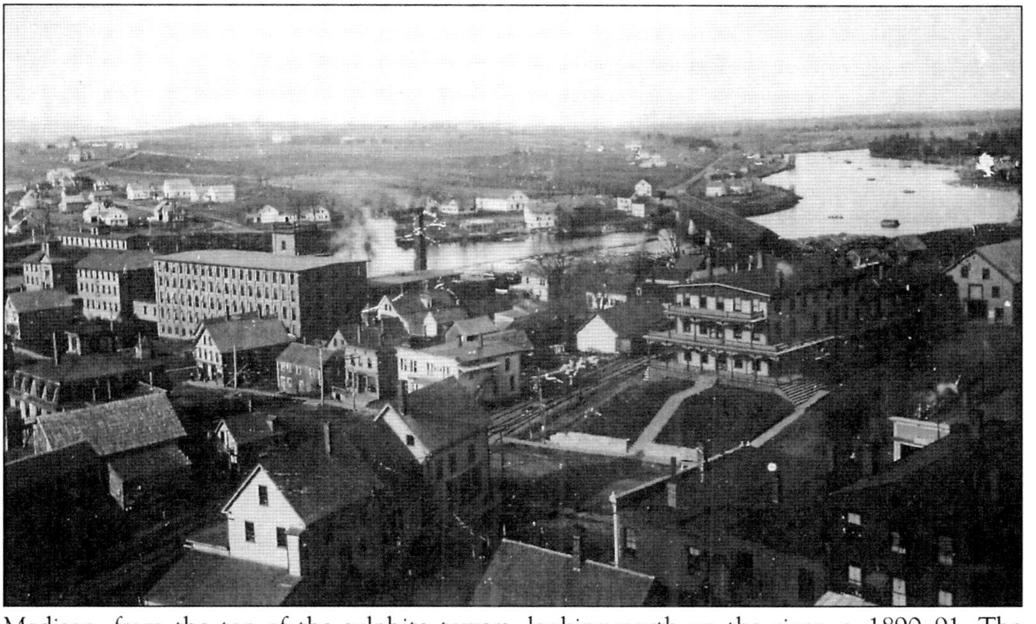

Madison, from the top of the sulphite towers, looking north up the river, *c.* 1890–91. The covered railroad bridge is right center, the woolen mill is at left center, and the Weston House is just below the railroad bridge.

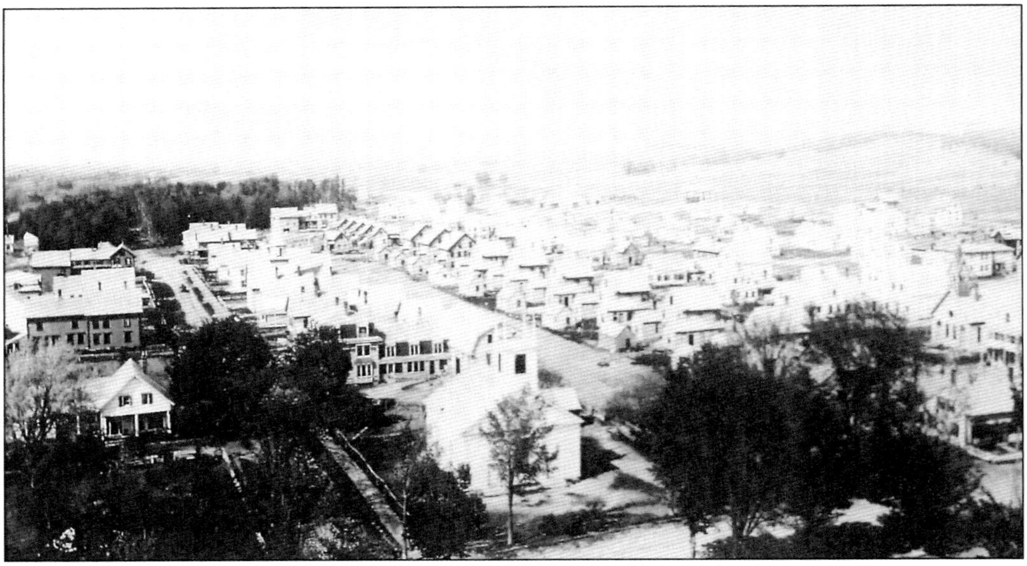

A bird's-eye view of Madison from the sulphite towers, *c.* 1890s. The old Congregational church on the corner of Main and Maple Streets is in the lower center. In 1893, this building was moved around onto Maple Street, raised 11 feet from the bottom, and fitted for two stores underneath with a hall and offices on the second floor. It was a period of very rapid building; the expansion of the village is well represented in this photograph of some of the many new homes. Note the lack of trees—a result of the new development.

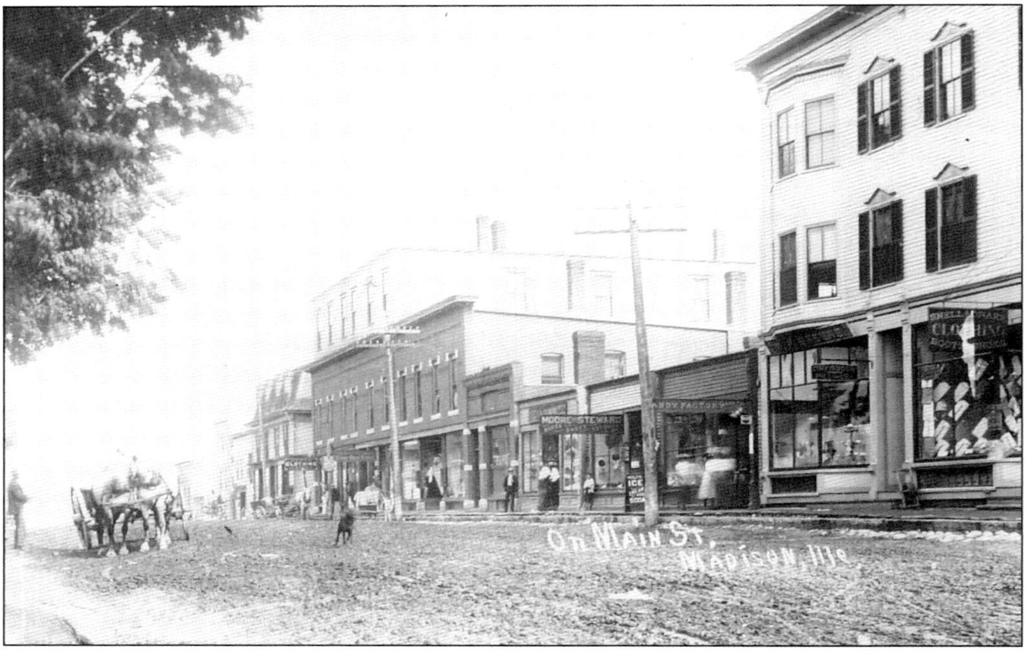

Main Street, *c.* 1900. The stores, from right to left, are Snell & Drake Clothing, W.F. Greene, Dry Goods & Millinery, the Candy Factory & Ice Cream Shop, and Moore & Steward Boots Shoes & Rubbers. The muddy street would be "macadamized" from the railroad crossing to Maple Street in 1908.

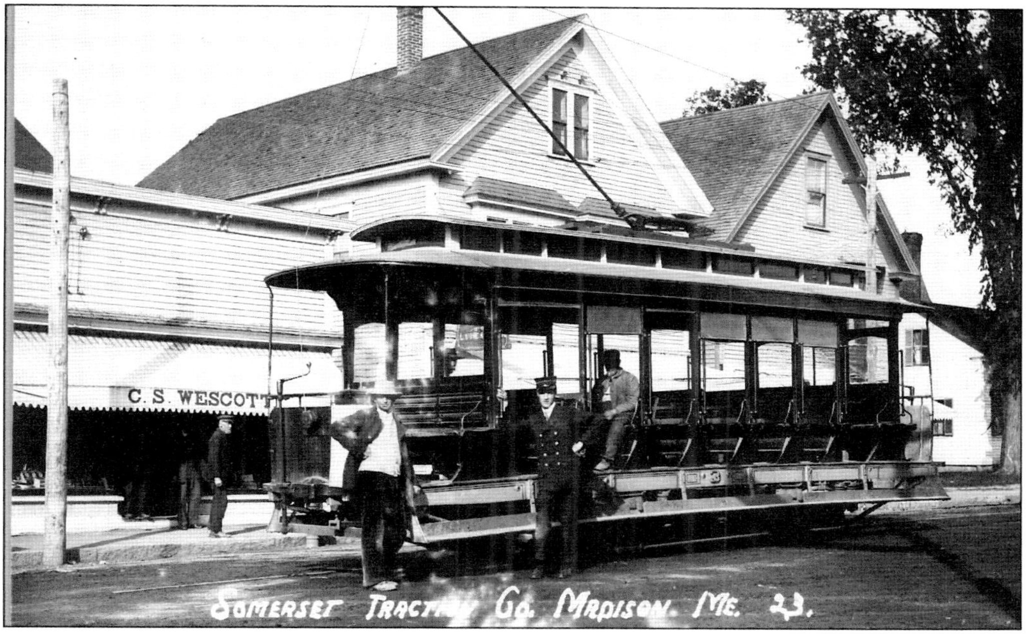

A Somerset Traction Company trolley, Madison, *c.* 1900. This line connected to Lakewood and Skowhegan. Typical of many trolley ventures, the company cultivated lodging and entertainment facilities at the end of their line (Lakewood in East Madison).

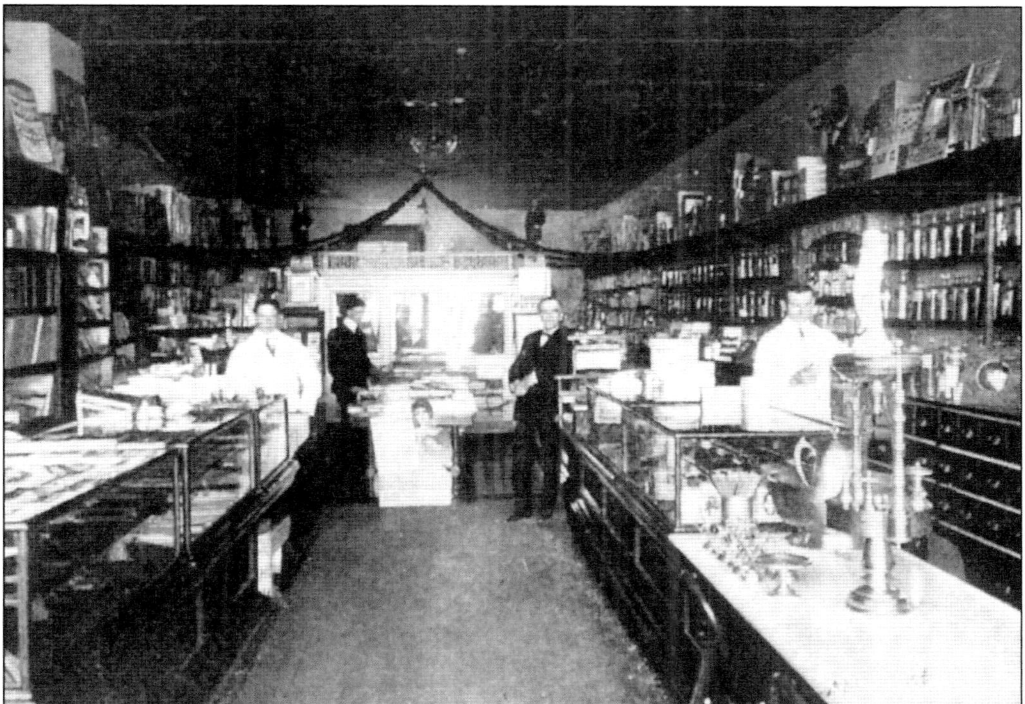

The interior of George Cushing's Drug and Book Store, February 24, 1906. Mr. Cushing is at center right.

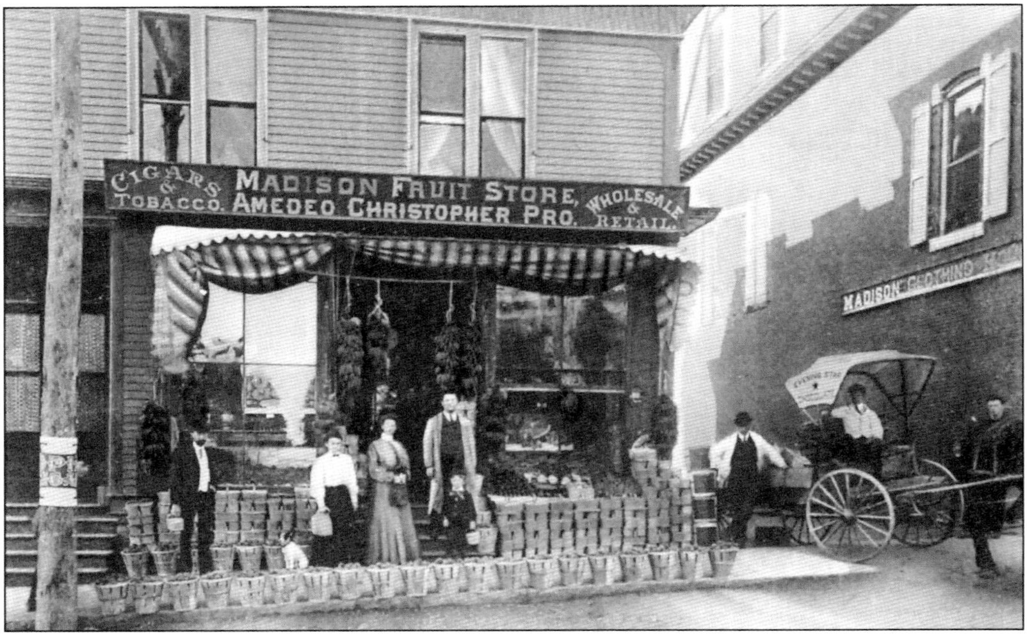

Amedeo Christopher's fruit store, opened on March 22, 1900. This turn-of-the-century postcard shows baskets of fruit and bunches of bananas, along with the store personnel. The store was located in the Simonds block, which had recently been moved.

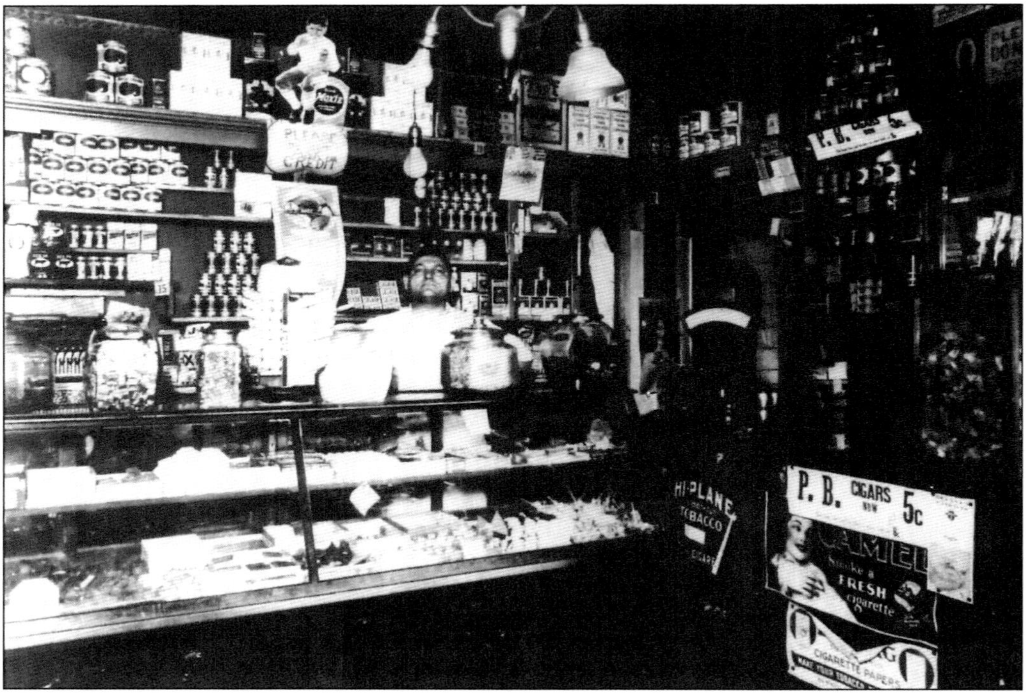

Frank Ventresco, inside his International Store on Old Point Avenue, *c.* 1936. During the heyday of the mills, there were several Italian stores in Madison, to cater to the needs of Italian mill workers.

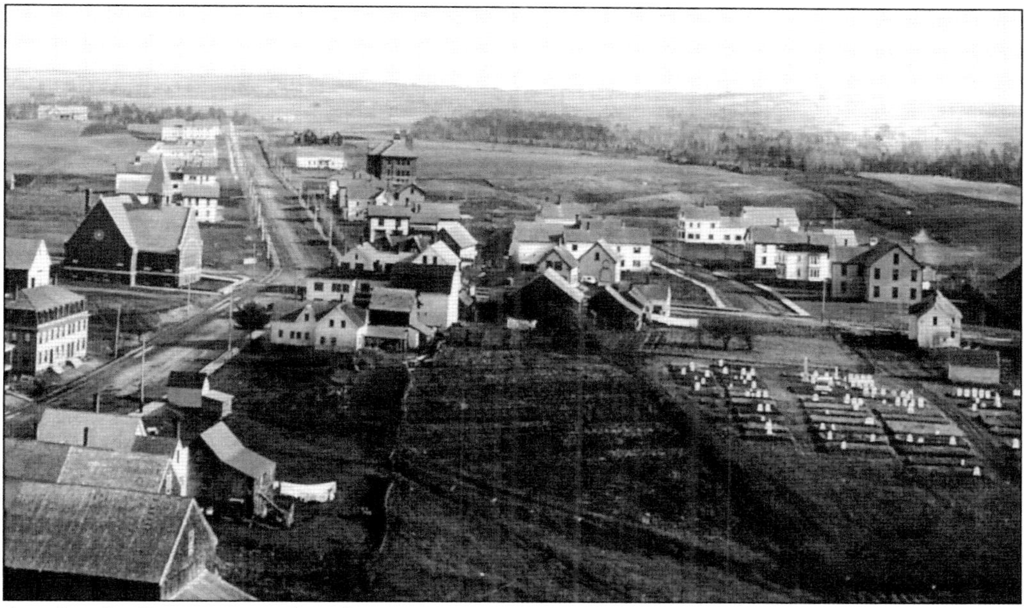

Another bird's-eye view of Madison, c. 1890s. It shows the present Congregational church at center left, and the old high school in the center distance.

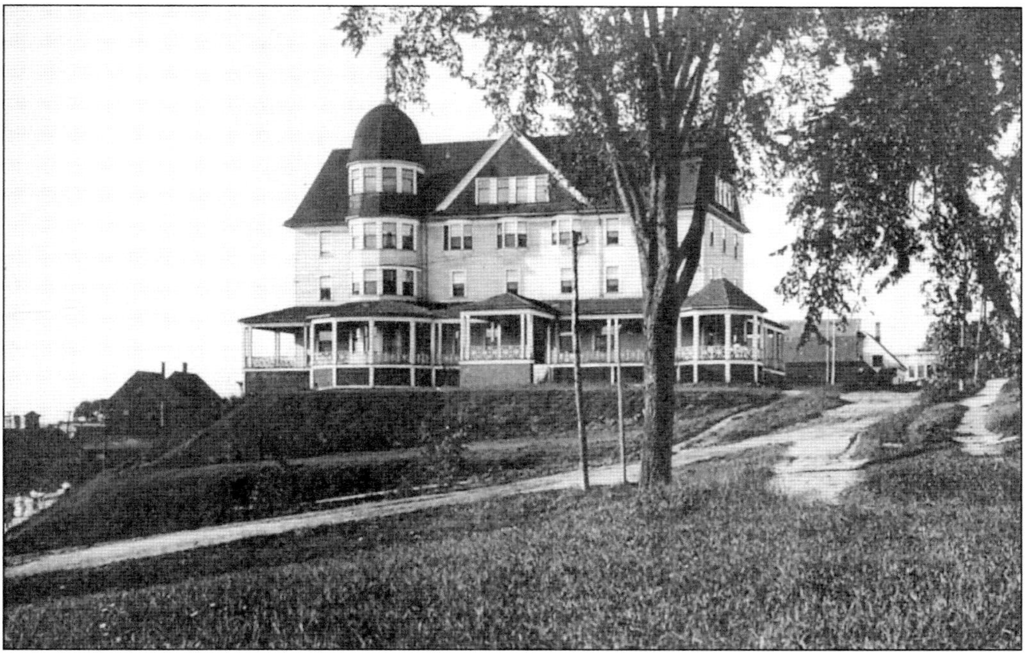

The Hilton House in 1899. Built on the former site of the sulphite towers, this hotel was run by Cephas Hilton (who had earlier run the Weston House). It burned on March 23, 1914.

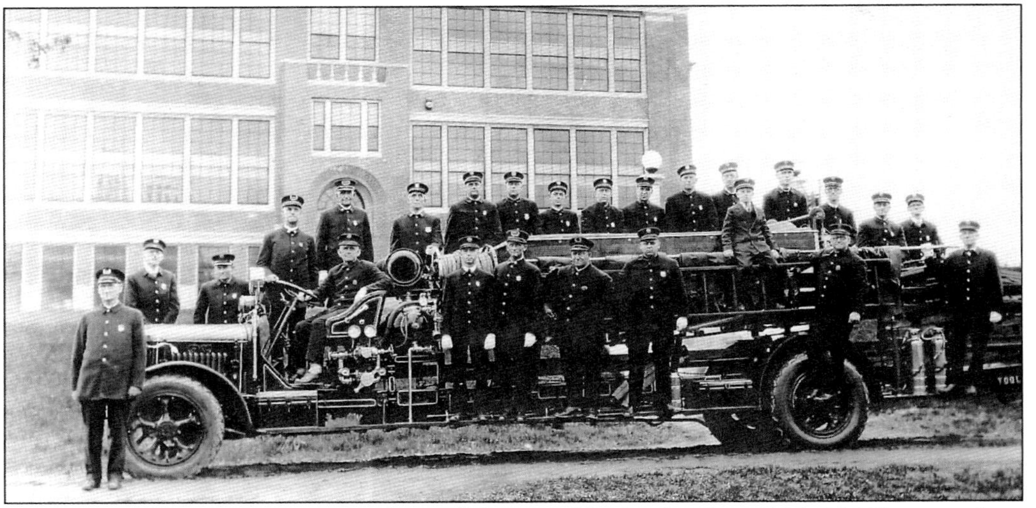

The Madison Fire Department, in front of the "new" high school, *c.* 1924–25. They are, from left to right, as follows: (front row) Duckworth, V. Williams, Caldwell, Nichols, Wescott, A. Williams, R. Heald, M.Cavanaugh, S. Golding, E. Moody, S. Wright, C. Daggett, E. Strickland, Duckworth, D. Warman, C. Sawyer, and G. Hill; (back row) F. Brackett, A. Burwood, R. Gilbert, J. Brooks, George Willis, W. Warman, A. Strong, and H. Lassan.

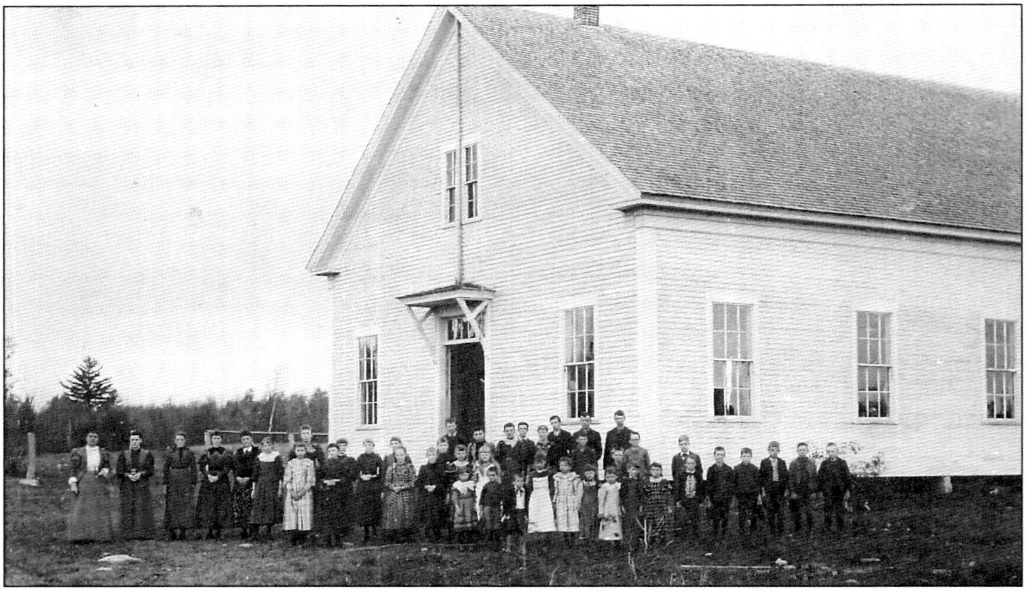

The schoolhouse at Blackwell Corner, *c.* 1896. This building was originally a town hall. It was replaced *c.* 1912–14. Shown here are Mittie Batchelder and May Holway (teachers), Edith Barron, Annie Turner, Nettie Holway, Lettie Rowe, Hazel Holway, Nettie Burnes, Grace Barrow, Gerrie Sawyer, Lottie Moore, Ethel French, Lona Moore, Mabel Davis, Daisy Holway, Nettie Moore, Elsie Jones, Beatrice Emery, Nellie Turner, Elsie Laurence, Guy Prince, Harold Danforth, Ethlyn Laurence, Ethel Davis, Alice Knight, Maud Holway, Lula Holway, Agnes Emery, Mabel Clough, Mahlon Welch, Truman Carl, Roy Danforth, Perley Adams, Gene Burnes, Leon Welch, Everett Salley, Allie Gilbert, David Holway, Elmer Salley, Mahlon Whipple, Leslie Holway, Manley Davis, Johnnie Sawyer, and Linwood Nutting.

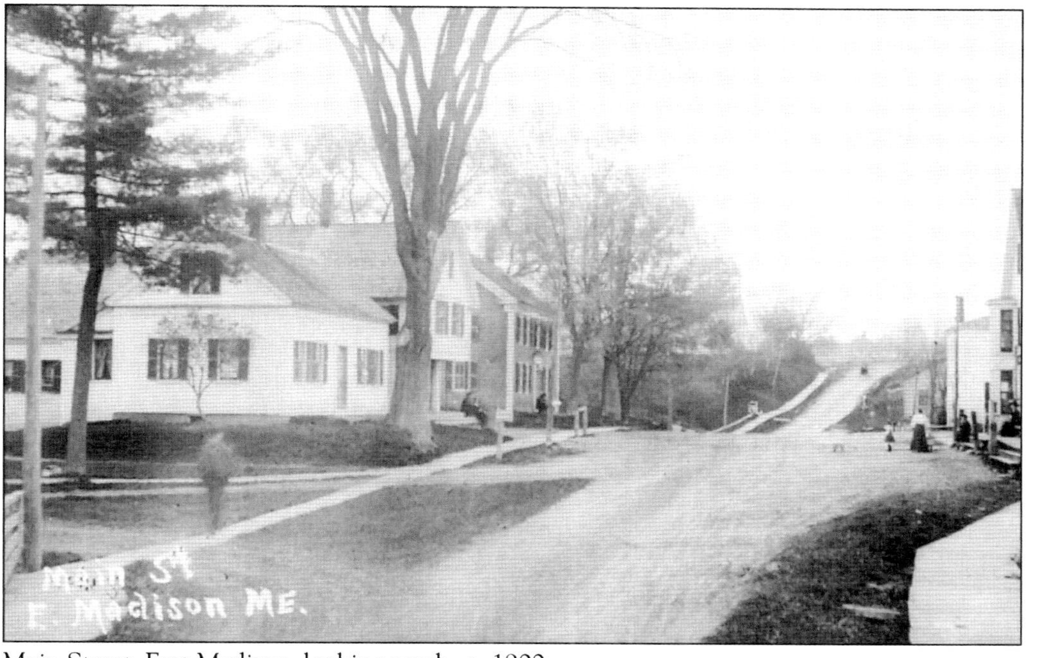

Main Street, East Madison, looking south, *c.* 1900.

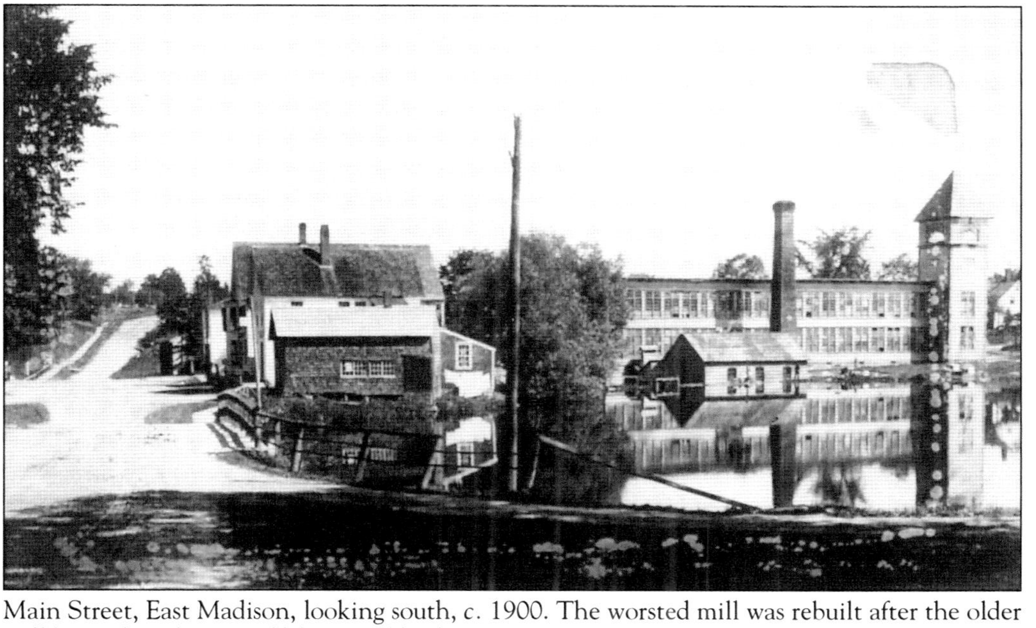

Main Street, East Madison, looking south, *c.* 1900. The worsted mill was rebuilt after the older mill burned, and was itself destroyed by fire in 1954.

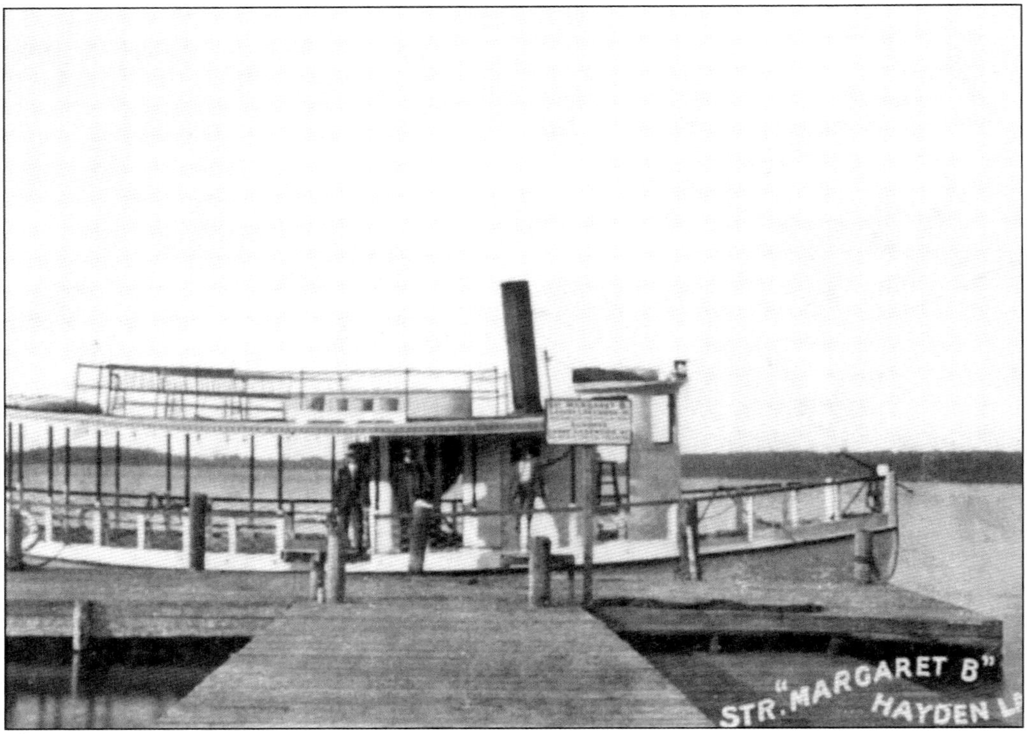

The steamer *Margaret B* at Lakewood, *c.* early 1900s. Known over time as Madison Pond, Hayden Lake, and now as Lake Wesserunsett, this was the popular end point of the Somerset Traction Company's trolley line.

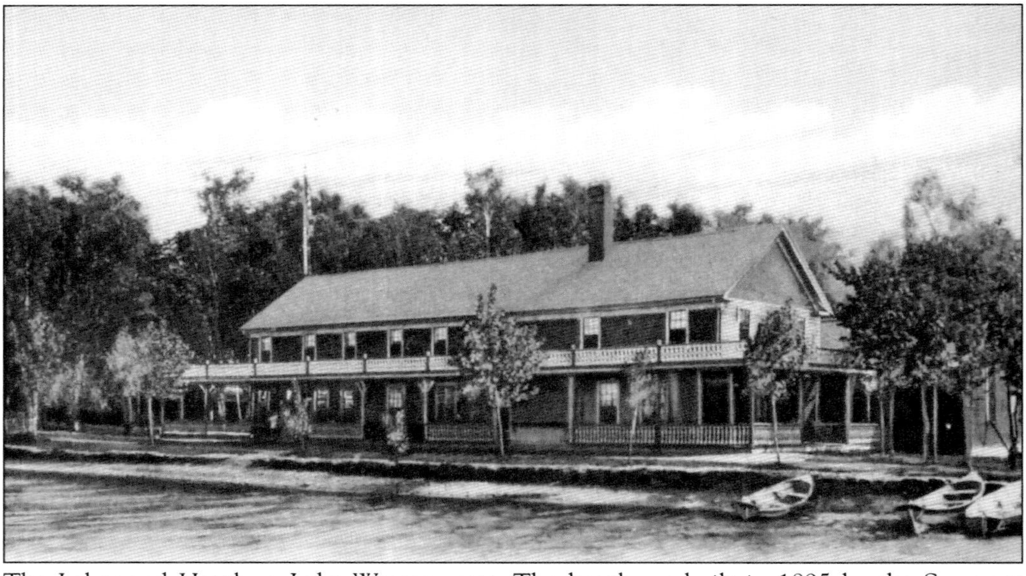

The Lakewood Hotel on Lake Wesserunsett. The hotel was built in 1895 by the Somerset Traction Company to encourage travel to the end of the line. The hotel opened on July 4, 1895.

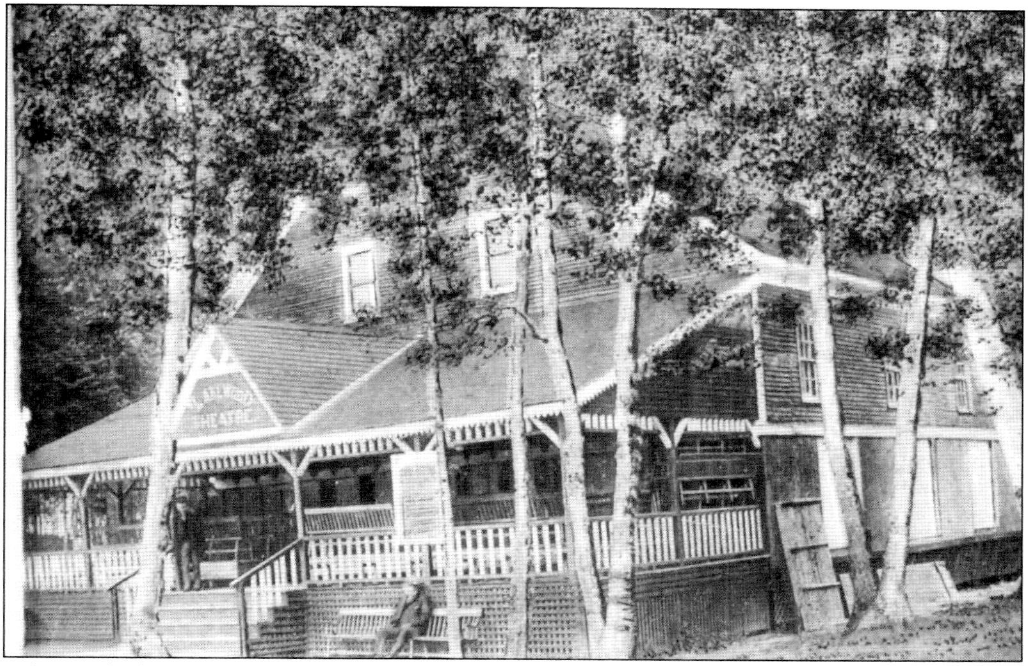

Lakewood Theater, postmarked 1906. Long a great summer draw, it offered excellent summer stock plays and shows, with major names from the theater and films.

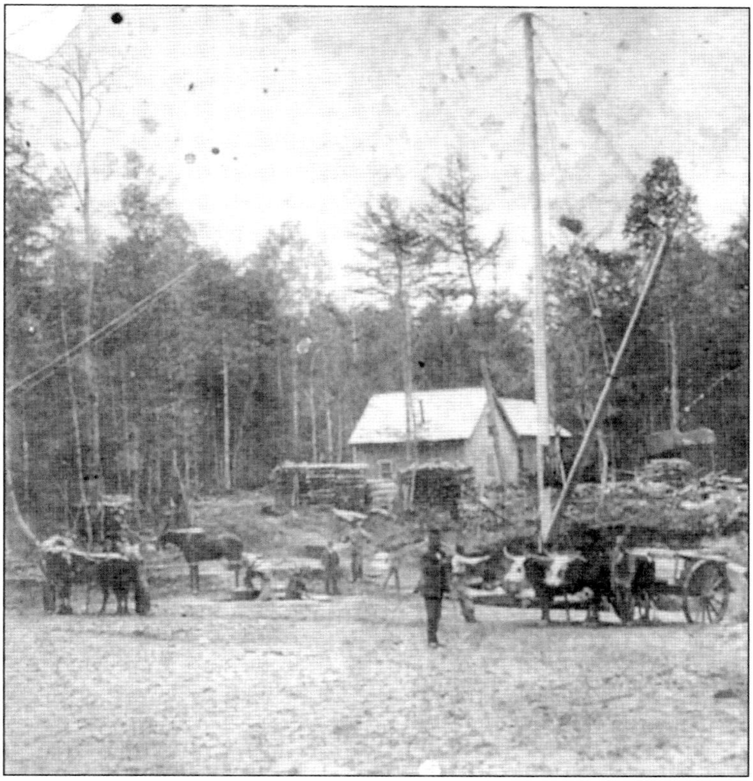

A stereo view of the Madison Pond Slate Quarry, c. 1880. Teams of oxen, cranes, and horses are helping with the heavy work.

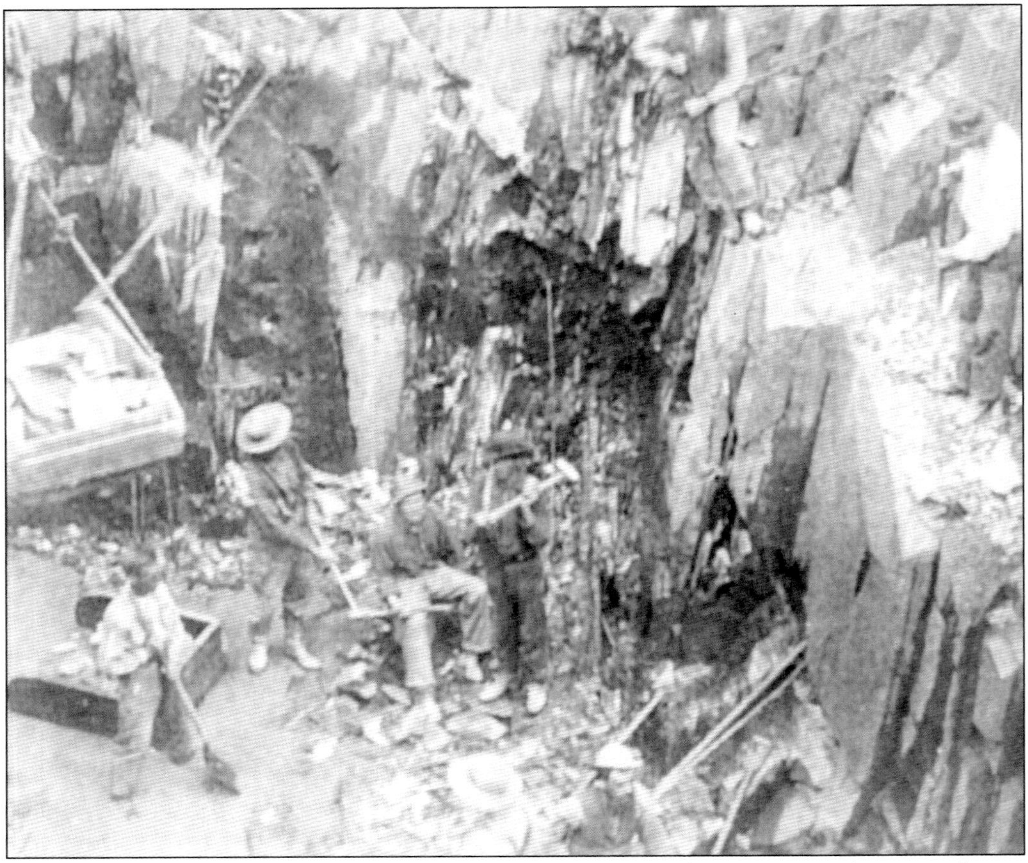

The Madison Pond Slate Quarry pit, *c.* 1880. Shown here are a hoisting rig and a crew splitting off slate.

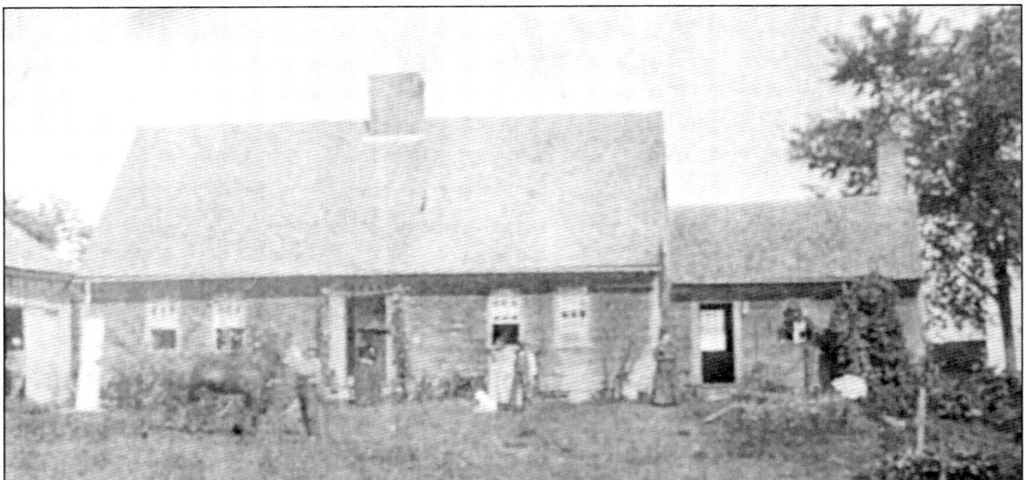

The Isaac Rowell farm, East Madison, August of 1880. This early Cape Cod-style farmhouse is now part of the Skowhegan School of Painting and Sculpture. Shown in front of the house, from left to right, are Rachel Rowell, Will Rowell, George Rowell, and Myra Rowell.